BOOKS BY HARLAN LEBO

Citizen Kane: The 50th Anniversary

Casablanca: Behind the Scenes

The Godfather Legacy

A FIRESIDE BOOK

PUBLISHED BY

SIMON & SCHUSTER

The Godfather

LEGACY

HARLAN LEBO

FIRESIDE
Rockefeller Center
1230 Avenue of the Americas
New York, NY 10020

FIRESIDE and colophon are registered trademarks
of Simon & Schuster Inc.

Designed by Richard Oriolo

Manufactured in the United States of America

10   9   8   7   6   5   4   3   2   1

Library of Congress Cataloging-in-Publication Data

Lebo, Harlan.
The Godfather legacy / Harlan Lebo.
p.   cm.
Includes index.
1. Godfather films—History and criticism.   I. Title.
PN1995.9.G6L4   1997
791.43'75—dc21   96-49984   CIP

ISBN 0-684-83647-5

Your comments and questions about this book are welcome.

Write to:

Harlan Lebo
c/o Fireside Books
1230 Avenue of the Americas
14th Floor
New York, NY 10020

Or E-mail: HLEBO@JUNO.COM

With Thanks

THIS BOOK could be created only because of the generous support of these wonderful people:

My editor, Cindy Gitter, who guided this project from the beginning, was endlessly tolerant of me in the middle, and made the manuscript readable at the end.

My agent, Felicia Eth, who I know takes a deep and cautious breath when I call, but is always there.

The librarians at the Margaret Herrick Library of the Academy of Motion Picture Arts and Sciences—terrific people at a truly incredible research center.

The Paramount folks—Paula Block, Jeff Baskin, and Mike Berman—who guided me through the maze.

The staff at Studio Photo Service—Jose D. Sanchez, Abel Gutierrez, Lauro Aguirre, Raul Alvarez, Chris Cormack, and Mike DiLeonardo—for work far beyond the call of duty to produce the nearly 700 photos that were used to select the final images for this book.

My doctor, Neil Parker, and my cats' veterinarian, William Carlsen, who took time when they shouldn't have to answer the medical questions for this book about both people and animals.

My old friend Neil Helgeson—an endless fount of useful information and abrasive inspiration.

My colleague Stuart Wolpert, who absorbs the brunt of my adventures in authorship with encouragement, patience, and class.

My wife, Monica Dunahee, who was involved every step of the way, is always there for me during the worst of it, and shows me how to appreciate the best of it.

And finally, Al Ruddy, Dick Smith, and Dean Tavoularis, three patient and generous gentlemen who gave so much of their time in discussions with me about their involvement in the creation of *The Godfather*. Their recollections provided the inside view that would have otherwise been impossible to capture.

HARLAN LEBO
Los Angeles

Contents

A NOTE ABOUT THE PHOTOGRAPHS

Most of the 125 photographs in this book are being published here for the first time. They were selected after a review of some 49,000 images from *The Godfather, The Godfather Part II,* and *The Godfather Part III* that are housed in the archives of Paramount Pictures in Hollywood.

Those Paramount files include dozens—often hundreds—of photographs of virtually every scene from these three films as they were being rehearsed and filmed. The thousands of images that were examined but not included here provided a bounty of visual references that helped to confirm—and in several cases to discard—some of the material that has gathered over the past quarter century about the making of *The Godfather.*

A NOTE ABOUT *THE GODFATHER* FILMS

This book refers to five different versions of *Godfather* films—first, the three motion pictures as originally released in theaters: *The Godfather, The Godfather Part II,* and *The Godfather Part III.*

The Godfather: The Complete Epic is the reediting of *Part I* and *Part II* into mostly chronological order as created to air on NBC in a four-part miniseries format in November 1977. The *Godfather*

Epic, also known as *The Godfather: The Complete Novel for Television,* as televised contained some edits for violence and one nude scene; the edits were restored when the chronological version was released on videotape.

The Godfather Trilogy, which was released in 1992, is the merging of all three films into a mostly chronological edition.

THE **GODFATHER** is the story of Don Vito Corleone, the head of a powerful New York Mafia family, and the rise of his youngest son Michael in the "family business." The Don is assisted in managing his criminal activities by Sonny, his eldest and most volatile son; Tom Hagen, his adopted son and consigliere (counselor); and his *caporegimes* (lieutenants) Peter Clemenza and Sal Tessio. The Don's middle son Fredo, tentative and weak-willed, serves only in menial roles in the family business; his youngest son Michael, a college student turned war hero engaged to outsider Kay Adams, loves his family but wants no part of a life of crime.

The film opens in August 1945 at the wedding reception for the Don's daughter Connie and her new husband Carlo Rizzi. Attending the reception is the Don's godson, singer Johnny Fontane, who begs his godfather for help getting a role in a film produced by studio mogul Jack Woltz. Don Vito dispatches Hagen to Hollywood to convince Woltz to cast Fontane in the film—"to make him an offer he can't refuse"—but the studio chief turns him down. Woltz awakens one morning to discover the head of his prize racehorse Khartoum in his bed; Fontane is cast in the picture.

Virgil Sollozzo, a drug dealer associated with the Barzini and Tattaglia crime families, comes to the Don for his assistance in setting up a large-scale drug trade; Sollozzo needs the legal protection the Don can provide through the vast network of judges, politicians, and police on the Corleone payroll. The Don declines, because his connections would desert him if he became involved in drugs instead of more acceptable vices such as gambling and union racketeering.

But Sollozzo is persistent. Just before Christmas, he plots to kill the Don, first murdering his chief assassin Luca Brasi, who "sleeps with the fishes." Following Brasi's death, the Don is gunned down but not killed. When Michael goes to visit his father at the hospital, he discovers that McCluskey, a corrupt police captain, has sent away the detectives assigned to guard the wounded man. Michael protects his father from a second murder attempt. Afterward, McCluskey arrives on the scene and angrily breaks Michael's jaw. Michael's love for his father quickly draws him into the family business; at a meeting intended to settle differences with the other crime families, Michael kills both Sollozzo and McCluskey, escaping to the relative safety of exile in Sicily and leaving Kay behind.

The murders of Sollozzo and McCluskey spark a war between the Corleones and their rival Mafia families, and Sonny, set up by Carlo, his own brother-in-law, is gunned down at a Long Island tollbooth. In Sicily, Michael falls in love with Apollonia, a local peasant girl, and they marry. However, Michael's bodyguard Fabrizio turns traitor and plants a car bomb meant for Michael but which kills Apollonia instead.

Sonny's death prompts the Don, who is recovering from his wounds, to negotiate a truce with Dons Barzini and Tattaglia, and the other crime families, and he agrees to cooperate in the drug trade. Michael, now committed to the family, returns from Sicily and assumes his place in the Corleone family business. He reunites with Kay, promising that the Corleone family will become completely legitimate within five years.

Three years later, Michael, now head of the family, initiates plans to expand his operations to Las Vegas. Fredo is already there, working in the gambling business under the tutelage of casino owner Moe Greene. Greene refuses to sell his hotel to the Corleone family despite Michael's personal offer. Vito, deteriorating but still acting as adviser to his son, counsels him about how their enemies will try to kill the young Don. Soon after, Vito dies.

Once Don Vito has died, Michael acts to solidify his position and exact revenge for Sonny's death. Against the backdrop of his nephew's baptism, he orchestrates the assassinations of Barzini, Tattaglia, Moe Greene, and other rival New York dons in one grand slaughter. He also orders the death of Tessio, who had betrayed the family and aided in an assassination plot against Michael, as well as his brother-in-law Carlo, who had admitted his involvement in Sonny's killing.

Michael, once the young, idealistic war hero, has become a powerful Mafia chief even more ruthless than his father. Maintaining his efforts to protect his family above all, he lies to Kay about his involvement in Carlo's death. As the film closes, she realizes the truth: Michael has become the new Don Corleone.

FRANCIS **FORD** Coppola has often said that the story of *The Godfather* is "a romance about a king with three sons." The story of the *making* of *The Godfather* films is anything but a romance. It is, in fact, three stories: the first, how a film project given no chance for success became the most popular and acclaimed motion picture of its age; the second, how Coppola revisited the original story to create a film statement about family and morality that has become one of the great achievements of cinema; and the third, how fifteen years later, after triumphs, defeats, and personal tragedy, Coppola reopened his saga, bridged two generations of cast and crew, and brought *The Godfather* story to its close.

But first came the story of the book *The Godfather* and Mario Puzo, an author whose life and times became one of the more remarkable success stories among twentieth-century writers.

"A Real
Terror
to the
Piece"

MARIO PUZO was born in 1920 and grew
up a child of Hell's Kitchen, the New York
district whose tenements housed the fam-
ilies of generations of immigrants. The son of Italian-born
parents, Puzo grew up with all the afflictions of New York—
slum poverty that would color his writing.

"As a child and in my adolescence, living in the heart
of New York's Neapolitan ghetto, I never heard an Italian
singing," Puzo wrote. "None of the grown-ups I knew
were charming or loving or understanding. Rather they
seemed coarse, vulgar, or insulting. So later in my life

when I was exposed to all the clichés of lovable Italians, singing Italians, happy-go-lucky Italians, I wondered where the hell the moviemakers and storywriters got all their ideas from."

Puzo's mother wanted him to become a railroad clerk, but Puzo had dreamed of being a writer. "At the age of sixteen, when I let everybody know that I was going to be a great writer, my friends and family took the news quite calmly, my mother included. She did not become angry. She quite simply assumed that I had gone off my nut."

After World War II, Puzo began to work his way into the world of writing—short stories, magazine articles, and rewriting—earning only a modest living while searching for the combination of work that could assure him success. His first two novels, *Dark Arena* and *Fortunate Pilgrim*, were both well received, but together they earned Puzo only a paltry $6,500.

In *Fortunate Pilgrim*, which explored the world of an Italian-American family living in New York, Puzo touched on a theme that would be the inspiration for his next book. A character in *Fortunate Pilgrim* was tempted by the lure of organized crime, and an editor at Puzo's publishing house mentioned that the book might have done better if there had been more of "that Mafia stuff."

Puzo set out to do what thousands of writers before him had attempted but few had successfully accomplished: to deliberately write a book that would make him financially secure for life. Puzo wasn't seeking to produce great literature—although he did want to produce a good story—he was looking to make a killing.

"I was forty-five years old and tired of being an artist. Besides, I owed $20,000 to relatives, finance companies, banks, and assorted bookmakers and shylocks. It was time to grow up and sell out."

For his next book, Puzo decided to write about a crime family in New York. He had never known a single gangster. Yet through exhaustive research, stories from his youth, and liberal doses of Italian culture and color, he began work on what would become a three-year effort: to produce a glorified, romanticized, thoroughly engrossing look at a fictional character named Vito Corleone and his family in America's criminal underworld. He called it *Mafia*.

Puzo's publisher, G. P. Putnam's Sons, wasn't alone in its interest in *Mafia*. While Puzo had received a modest advance from Putnam, he had also interested Paramount Pictures in his evolving book—a full two years before it reached the bookstore shelves.

One of the grand old studios of Hollywood, Paramount had never developed the glitzy reputation of MGM or the slam-bang edge of Warner Bros. But it had, since 1912, been a productive and versatile studio and for years the largest and most profitable company in the business. By the early 1960s, though, the studio's fortunes had begun to decline. The studio recorded modest profits, but never with the strength of its earlier years; its production schedule was marked by occasional successes, but even larger flops. In the mid-sixties, with profits stagnant, Paramount was vulnerable to a takeover. In 1966, the studio was purchased by Gulf+Western, a diverse holding company that had business interests in, among other ventures, industrial products, auto parts, paper, and engineering; Paramount formed the core of G+W's Leisure Time group. At the head of Gulf+Western was Charles G. Bluhdorn, the company founder and chairman of the board, a hard-edged and hot-tempered executive who had no experience in filmmaking but plenty of interest in reviving the fortunes of one of its smallest and most problematic subsidiaries.

"Everyone's other business is show business," said Al Ruddy, who would soon become the producer of *The Godfather.* "Charlie finally got the ultimate toy. He loved it. He was an amazing man."

Regardless of Bluhdorn's enthusiasm, however, Paramount was in jeopardy. Although the studio continued to produce the occasional solid hit in the sixties—*The Carpetbaggers* in 1964, *Barefoot in the Park* in 1967, and *The Odd Couple* and *Rosemary's Baby* in 1968—the successes were few and far between, and the studio contributed little to Gulf+Western's profits; in 1970, G+W made five times more money selling cigars than movies. In the halls of G+W, Bluhdorn pondered that his Leisure Time subsidiary might be more valuable as a vacant lot than as a creative enterprise; there was frequent talk of disbanding the company, disposing of its assets, and selling the studio on Melrose Avenue as prime commercial space.

Paramount's problems were also Hollywood's problems. By the 1960s, the motion picture industry had gone soft and stale. Hollywood had always shown an extraordinary resilience to economic downturns and evolving tastes, but in the 1960s, with few major hits and little energy for change in the business, moviegoing wasn't the regular treat it had once been. In 1963, all of the major Hollywood studios combined released only 142 pictures, and movie attendance had declined to 18 million per week—both the lowest figures since the invention of sound films. As one writer put, "Hollywood died a couple of years ago, and nearly all the media carried the obituary."

In spite of the industry's troubles, however, some of the Hollywood studios—including Paramount—still strove for innovation. While all movie studios bought original scripts or sought pretested ideas, some continued to develop new projects from scratch and provided financial backing to support them. Paramount was one of the few studios that nurtured an idea through formative stages by collaborating with authors, even if they weren't working on a screenplay. Paramount executive Peter Bart would guide a project through development over a period of years, supporting writers through the lean times with an advance or a payment for rewrite.

"What I've tended to do was, say, twice a year, take projects that really interested me and work on them with a writer alone, functioning basically as a producer does," Bart said. "The writer and I will try to figure out the construction of the story, figure out, most important, what story we want to tell."

In March 1967, *The Godfather* became one of those projects.

" 'Paramount,' an executive of the company admitted last week, 'has been actively searching out material, often before it is in completed form, and backing it with impressive money because this is the proper initial approach to moviemaking these days,'" reported the *New York Times* in March 1967. "'We've just bought two novels before publication we're convinced will be both bestsellers and fine films.'"

One of the projects, reported the *Times*, was *Mafia*, identified inaccurately by the *Times* as "a first novel," which Bart bought on the strength of 114 pages of manuscript and an outline. "*Mafia*," reported the *Times*, "deals sympathetically with an American Mafia leader and a singer–movie star he aids."

"'The 114 pages convinced us it would make a fine movie and the price we paid could go as high as six figures, depending on the book's sale,' said the executive" (later identified as Bart).

Developing film projects in this way may indeed be the "proper initial approach," as Bart put it, but it was still rare in Hollywood—or at least rarely successful.

Considering Paramount's precarious position, it remains a wonder that the studio would risk seed money at all on an original script, let alone an undeveloped story. Yet at Bart's direction, and with support from his boss Robert Evans, Paramount's vice president in charge of production, the studio produced two of its greatest successes—*Love Story* and *The Godfather*—by carefully nurturing projects until they were ready for filming.

So in 1967 and 1968, Paramount helped Puzo along, bringing him to the West Coast from time to time, buying development rights to the project, and keeping the author afloat with occasional checks to support his efforts.

"We had to give Puzo the bread to keep him alive while he was writing the book, with $5,000 here and $7,500 there," said Evans in 1970.

Despite Paramount's interest in *Mafia*, the book wasn't yet published. In 1968, after three years of work, Puzo finished *Mafia*, which was by then renamed *The Godfather*. Without waiting for his publisher's reaction to the finished work, he took his family on a celebratory trip to Europe with the last of his advance money and a wallet full of credit cards.

Puzo returned to excitement at his publisher's office. Not only was Putnam ready to produce a massive first printing, but Puzo's agent was negotiating a sale of paperback rights to Fawcett that would eventually net $410,000—at the time the largest paperback advance in publishing history.

The Godfather seemed on its way to publishing acclaim, bestseller lists, and a quick transfer to the screen, until two seemingly unrelated events occurred within three months of each other: The Mafia film *The Brotherhood* came to America's theaters and *The Godfather*-the-book burst on the scene.

"To Know Him Is to Love Him. To 'No' Him Is to Die," declared advertisements for *The Godfather* in book review sections of newspapers across the country. "It's here—the book you've been hearing about, the year's greatest reading experience! The most revealing novel ever written about the criminal underworld of the Mafia."

The ads for *The Godfather*, which began to appear in March 1969, carried a long list of rave

reviews, as well as the distinctive design that would soon become forever associated with the book and the film: the "puppet on a string" logo with *The Godfather* lettering dangling beneath it.

Superficially, *The Godfather* was a pulp novel about sex, violence, and crime in America's gangland underworld. But at its core were solid storytelling and vivid characters. More than just a superficial summer page-turner, in *The Godfather*, Puzo treated readers to an inside look at an imaginary world filled with real-life issues, corruption, and dynamic personalities.

The critics were wildly enthusiastic.

"As engrossing as it is terrifying, as frank and graphic as it is powerful—a book that explodes with the staccato gunfire it describes," said *Literary Guild* magazine.

"I'm not sure America is ready for this book . . . the plot itself is remarkable. It comes with the force of a mugger in a midnight alley."

From the publishing industry perspective, the book was solid gold. "This is the stuff of which best-sellers are made," crowed *Publishers Weekly.*

"Mr. Puzo's novel is a voyeur's dream, a skillful fantasy of violent personal power without consequences," said Roger Jellinek in his *New York Times* review. "The victims of the Corleone 'family' are hoods, or corrupt cops—nobody you or I would actually want to know. Just business, as Don Vito would say, not personal. You never glimpse regular people in the book, let alone meet them, so there is no opportunity to sympathize with anyone but the old patriarch, as he makes the world safe for his beloved 'family.'"

Readers, too, loved the book and bought it by the thousands. And then by the hundreds of thousands. And then by the millions.

Although Puzo had never had firsthand experience dealing with the Mafia, his extensive research brought him inside the real circles of crime—at least as reported in documents, articles, and FBI reports. Advertisements touted the book as "revealing" details about the inner workings of the Mafia—implying the *real* Mafia. (Those same claims would later haunt production of the movie, when Paramount was accused of slurring real-life Italian Americans and their culture.)

Such promises were the stuff of hugely popular fiction and the foundation for a potentially gold-plated motion picture script. And it all came to Paramount dirt cheap. In January 1969—three months before *The Godfather* was published—Paramount sewed up the movie rights to developing the film for $80,000. It would turn out to be Hollywood's find of the century.

"Paramount Pictures probably made the prime deal for a bestseller in modern film history," *Variety* wrote. "Par's deal is a bargain-basement literary buy."

For only a few thousand dollars, plus some care and feeding of a struggling author, Bart and Paramount found itself controlling the rights to a book that was not only a blockbuster, but potentially *the* blockbuster of the decade. The deal looked even better when compared to other big-dollar deals for books, such as the $1 million–plus rights that producer Mike Frankovich paid for Jacqueline Susann's *The Love Machine* or the $400,000 paid to Philip Roth for *Portnoy's Complaint.*

Looking back at Paramount's $80,000 deal for *The Godfather,* one can only wonder how Paramount purchased the project so cheaply. But the deal had actually been handled two years before, when Paramount offered Puzo a $12,500 payment for an option on the book, against $50,000 if the studio exercised the feature rights. His agency, William Morris, advised against the deal.

"That was like advising a guy underwater to take a deep breath," Puzo recalled. "I needed the cash and the $12,500 looked like Fort Knox. But I never held it against Paramount that they got *The Godfather* so cheap."

Six months after it was published, *The Godfather* had passed the 400,000 mark in hardcover sales—a huge success by any standard—and was selling between 15,000 and 20,000 copies a week. By mid-September, after twenty weeks as America's number-two bestseller, *The Godfather* passed Jacqueline Susann's *The Love Machine* to move into number-one position. At the time, *The Godfather* was the longest-ranked bestseller except for Philip Roth's *Portnoy's Complaint,* which at the same time was entrenched in the number-three position. Eventually, *The Godfather* would remain on the bestseller list for sixty-seven weeks.

Puzo was earning a fortune as *The Godfather*-the-book was on the rise. Meanwhile, Paramount's interest in producing *The Godfather*-the-film was rapidly waning. While having made only a minimal investment, Paramount faced a serious quandary. In one hand, the studio held *The Godfather* property and a potential audience of millions of readers who would want to see the film version of the book. In the other hand, it held *The Brotherhood*.

The Brotherhood, a rare Paramount venture into organized crime, was released in January 1969. Directed by Martin Ritt, starring Kirk Douglas in his middle-aged prime, and featuring a strong supporting cast, *The Brotherhood* had all the makings of a hit. *The Brotherhood* had only one problem: No one went to see it. For whatever reasons, *The Brotherhood* didn't interest audiences in 1969. It came to America's theaters and left with little fanfare, creating yet another financial loss and a bad feeling about taking on another picture about the Mob.

Of course, the success of Puzo's book was not lost on Paramount as it planned to launch *The Godfather* into production. With *The Godfather*, Paramount not only had a great story, but also a book that was already the king of bestsellers; with paperback sales, *The Godfather* became for several years the all-time bestselling novel in publishing history. To the rest of the motion picture industry, Paramount's ownership of *The Godfather* placed the studio in the most enviable position imaginable, unlike anything since David O. Selznick acquired *Gone With the Wind*.

But at Paramount, no one felt enthusiastic about the project. True, the studio's deal for *The Godfather*—the nation's number one bestseller—had cost virtually nothing. But sour memories of *The Brotherhood* lingered. That film's failure, combined with Paramount's precarious financial position, actually forced Paramount to shelve *The Godfather* in mid-1969, in spite of the book's position on the bestseller list.

In the film business, it is always the specialty subjects that ride cycles of popularity and disinterest. Like westerns, gangster pictures have moved in and out of vogue in Hollywood with the regularity of tides, often disappearing for years before suddenly returning in the form of a smash hit. Of course, the failure of a romantic comedy or turgid drama has never turned away the studios from those genres, but as far as gangster pictures were concerned, with the exception of the 1967 Warner Bros. hit *Bonnie and Clyde*, gangster pictures had all but disappeared from studio lineups late in the decade.

If *The Brotherhood* had simply been a bad film, Paramount might have had fewer concerns about *The Godfather*. But it was a strong picture. Reviews had ranged from good to excellent; the *New York Times* called it "a blunt, square, and sentimental Mafia movie." If *The Brotherhood* couldn't succeed with Kirk Douglas and solid reviews, could *The Godfather* have any better chance, even with its bestseller status?

"'Sicilian mobster films don't play' was distribution's bottom line," Evans recalled. "When you bat zero, don't make another sucker bet. *The Brotherhood*, a perfect example—no biz, not even a good first weekend."

The prospect that *The Godfather* could be the financial triumph and cultural phenomenon it became had all the potential of a ticket in a billion-dollar lottery. But slowly the odds began to improve, thanks to the interest of every studio in Hollywood—other than Paramount. Recognizing the book's continuing strong sales, virtually all of Paramount's competitors and several independent producers made offers to the studio for the property—some of them, one studio official admitted, were "staggering." It was those offers, buttressed considerably by the rock-solid position of the book on the bestseller list, that eventually switched the production light from red to green.

Evans and Bart brought the project off the shelf. Late in 1969, the studio announced that it would proceed with its plans to produce *The Godfather*. None of the key figures in the production were involved in the announcement, since hiring a producer, a writer, and a director was still months away.

Indeed, Paramount would produce *The Godfather*, but initially the studio's vision of the film would be Puzo's book in name only. To limit its risk, Paramount wanted only to capitalize on *The Godfather* name and create a quickie gangster film that would hook the millions of readers who had purchased the book.

The film, Evans said, would be made with a "few" changes: Use the name, to be sure, but make the film on a shoestring budget of $2 million—cheap even by 1970 standards; change the setting to contemporary—period films cost more to produce; shoot it on the back lot or use any city in America other than New York, because filming costs are sky high in Manhattan; bring in a producer who could ensure the project would remain cheap and hire a director who could do the same; and finally, bring in a finished product that ran only one hour and forty-five minutes.

Today, it is easy to conclude that Paramount was overly cautious in its early plans for *The Godfather*. But there was plenty of evidence in the late sixties that a bestselling book was no guarantee of box office success. *Portnoy's Complaint*, *The Love Machine*, and other literary translations to the screen did only modest business at the box office; some, like perennial bestseller *Catch-22*, bombed outright.

In the end, however, financial and creative restrictions did hamper the search for a producer. Through the fall of 1969 and the winter of 1970 as the hunt for a production team for *The Godfather* began, the only response Bart and Evans heard was "no." Established producers had little interest in a project they thought would romanticize the Mafia, and even less in shredding the story of the most popular book of the year to meet the studio's constraints about budget and length. Finally, Evans and Bart turned to an acquaintance who had developed a network of contacts in Hollywood and a reputation for production savvy—but little more than that.

Years after *The Godfather*, when Al Ruddy was asked why a producer with a single TV show and three unsuccessful pictures to his credit would be asked to produce the film that became one of the most acclaimed pictures ever made, he would have a simple answer: "They knew I could make it cheap."

In Ruddy, Evans and Bart found a street-smart producer of the classic Hollywood school—a friendly, straightshooting schemer with charm, horse sense, and a tremendous drive to succeed.

Ruddy's rise in the entertainment business demonstrated how a self-taught novice could jump into television and motion picture production with virtually no experience or background in the business. A graduate of the University of Southern California with a degree in architecture, Ruddy chose to work briefly in construction and then in technology consulting as he developed an interest in the entertainment business. He made slow but steady inroads into movies and television: He worked briefly at Warner Bros., and as part of a training program at Universal studios produced *Wild Seed*, which his friend Brian Hutton directed as his first feature film (Hutton would go on to direct two of Clint Eastwood's biggest hits: *Where Eagles Dare* and *Kelly's Heroes*). His big break came while he was working full time during the day and began developing television shows with a cowriter at night. Ruddy, with writing partner Bernie Fine, eventually created *Hogan's Heroes*, the half-hour comedy about Allied soldiers in a German POW camp that became one of CBS's biggest mid-sixties hits.

AL RUDDY, PRODUCER OF *THE GODFATHER*. "THEY KNEW I COULD MAKE IT CHEAP."

Practically overnight, Ruddy went from Hollywood novice to creator of a hit TV show, and he began to extend his reach into films.

"When the show became a smash, I got calls from every studio in town, asking for meetings about other ideas I had," Ruddy said. In one of those post-*Hogan* meetings, Ruddy was introduced to Robert Evans and Peter Bart, to whom he pitched several stories. They liked several of his ideas, including a story about motorcycle racers called *Little Fauss and Big Halsy* and a youth-oriented picture called *Making It.*

"The next thing I knew," Ruddy said, "I had an office on the lot."

Ruddy was able to attract Robert Redford to *Little Fauss and Big Halsy*, as well as Michael J. Pollard, who had risen quickly to film prominence on the strength of his supporting role in *Bonnie and Clyde*. Working on a shoestring budget and personally hustling free props and extras, Ruddy completed *Little Fauss and Big Halsy* $200,000 under budget.

Although the picture wasn't a success, the timing of its release was perfect in furthering Ruddy's career. He brought in his film with money to spare during a period that saw the production of the worst financial disasters in Paramount's history. While Ruddy was producing a picture starring Robert Redford for $2.5 million, the studio was hatching a flock of turkeys: *The Molly Maguires*, which cost $11 million; *Paint Your Wagon* ($20 million); and *Darling Lili* ($22 million); along with several other megabuck pictures that all lost money.

Making It wasn't any more successful than *Little Fauss and Big Halsy*, but it, too, was inexpensive and on budget. With only a TV series and three pictures on his resumé, Ruddy had already managed to establish a reputation for being an innovative Hollywood ideamaker, a well-heeled, well-connected producer. Polite, friendly, and easygoing, by 1970, at thirty-four years old, Ruddy had become a charming raconteur who could entertain for hours with industry gossip laced with bushels of profanity.

In spite of his connections and emerging reputation, it was still a shock when Evans and Paramount president Stanley Jaffe called and offered the opportunity to produce *The Godfather*.

"I almost dropped the phone," Ruddy said. "Needless to say, my answer was yes."

Before Ruddy could be signed to produce the picture, he had to face the dreaded Charlie Bluhdorn, who, in the words of Peter Bart, was often like "Hermann Göring on a bad day."

"I prepped for my meeting with Charlie for days, analyzing the book, taking notes about what to cut and what to use," Ruddy said. "I worked all weekend, went to Paramount and wrote out pages of notes about how I'd cut down the book. Then I went to New York ready to tell Bluhdorn how bright I was."

Ruddy flew to New York to meet with the chief executive at his office in the G+W Building at Columbus Circle. He waited in a conference room for the frenetic executive to arrive.

"Charlie bounced in yelling, '*Ruddy, vat do you vant to do with this movie?*' I looked at him and I figured if I start boring this guy with my ideas, I'd lose him.

"This is what got me the job: I looked at him and said, 'Charlie, I want to make an ice-blue terrifying movie about people you love.'"

'*Genius. Fantastic.*'

"Charlie bought it. He banged his fist on the fucking table and walked out."

Ruddy, the consummate storyteller, would recall several variations of this story over the years: He would describe his early vision of *The Godfather* with such sound bites as "The audience should feel they're looking through the keyhole into a dark world filled with violence and interesting people," or "A terrifying movie about people you like."

Regardless of his description, Ruddy had started down the right track. There was no question among any of the principals involved in the production of *The Godfather* that the picture would be about crime and criminals. What would distinguish it from the pack would be its ability to touch on other emotional elements as well.

"You had to walk both sides of the street on *The Godfather*," Ruddy said. "It would be a movie about a family and individual personalities. But there had to be a real terror to the piece, a real fear to this thing, because this was the world in which these people lived, no matter how you coated it over."

Ruddy had the germ of an idea that had the potential to transform *The Godfather* from a modest gangster flick into a very different kind of project.

On March 23, 1970, Paramount announced that Ruddy would produce *The Godfather* through his company, Alfran Productions. His first act as producer was to tamper with one of Hollywood's oldest laws: Don't hire the author to write the screenplay.

"The film business is biased against the novelist doing the script because most producers think the author can't let go of their original work," Ruddy explained. "But because the book was so popular, I thought it was important to keep Mario involved—to millions of readers, he was *The Godfather.*

"Regardless, I had to meet Puzo, so in New York we had lunch at the Plaza. He had a copy of the book with him. I told him that authors don't make it in Hollywood because they have too much ownership of their work. Mario took the book and threw it on the floor and said, 'I never have to read that book again. I can do the screenplay.' I said, 'OK, you're on.'"

Puzo was as surprised as anyone that he was hired for the production. Although he had set out to deliberately write a novel that would make him financially secure, he was remarkably shortsighted about a sale to Hollywood.

"At that time," Puzo said, "I was only thinking in terms of a novel. I had no notion of a motion picture when I began."

On April 14, the studio announced that Puzo had been hired to write the first draft of the screenplay for *The Godfather* for $100,000 and a percentage of the net profits—more than the studio had paid for the original rights to the material.

Puzo had never before written a screenplay. Although more familiar with the material than anyone else, his biggest job was stripping away the parts of the book that—while the essence of a first-class novel—would mean little on film.

By the spring of 1970, Puzo began his work on a project that the studio only grudgingly wanted, written by an author who had never created a screenplay, and coordinated by a producer who had never brought a successful picture to the screen. The studio would soon discover yet another problem: No one wanted to direct it.

In the fall of 1970, the early stages of preproduction proceeded for *The Godfather.* Puzo had been working on the script for six months, alternating time at the typewriter with trips home to Long Island.

Creating an acceptable script was, of course, critical to moving forward with production.

But the key issue remained: Who would direct the film? With Ruddy on board as producer and Puzo moving ahead on the screenplay, it was imperative to bring a director into the project as soon as possible.

"Soon" turned out to be more than five months after Puzo was assigned to write the script. Still budget-conscious while it searched for a known name to direct the film, the studio had not yet decided how closely the film would follow the book. By making decisions about the budget to keep costs low, Paramount made it all but impossible to attract a top-flight pilot to the project. Knowing that a hatchet job of such a popular book would launch a deluge of criticism at any director who attempted it, the most sought-after directors of the day avoided the assignment.

"Paramount felt comfortable thinking of *The Godfather* as a $2 to $3 million movie—but this was a cheap picture being made about the world's most popular book," Ruddy said. "Before I got there, they went to a number of big producer-directors like Richard Brooks and Fred Zinneman, who for a lot of reasons didn't want to do the picture. They thought it was just a big commercial project about gangsters and didn't see it as a film with redeeming social or any other value. They got me cheap because of the original idea of making a quickie shoot-'em-up, and they knew I could bring the picture in cheap."

Beyond that, Paramount could not interest a director in creating the film version of a book by many considered to be—in spite of its high-quality storytelling—nothing more than pulpy sex and violence. Yet despite its more sensational elements, the book clearly contained all the elements of a study of power and personality. Just as clearly, no one yet recognized its potential or was encouraged to view the project that way.

On the other hand, Paramount sought only the best directors—perhaps an early indication that the studio *did* take the project seriously. But time after time, Paramount was turned down. Besides Zinneman and Brooks, Costa-Gavras, the Greek director of *The Sleeping Car Murder* and *Z*, also declined the directing assignment. Even the legendary Otto Preminger, the director of such hard-edged thrillers as *Laura* and *Stalag 17*, was approached and turned down the directing job. Peter Yates, riding the crest of his early success after directing Steve McQueen at his supercool best in *Bullitt*, also refused *The Godfather*.

Finally, Ruddy offered the job to a young director who was just beginning to make his mark in Hollywood as a talented writer and director who wanted to steer clear of the moviemaking mainstream. His name was Francis Ford Coppola, and he, too, said no.

The Great Seducer

FOR FRANCIS Ford Coppola, 1970 should have
been the year he wrote and directed yet another
modest motion picture, working cozily in his
San Francisco studio as he built a reputation for creating
imaginative and insightful art films. But the benefits of success, and the penalties of failure, would forever conspire
to take him in other directions.

To think that Coppola, with only three major directing credits in his portfolio—none of them financial successes—would have even been a candidate to direct *The
Godfather,* let alone actually chosen, still seems far-fetched.

"WHAT DO YOU WANT
FOR YOUR BIRTHDAY,
FRANCIS?" A YOUNG
FILM EDITOR ASKED
FRANCIS FORD
COPPOLA IN 1975.

"ENLIGHTENMENT,"
ANSWERED COPPOLA.

But the journey that would lead to Coppola's selection to direct *The Godfather* transcends his ability as a director. The film as he envisioned it was the product of a childhood, a culture, a self-styled training in filmmaking, and an attitude about motion pictures that would result in *The Godfather* becoming that rarest commodity in filmmaking: An overwhelming financial success that is also a creative masterpiece.

Coppola was born in Detroit on April 7, 1939, where his father Carmine was conductor and arranger for the radio program *The Ford Sunday Evening Hour.* Through the first two decades of his son's life, Carmine served as a musician and conductor on Broadway and in traveling musical companies; the family was endlessly on the move to follow his assignments. Despite the nomadic existence, the Coppolas were a closely knit Italian-American family: Father Carmine, mother Italia, brothers August and Francis, and sister Talia—known as Tali. "We were constantly moving," Coppola said, "within a warm, loving, and active environment, replete with upheavals, shouting, and passion."

Carmine longed for greater success; even as the principal flutist in the NBC orchestra, under the direction of Arturo Toscanini, Carmine hoped for greater opportunities. The family was preoccupied by his quest.

"I lived in the household of a jealous man, and it changed me," said Coppola. "I said I'm never going to sit around waiting for my break to come. I said I'm going to make it, and I did."

The Coppola children grew up as Italian Americans with a strong infusion of Italiana. "We were taught," Coppola said, "that Italians had great culture: Like Fermi, Verdi, and so on." What wasn't explicitly taught was acquired. Coppola absorbed the Italian heritage of his parents and grandparents: The food, the clothes, the language, and the music—all the colors and textures of a heritage that would one day figure so prominently in his films.

When Coppola was nine years old, he was struck with polio. For a year he was confined to his room and the world of make-believe, watching television, and tinkering with gadgets and toys. His early fascination with contraptions both mechanical and electrical left him with a lifelong interest in high-tech toys and emerging technology, a passion that would mark the most notable film ventures of his career.

"I was lost in a fairy world. The popular kids are playing outside, not lost in introspection. But the lonely ugly duckling is inside, sick and sad and thinking."

Coppola's confinement produced a level of introspection uncommon in nine-year-olds. He wrote a note to his mother: "Dear Mommy, I want to be rich and famous. I'm so discouraged. I don't think it will come true."

"I always felt I had a lot of gifts," Coppola recalled, "but that my gifts were somehow not easily showable. I always felt I had a lot of stuff in my heart, but that I didn't have the skills or the obvious talents of kids who can play an in-

FRANCIS FORD COPPOLA ON THE LAKE TAHOE SET OF *THE GODFATHER PART II.* "HE WAS THE MOST EFFECTIVE FIGHTER AGAINST THE STUDIO HIERARCHY I'VE EVER SEEN," SAID FRED ROOS, CASTING DIRECTOR ON *THE GODFATHER* AND CO-PRODUCER OF *PART II* AND *III.* "HE DID NOT DO IT BY YELLING OR SCREAMING, BUT BY SHEER FORCE OF WILL."

strument, tap-dance, or draw. I always felt like I had a little vein of gold, and that if I could follow it further down I'd find a deposit of it."

Coppola's interest in things visual, plus a year's worth of nonstop viewing of television programs and movies on TV, inspired an early interest in film. He is said to have acquired his first 8 mm camera and made his own "professional" films at age ten. "I starred in them and I even made some money with them, as I would show them to the kids in the neighborhood."

This early interest was only a child's hobby; the seeds of a movie director were yet to be planted. Coppola's wife Eleanor would recall being told that he first thought about being a film director when he was fourteen. Coppola was in the family kitchen with his brother August and August's wife. As they danced scenes from a romantic movie, Francis looked through his fingers as if following the action through a viewfinder and pretending to operate a camera. About the same time, an even stronger desire for Coppola also began to take root: His lifelong interest in owning a studio.

"I wanted to be Captain Video," Coppola remembered. "I wanted to have a TV studio. I built out of wood the sound booms and the television cameras and a window, where you could 'play' the television."

Every creative fire needs a spark; for Coppola, it was the discovery of the films and the career of Sergei Eisenstein, the legendary Russian motion picture director. When Coppola was seventeen, he saw *October/Ten Days That Shook the World*, Eisenstein's masterful account of the Russian Revolution. "On Monday I was in the theater," he said, "and on Tuesday I wanted to be a film-maker."

After a youth filled with television, movies, music, and the arts, it is not surprising that Coppola would turn to filmmaking due to Eisenstein's influence. The master storyteller, who painted the screen with vivid, dynamic images, was the perfect catalyst for a teenager who wanted to communicate but had yet to identify a medium. Thanks to Eisenstein, Coppola discovered the film screen was his canvas and learned to understand how imagery, power, and personality could form his palette.

"I was dying to make a film," Coppola remembered. "So, following Eisenstein's example, I studied the theater and worked very hard. I could build and light a set. I wanted to know everything, from every aspect, to have the same breadth of knowledge as Eisenstein did, for that was how he began."

Coppola became a self-taught film theorist and a regular at screenings of classic films at New York's Museum of Modern Art. He enrolled as a theater arts major at Hofstra—where he met fellow student James Caan—and immediately began to display the creative drives that would mark his professional career and personal ambitions.

"I became a powerful and dynamic student," Coppola said of his time in theater arts at Hofstra. "The whole tone of my regime—and it was a regime—was to turn control of the theater arts department in the hands of the students. I controlled thousands of dollars and became the first student to direct major productions. It was a helluva three years. I sometimes think that was the most powerful period I had."

After Coppola graduated from Hofstra in 1960, he enrolled at UCLA in the university's theater arts department to earn a master's degree in fine arts. Coppola again began to expand his interest beyond his personal education. He founded the Cinema Workshop, and he bought his first 16 mm camera. While Coppola began to make an impression at UCLA, his work drew the interest of producer Roger Corman. Corman had justifiably earned the title of "king of the cheapie films" and was best known for horror, terror, and youth exploitation pictures. But he was also a success in an industry dominated by big studios and big budgets; it was Corman's films that regularly produced the highest financial return for each dollar spent. He became the youngest producer to ever have a major film retrospective of his work at the Museum of Modern Art, as well as the National Film Theater in London.

The publicity hype surrounding one Corman film that Coppola worked on without credit gives a sense of the tone of the producer's work: *"The Terror*—from the depths of an evil mind came a diabolical plan of torture . . . Inconceivable, unbelievable!"

In the early 1960s, Corman was also a magnet for future mainstream Hollywood talent. Among those who worked on Corman productions either in front of or behind the cameras were Jack Nicholson, Robert De Niro, Peter Fonda, Ellen Burstyn, Diane Ladd, Martin Scorsese, Haskell Wexler, and Coppola.

Corman used the film programs at UCLA and USC as minor-league training grounds for his own operation. When he asked Dorothy Arzner—a UCLA faculty member who had been one of the few women directors in Hollywood during the studios' golden age—for talented prospects, she suggested Coppola.

Coppola immersed himself in the Corman operation, just as he had at Hofstra and UCLA. "He had me doing everything," Coppola recalled of Corman. "I did a little bit of editing, a little bit of writing. I did some second-unit photography; on Roger's films, everyone got to do everything. It was really like an intensive course in the mechanics of putting a film together.

"I tried to impress Roger every way I could. I purposely worked nights, so that he would find me the next morning, bleary-eyed, working with the Moviola."

Coppola worked on an English-language version of a Russian science-fiction film, *Battle Beyond the Sun,* "getting about $200 for a million weeks of work." For the first time, he was paid to work in movies.

Coppola soon became heavily involved in Corman productions. He asked to serve as sound technician for *The Young Racers,* which was shot on location in Europe and Ireland. Coppola had no experience as a sound engineer; he learned the basics of the profession by reading the equipment manual.

Also on location in Ireland with Coppola on *The Young Racers* was Robert Towne. Later, in one of the most critical moments of *The Godfather,* Coppola and Towne would collaborate again.

While working on *The Young Racers*, Coppola convinced Corman to give him the time and start-up to make his own movie, *Dementia 13*. It was Coppola's first professional directing assignment, and he remembered it as "the only film I ever enjoyed working on," perhaps because on that project Coppola had nearly complete creative freedom, the guidance of a patient mentor, no studio pressure, and no fussy stars. (While working on *Dementia 13*, he got better acquainted with Eleanor Neil, a fellow graduate of UCLA. Their relationship blossomed, both in Europe and back in Los Angeles, and they were married in February 1963.)

Dementia 13 was a wild venture—even by Corman standards—and hardly a bellwether of Coppola's career to come. Said one critic: "The photography's better than the plot, the plot better than the dialogue, and the dialogue better than the recording. The latter is something very hard to distinguish, which may be a mercy." But it was a useful education for Coppola, as were the nudie films he also directed, which all provided useful filmmaking experience. At a time when the film business was slowly dying and opportunities to break into the business were rare, Coppola welcomed the opportunity to make films—any films.

For Coppola, his early years in the film business must have been an experience unrivaled in Hollywood history and an odd training ground indeed: On one hand, he was a graduate student, learning the theory and criticism of film; on the other, he was hip deep in the day-to-day reality of filmmaking at its most raw and enlightening. Coppola was one of the few film students who was making his own way outside of school. He was quickly developing the tools of his trade in a working setting, in collaboration with some of the busiest people in Hollywood.

Before he worked on *Dementia 13*, Coppola participated in a screenwriting competition; his script for *Pilma Pilma* won the Samuel Goldwyn Award in 1962; early in 1963, Seven Arts Productions, the company founded by producer and power broker Ray Stark, offered Coppola a job as a contract writer.

Coppola left UCLA shy only his thesis to earn his master's degree. In characteristic fashion, he would later complete his graduate work in a manner unlike any of his peers.

Coppola's first screenwriting job was the uncredited screen adaptation of the book *Reflections in a Golden Eye*. The film version of Carson McCullers's novel starred Marlon Brando and provided Coppola's first experience of seeing his words spoken by the man considered the world's greatest film actor.

While at Seven Arts, Coppola worked as writer, cowriter, or script polisher for more than a dozen projects. While he received few screen credits during this period, he gained credibility as a dramatist with a flair for writing and a deep interest in all aspects of film.

For a filmmaker who was self-described as "a writer who directs," it would have seemed an ideal start to a career in the Hollywood mainstream. By the end of his first year at Seven Arts, he was being paid $1,000 a week. Yet the money and the assignments weren't enough. By then, Coppola had seen a year's worth of work go largely uncredited or reach the screen under someone else's supervision. Coppola had become, by his own admission, "horny to direct a film."

Coppola's career began to advance more rapidly with other writing assignments. In 1965, he was assigned to work on *Is Paris Burning?*, the story of the liberation of Paris during World War II. Coppola became one of more than a dozen writers who eventually produced material for the film, which wound up a muddled flop. But his work on the project gave him the experience—or at least the perceived experience—to snare a far greater prize: The screenplay for the mammoth film biography of General George Patton.

Writing the script for *Patton* provided Coppola with the ideal opportunity to explore the character of a man who was as loved as he was reviled. Coppola painted a portrait of, as he described it, "a man out of touch with his time, a pathetic hero, a kind of Don Quixote." In Patton's case, however, it was a Don Quixote with an army, so Coppola created an extraordinary leader of men, a confounding character of intriguing complexity, conflicts, and magnetism whom audiences would admire one moment and despise the next. In *Patton*, Coppola created the character of a general whose motivations for slapping a shell-shocked soldier were as easy to understand as were his emotions when he kissed a battle-weary veteran in the field. With the swirl of the World War II Allied conquest as a framework, Coppola deftly explored both the glory and the frustrations that power can provide.

The script for *Patton*, like many other milestones in Coppola's career, was perfectly timed; bad investments left him in desperate need of cash, and the $50,000 paycheck would, for a time, keep him and his many interests afloat. Four years later, when *Patton* was released, the film would be a motivating factor in Paramount's decision to ask Coppola to direct *The Godfather*.

By the time he completed his six-month assignment on *Patton*, Coppola was twenty-seven years old. Long before the era when music video directors scarcely old enough to vote were crossing over to mainstream films, Coppola was already being perceived as a young legend—a talented writer whose abilities were only beginning to be tested.

In his free time while assigned to *Is Paris Burning?*, Coppola wrote a screenplay based on *You're a Big Boy Now*, a novel by British author David Benedictus. Coppola revised the story of an English shoe salesman by moving the story to New York and transforming it into a young man's adventures while working at the New York Public Library.

Coppola piqued the interest of several studios with his innovative rite-of-passage film. However, because he wrote the script while working on *Is Paris Burning?*, Seven Arts took control, claiming ownership of the project because it had been completed while he was working for the company. With *You're a Big Boy Now*, Coppola would get his first big-league directing assignment, but not without the frustrations. Coppola directed *You're a Big Boy Now* for Seven Arts for $8,000 for his combined writing and directing efforts—far less than the $1,500 to $2,000 a week that he could earn for straight screenwriting. His experience with the project would provide yet another reason why he wanted to work outside of control by the Hollywood mainstream. Coppola craved freedom.

Shot mostly on location in New York, *You're a Big Boy Now* starred Peter Kastner and Elizabeth Hartman, with Geraldine Page in a strong supporting role. The film received mixed reviews at the time—it is better regarded now—but it was nevertheless a substantial career booster for

Coppola. Geraldine Page was nominated for an Academy Award for Best Supporting Actress, and the film was presented at the 1967 Cannes Film Festival as the only American entry. Both achievements helped establish Coppola as a proven director who was ready for other larger assignments.

Further, the film provided an educational bonus for its young director. When Coppola left UCLA, he was shy only a completed film to fulfill the requirements of his thesis. For most students, that meant creating a short subject or a documentary. For Coppola, it could mean only a full-length feature—and one submitted to the Cannes Film Festival, no less. *You're a Big Boy Now* was submitted and accepted for completion of Coppola's MFA—perhaps the only time an actual Hollywood production has been submitted for a master's program degree and no doubt the only thesis that had ever represented America at the Cannes Film Festival.

Coppola set up his own office and began to write a screenplay which, seven years later, would become *The Conversation*. His new notoriety attracted Warner Bros., and the studio asked him to direct the screen version of the Broadway musical *Finian's Rainbow*. Knowing that he needed to prove himself within the mainstream before he could develop the influence to work independently, Coppola took on the assignment, even though he had little enthusiasm for directing a musical.

Work on *Finian's Rainbow* provided a vivid indication of the business and creative climate in the motion picture industry. When production began, the picture was the only project in production on the Warner Bros. lot. It was a desolate time in Hollywood, but there were indicators of changes to come; while Francis Ford Coppola was directing his big-budget production, a student named George Lucas arrived at the studio.

Coppola struggled mightily with the outdated civil rights themes from the 1947 theatrical production, and the picture was a flop (one critic called it "embarrassingly dated"). For Coppola, it was not the failure of the film that concerned him, but rather the feelings of enthusiasm at the studio as executives assured him the picture would be a hit.

Still, *Finian's Rainbow* was not without its benefits for Coppola. The film connected Coppola and Lucas in a productive relationship that would lead to the creation of the director's dream enterprise outside of Los Angeles. Both Coppola and Lucas were interested in working outside the traditional studio mill. Finding in Lucas a kindred spirit—and a fledgling filmmaker with ambitions similar to those of his mentor—provided Coppola with another reason to break away from the Hollywood mainstream. Seven Arts' successful acquisition of *You're a Big Boy Now*, distrust of studio opinions that developed with *Finian's Rainbow*, and the uninspiring life in the studios provided Coppola with more than enough reasons to seek a creative base outside of Hollywood's influence. Beyond that, he still dreamed of creating his own production center and training ground.

At twenty-nine, Coppola was still young, even by Hollywood standards. He knew he would have to make his move soon, or he might never make it.

"People said take the money and then make a personal film, but when they get the money, they're too terrified to do it," Coppola said later. "If you're not prepared to risk some money when you're young, you'll never risk it."

Even then, Coppola's career was marked by a roller coaster of conflicts. Coppola was obsessed by success and, even more, by having his talents recognized. Yet he constantly sought refuge from the tumult of his success; he spoke often of "retiring" from the mainstream and directing less lucrative but more creatively invigorating projects. As early as 1968, on the eve of the release of *Finian's Rainbow,* he said, "What I'm thinking of doing, quite honestly, is splitting. I'm thinking of pulling out and making other kinds of films. Cheaper films. Films I can make in 16 mm. No one knows whether there's a viable market for that kind of film yet. All I know is that I'm tired. It's not just opening-night jitters. I've been thinking about this now for six months. I'm tired. I never knew that so many people wished you failure. I didn't realize. Let somebody else have the headaches."

As a first step in his plan for independence, Coppola directed *The Rain People,* his first opportunity to create a major film from his own original screenplay. The film, about a young woman who runs away from her husband, was shot in a roundabout voyage across America that took advantage of sights and locations along the way as the backdrop for the ever-evolving film. Coppola found locations to shoot in eighteen states, often changing his script to accommodate local events or scenery. Included in the cast were James Caan, his former Hofstra classmate, and Robert Duvall, both of whom were already becoming members of the loosely knit Coppola family of actors and crew.

The Rain People would add a near-mythic quality to Coppola's growing reputation. While not financially successful, the film was noted by critics, who also appreciated the odd nomadic odyssey that led to its creation. "*The Rain People* is not only a lovely film to watch," said one film writer, "but it is also one of the deepest studies about responsibility and independence, about the moral implications and the ambiguities of love and sin, ever brought to the screen." The motion picture, along with the stories of the freewheeling anti-Hollywood wanderings that created it, helped build Coppola's reputation by creating an almost romantic perception of the young filmmaker's abilities.

The independence of the road made Coppola more anxious than ever to sever his Hollywood ties. After the filming of *The Rain People* was completed, he traveled with his wife and Lucas to visit independent filmmaker John Korty at his home and studio in Stinson Beach, a town on the Northern California coast. Korty had been making films since he was sixteen and had established an independent artistic life for himself primarily by creating low-budget features from his own screenplays and employing largely unknown actors. In Korty, Coppola saw that the independent filmmaker's life was possible. "He said, 'If you can do it, I can do it,'" Korty recalled.

For all of Coppola's disinterest in Hollywood, he was becoming well known around town. He had been showcased in the *Los Angeles Times* and *Variety* as an up-and-comer. *Time* magazine, in its review of *The Rain People,* would describe the film as the product of "the vast, undisciplined energy of its writer, producer, and director—all of whom happen to be Francis Coppola."

Coppola himself had become the subject of a motion picture. George Lucas, who had worked on the production crew of *The Rain People,* also shot a documentary about the making of the film. Lucas's two-hour documentary, titled *Filmmaker,* was his first full-length production. He described the documentary as "a personal viewpoint on the daily tensions and stress occurring during a film production."

Coppola decided the time had finally come to move on. "I don't dislike LA, but I figure at this age I should find out where I'm going," Coppola said in 1968. "I'm from New York, but I wouldn't want to live there. Los Angeles, I like it—but I want to do what Jack Warner and Harry Warner did forty years ago. Find the place."

For Coppola, "the place" turned out to be San Francisco. Taking a lead from Korty, Coppola settled on Northern California for his base of operations. His reputation helped him secure financial support from Warner Bros., which provided a loan for start-up funds and agreed to consider his first projects.

After a lifetime of dreaming, Coppola would finally get his wish. At the height of flower power, Haight-Ashbury, and the "Make Love Not War" period in San Francisco, Coppola moved north. On November 19, 1969, his new company was officially incorporated under the name American Zoetrope. In Greek, *Zoetrope* means roughly "movement of life"; it was also the name of the first handheld viewer that could create the illusion of motion from still images.

"The main objective of this company," said a press release from the new organization, "will be to undertake film production in several different areas by collaborating with the most gifted and talented young people, using the most contemporary and sophisticated equipment available."

American Zoetrope moved into a former warehouse at 827 Folsom Street. With a load of new equipment and an eager young staff, it soon became a haven for Coppola's utopian vision of how filmmaking could be accomplished outside the traditional Hollywood realm.

The creative euphoria at American Zoetrope would last scarcely nine months. Production was erratic, freely offered equipment soon disappeared, and planning was nonexistent.

Coppola had hoped that the first film produced by his own studio would be *The Conversation,* a brooding message film about surveillance bugging and personal privacy. Instead, Coppola agreed to Lucas's idea of expanding *THX-1138,* a student project Lucas had created at USC, into a full-fledged feature. Starring Robert Duvall and Donald Pleasance, *THX-1138* was shot in the under-construction tunnels of San Francisco's Bay Area Rapid Transit system. The picture has since become a cult classic, due largely to its connections to Lucas, *Star Wars,* and other more prominent projects. However, at the time, Warner Bros. considered the film a creative and financial disaster, and the film received only modest theatrical release. More significantly, *THX-1138* nearly sank American Zoetrope. Warner Bros. canceled its involvement in other Zoetrope projects, simultaneously reminding Coppola that its financial backing of some $600,000 for the new company was a loan that had to be repaid.

For Coppola, it was the hardest lesson of his career. "My enthusiasm and my imagination had simply gone beyond any financial logic," admitted Coppola.

Coppola quickly regrouped to tackle his financial obligations. The company branched out into television commercials and educational films, and Coppola continued to try to develop feature material for motion pictures. (Perhaps most notably, Coppola did not try to raise cash by selling stock or relinquishing any level of creative control, even if that meant potentially forfeiting the company.) All of his efforts merely postponed confrontation with a problem that could only be solved by closing the company or acquiring a massive infusion of cash. By the fall of 1970, Coppola was in debt and desperate.

Then, as with *Patton* four years before, a lucrative offer came to Coppola just at the point when he needed it the most. It was a job he had already turned down: directing *The Godfather*.

Coppola had first been offered the job in the spring of 1970, soon after Al Ruddy was named producer. To any other ambitious young director, the job would have been considered a career-making plum. But philosophically, it represented a step backward to Coppola, a return to a typical Hollywood project under tight studio control. Nevertheless, given his worrisome financial position, Coppola had agreed to consider the project and started to read the book. He struggled through the first fifty pages and gave up, calling it "cheap and sensational."

"I got to the part about the singer supposedly modeled on Frank Sinatra and the girl Sonny Corleone liked so much because her vagina was enormous—remember that stuff in the book? Anyway, I said, 'My God, what *is* this—*The Carpetbaggers* (a leaden melodrama starring George Peppard as a Howard Hughes–type tyrant)?' So I stopped reading it and said, 'Forget it.'"

After the money problems at Zoetrope had worsened considerably and the company's fate literally hung in the balance, Coppola was again asked to direct the picture. He wisely reconsidered, and this time, he read the entire book.

"I got into what the book is really about—the story of the family, this father and his sons, and questions of power and succession—and I thought it was a terrific story, if you could cut out all the other stuff. I decided it could be not only a successful movie but also a good movie. I wanted to concentrate on the central theme, and that's what I tried to do."

Coppola, like Ruddy, was already thinking about building up the key plot and character elements and "eliminating everything else." Certainly *The Godfather* could turn into an Italian-American version of *The Carpetbaggers* if the producer and director wanted to bring out the more turgid elements of the book, but fortunately both Ruddy and Coppola had different ideas in mind.

Peter Bart was already familiar with Coppola and his work when problems finding a director for *The Godfather* began to crop up.

He also understood the director's strengths and limitations. "I thought Francis Ford Coppola was perfect for *The Godfather*, and I fought like hell to get him," Bart said. "Objections? Little details like he had never done a successful picture, he wasn't disciplined enough, and he wasn't experienced enough."

Nevertheless, Bart asked Ruddy to speak to Coppola.

"'The guy's Italian, a great writer, and he's an interesting director,' Bart told me," Ruddy said. "I went to San Francisco, I met Coppola, and it was obvious he was perfect for this project."

With money problems looming—and persuasive arguments from Lucas that the job could be his only hope to save American Zoetrope—Coppola agreed to meet with the Paramount brass. But regardless of his financial problems, if he was going to accept another studio project, he was going to do it *his* way.

"I told Francis, 'I think you're right for the job, but you've got to talk to Bob Evans and Stanley Jaffe,'" Ruddy said. "Francis came down from San Francisco, and when I met him at the airport, I gave him all the lines they were going to want to hear: We'll do the picture at a price, we'll finish it on budget, everything I can think of.

"I was in for the shock of my life. We went to the meeting. I thought Francis was a quiet artiste. Ten minutes into the meeting he was up on the fucking table, giving one of the great sales jobs of all time for the film as *he* saw it. That was the first time I had ever seen the Francis the world got to know—a bigger-than-life character. They couldn't believe what they were hearing—it was phenomenal."

Evans agreed with Ruddy. Long after *The Godfather*, Evans described Coppola as Hollywood's "greatest seducer." In terms of persuasive power, Evans said of Coppola, "he makes Billy Graham look like Don Knotts."

Coppola had outlined a vision for *The Godfather* that was nothing like *The Brotherhood*, not even like most of Puzo's book—not by a long shot. He had no interest in the budget; he was focused entirely on character, on the family, and the exploration of power and the human condition.

"Even though Francis was the underdog in *The Godfather*, he took a strong position right away," said Fred Roos, the casting director of *The Godfather* who would become coproducer of both *The Godfather* sequels. "Francis said, 'I can't do this as a Harold Robbins–type of movie.' He was the most effective fighter against the studio hierarchy I've ever seen. He did not do it by yelling or screaming, but by sheer force of will. He would go into a kind of performance, pace around the room and convince people by the logic of his arguments."

Evans, Bart, and Ruddy quickly realized that in Coppola they would be working with a very different kind of director. True, he did not have a financially successful picture under his belt, but at least he was available and willing to take the job, a distinct improvement on some of his colleagues. Moreover, his background developing screenplays could provide invaluable aid to Puzo as a cowriter. And, as the studio chiefs discovered in their first meeting with him, the director had a clear vision for the project. Even better, he came cheap.

"Sure he was a renegade, and not particularly bankable," said Ruddy. "It didn't matter. I was looking for a guy I could trust who would direct the fucking picture for $125,000."

Perhaps most important, Coppola was an Italian American. Evans was glad to have a director with the strong knowledge of Italian heritage that only a lifetime of cultural immersion can create. Coppola, Evans said, "knew the way these men in *The Godfather* ate their food, kissed each other, talked. He knew the grit." And Coppola's Italian name could also serve as a useful insurance policy. Paramount had already heard the first rumblings that *The Godfather* might be disturbed by the Italian-American organizations protesting the portrayal of Italian Americans in a stereotypical fashion. The rumblings would soon become full-scale shouting; to have an Italian-American director on the project, the studio believed, could help ease some of the pressure.

In 1970, it would have been too convenient to assess Coppola as an out-of-step filmmaker with limited success. He was, in fact, a creative tornado waiting for the proper conditions to be unleashed, a director intrigued by power and the complex frailties of the human personality—especially the powerful male personality. He was a self-described "writer who directs," a filmmaker who spoke in absolutes about the most important elements of his work. He was at once two distinct professionals: Coppola the director, caught up in the excitement of the filmmaking process, in command of a small army of artisans working toward a common goal; and Coppola the writer, often at his creative best while hidden away in a hotel room with a typewriter or sitting alone editing manuscripts in a North Beach coffeehouse, the solitary creative spirit in complete control of his work. But most of all, at thirty-one, Coppola had already become a cinematic visionary, a director who understood the power of the medium as a communications tool with a formidable global reach. *The Godfather*, even though a product of mainstream Hollywood, would give him an opportunity to test that power.

On September 27, 1970, Paramount publicly confirmed the rumors that had for days been floating around Hollywood: Coppola was signed to direct *The Godfather*. The picture, the studio reported, would be the studio's major Christmas release for 1971.

Coppola signed for $125,000 and 6 percent of the gross rentals. Given the limited ticket sales expected by the studio, the percentage probably wouldn't add up to much, or so everyone thought. But there was at least one party no doubt eager for Coppola to succeed. As long as he owed Warner Bros. $600,000, that studio would remain intensely interested in the potential success of *The Godfather*.

To kick off the production, on September 29 Evans held a press conference at Paramount's Beverly Hills offices to introduce Ruddy, Puzo, and Coppola to the entertainment media. *Variety* called it "that old *Gone With the Wind* buildup," but Paramount had to do nothing to encourage reporters to attend; by the time of the press conference, *The Godfather* had sold more than one million copies in hardback and six million in paperback. *The Godfather* was also beginning to move up the bestseller lists throughout Europe with overseas editions in every major language. Clearly, worldwide interest in *The Godfather* and the film version of the book was cresting.

The press conference would also provide the first public hints of how the creation of the film would proceed. Ruddy and Coppola had prevailed: *The Godfather* would be no shoot-'em-up in a modern setting; the studio had given the go-ahead to produce the film as a high-quality production.

"*The Godfather*," Evans said, "will be our big picture of 1971."

Although Evans had to acknowledge that the budget had not been established, he did confirm that the film would be shot on location—a concession to Coppola, a stickler for realism throughout the production. The film would be shot in Sicily, Las Vegas, Los Angeles, and New York. The statement also helped Ruddy gracefully back away from interviews earlier in the month, in which he said *The Godfather* would not be filmed in New York because of the high costs and "because the International Alliance of Theatrical Stage Employees and the Teamsters are much tougher to deal with in New York than they are in other cities." However, Evans quickly added that if New York proved to be "too inconvenient or uneconomical," then a midwestern city with similar old Italian sections would be used.

The press conference then turned to questions about casting, at which time Evans gave a statement that would create instant problems for everyone involved in casting. "We're going to cast real faces, people who are not names; nor are we going to have Hollywood Italians," he said.

"We would rather go with unknowns than big-name actors and actresses," said Evans. "We want it to be authentic. The characters will have to look like Italians and Italian Americans, so there is a good chance we will use Italian performers."

Evans should have regretted his statement about "unknowns" the moment he said it. He and Ruddy both reinforced the comment in other interviews, when they were quoted as saying *The Godfather* would be cast with "unknowns." What both of them meant to say—and later emphasized as often as they could—was *relatively unknown faces among established actors.* But by then it was too late. Paramount was already receiving inquiries from virtually every actor in Hollywood about *The Godfather*, and the statement about unknowns created an inundation of applicants unlike anything that had hit Hollywood since David O. Selznick hunted for his Scarlett O'Hara.

The film was scheduled to go before the cameras on January 2, 1971—a delay from the previously promised start time of November. Even with such a delay, a January start date would provide Coppola with only three months to handle all aspects of preproduction: auditions, casting, rewrites with Puzo, hiring key off-camera personnel, and most important, developing an overall tone for the production.

The press conference ended with smiles all around and an excitement in the air now that the nation's top-selling book was being prepared for the screen. The honeymoon would last only nine days.

Bob Evans's press conference demonstrated that Paramount was willing to go the extra mile with *The Godfather*. Gone and forgotten was the idea for a quickie gangster flick; in its place the project as Ruddy and Coppola envisioned it: an in-depth feature about the powerful personalities in a crime family photographed in a period setting. The studio and Gulf+Western revised their thinking about money and added substantially to the budget. What had been a $2 to $3 million project was revised at the time of the press conference to at least $4 million and would eventually go before the cameras with a $6 million cap.

"By then we knew that the studio wanted to do more than just 'ride the title' of the book," Ruddy said. "Once Charlie Bluhdorn bought into the fact the movie could be done on a tight budget, he agreed to let us do it in period and on location."

But which location? Bob Evans had promised New York for the location shooting, if New York was viable. But no one was convinced that a tightly budgeted film could be shot in New York—except Coppola. The director was convinced that to capture a visual sense of New York, he would have to shoot *in* New York—yet another of his absolute declarations. "Once I saw the picture as being shot in New York," Coppola said, "I couldn't get it out of my head."

As Ruddy considered other locations and sent location scouts to St. Louis and Kansas City, Coppola shared his frustrations about shooting on location with entertainment reporters on October 8, barely a week after the press conference.

"As far as I'm concerned, the odds favor New York," said Coppola. "I very much want to do it in New York. The atmosphere is strictly New York, and since I want to do the film as a period piece, if possible—say the 1940s—any other locale is going to make it more difficult to capture the special flavor of New York."

Replied Ruddy, "We're watching the pennies, and we think we can make the picture for much less in other locations and not sacrifice quality."

Then, as now, several other cities in America and Canada could substitute for New York City in the 1940s. As major urban centers began to recognize the financial benefits of accommodating a motion picture production, many municipalities—such as Toronto, Montreal, Kansas City, and St. Louis—proved that they could provide a safer and cheaper "New York" than New York could. But there was a much more important reason besides "watching the pennies" for considering cities other than New York. Al Ruddy knew that the issue might not be whether or not it was too expensive to shoot in New York—rather, it was whether it would be possible to shoot in New York at all.

Even with the start of production still months away, Paramount was already getting pressure from Italian Americans. The New York–based Italian-American Civil Rights League joined the fight against *The Godfather*. The League—as it was known to its membership—was organized and well equipped with a war chest of cash that it would use to back its efforts to stop the film. Concurrently, there were rumblings that other influential organizations with less-than-legal interests might also move against the production.

"I always wanted to shoot the picture in New York," Ruddy said, "but we all knew what the problems were. It was never really a budget issue.

"The League had a big rally at Madison Square Garden to raise money for the sole purpose of stopping the film," he explained. "It was very obvious that there was a strong possibility, if no accommodation could be made, we were not going to shoot in New York. If certain people don't want you in New York, you're not going to get a truck loaded. So I insisted that we scout St. Louis and Kansas City as a backup.

"We were going to shoot in the really rotten part of Kansas City that does look a lot like old New York. But we all wanted to shoot in New York from a very selfish standpoint—New York is still New York City. But we knew what the problems were. Whether these problems could be solved without compromising the material was something else. So we had to have an alternate."

Just how serious the rift might become between Italian Americans and the production was vividly demonstrated during an accidental confrontation between author Puzo and the world's most famous entertainer. When Ruddy, Puzo, and others went to a birthday party dinner at Hollywood's famous nightspot, Chasen's, they found they had been seated within viewing distance of Frank Sinatra, presumed by most to be the model for the Johnny Fontane character in *The Godfather.*

Puzo and Sinatra had never met. A friend of Puzo's who has mercifully remained anonymous through the years insisted on introducing the author to Sinatra, but Ruddy and others diplomatically suggested otherwise.

"I said, 'Are you brain-dead? Frank will go nuts,'" recalled Ruddy. "We all thought it had been settled, so I went to another table to say hello to some friends. Then all hell broke loose."

While Ruddy visited another table, he heard a disturbance. He turned back to his table to see Puzo's chair empty and the author standing in front of Sinatra, having been dragged into an introduction by his friend.

"The next thing I know a fight almost broke out," Ruddy said. "Sinatra was yelling and shouting, and my friends were holding Mario."

Puzo, who knew the encounter was not Sinatra's fault, stood and took the abuse.

"What hurt was that here he was, a Northern Italian, threatening me, a Southern Italian, with physical violence," Puzo said. "This was roughly equivalent to Einstein pulling a knife on Al Capone."

Ultimately, the decision to proceed with New York location shooting was made without resolving the protests—that problem would linger until the cast and crew were settled in New York, and the issue of Italian Americans and *The Godfather* became a national news story. Coppola would not budge on the issue of shooting in New York—a stance he would have to defend again and again over the course of the production.

A Portrait of Treachery

WHILE **RUDDY** grappled with the New York issue, Coppola began to involve himself in writing the script with Puzo. As Coppola started work on *The Godfather*, Puzo, by his own admission, had alternated between "writing and goofing off" for nearly five months. But in spite of his somewhat undisciplined style, Puzo had accomplished a great deal: By the time Coppola arrived, he had made most of the necessary cuts—trimming a 446-page novel down to something closer to a 150-page script—and dealt with principal structural work. It was time for writer and director to begin work together.

"One of the biggest attractions of Coppola, aside from the fact that he was a fine director and understood production problems, was that he was a very gifted writer," Ruddy recounted. "It became easy at that point to have the director—and not another writer—work with Puzo. Not that Mario Puzo's screenplay needed that much help; it was, basically, very good, but it wasn't in perfect screenplay form. When Francis was hired for the film he went to work immediately with Mario and really slicked it up, brought it up to shooting form. But many of the bones, the architecture of the script, had been settled by Mario before they had worked together."

In the case of Puzo and Coppola, working together really meant working separately and revising each other's work. In a creative relationship that remains a rare occurrence in Hollywood film writing, Coppola and Puzo did not physically write together or work face-to-face with a typewriter between them. The director worked in San Francisco, the author in Los Angeles or New York; when each of them finished a draft, he would send it to the other for revision.

"He rewrote one half and I rewrote the second half," Puzo said. "Then we traded and rewrote each other. I suggested we work together. Francis looked me right in the eye and said no. That's when I knew he was really a director."

Somehow, the pair of writers managed to work well together—in spite of Puzo's lack of experience, Coppola's tendency to swallow up projects, the physical distance between them, and the vast amount of material to consider. In part, the process succeeded because Coppola had plenty of sympathy for writers. "The position of the screenwriter is an absurd, ridiculous one," Coppola said. "He earns a great deal of money but has no say whatsoever about the film, unless he is one of the more famous screenwriters."

Coppola recognized the critical role of the writer—especially on a project with the delicate balance of elements such as in *The Godfather:* "When people go to see a movie, 80 percent of the effect it has on them was preconceived and precalculated by the writer." With a screen adaptation of a book as popular as *The Godfather,* that balance was especially important.

The principal philosophical difference that emerged in writing the script was Puzo's interest in retaining and condensing many elements from his book while Coppola wanted to amplify specific plot lines—in particular the issues of power, character, culture, and family. Beyond the exhaustive detail and plot development in the book, Coppola saw the true heart of the story: "I saw important ideas in this book that had to do with dynasty and power."

Coppola focused on developing those ideas. "It was my intention to make this an authentic piece of film about gangsters who were Italian, how they lived, how they behaved, the way they treated their families, celebrated their rituals."

Puzo, too, encouraged development of the undercurrent of personality that was more important in the movie than the book. "*The Godfather* is about more than the Mafia; it's about conflicts in American culture. It's about a powerful man who builds a dynasty through crime—but he wants his son to be a senator, a governor. It's about the very nature of power. What it does to you. Who survives. I think it's a tragedy."

Coppola took Puzo's basic structure and beefed up the elements that were particularly important to his vision for the project. That process would continue long after shooting of the film was under way.

The writers' work on the character of Vito Corleone was the most important of their collaboration. Although other characters would consume most of the screen time—Vito is severely wounded only forty-five minutes into the film and spends most of the picture recovering—the power and influence he suggests needed to pervade the entire picture. In the book, Vito Corleone is occasionally animated and often chatty; in the script, he suggests power rather than displaying it—an ideal canvas for an actor willing to underplay his role, yet capable of stealing every scene.

By the time the script was in shape for readings and auditions, most of the principal elements that viewers know from the film were in place, and nearly all of the cuts from the book were complete. What remained was a plotline that focused almost exclusively on the world of Vito Corleone and the emergence of his youngest son Michael as a central figure. Jettisoning most of the other major plotlines from the book, the film would center on the incidents that pulled the Don's youngest son into the family business in spite of his best efforts to avoid it, his maturing into the role as an underworld leader, and the eventual transfer of power from father to son.

Gone entirely were other elements that had dominated the book, including several characters and plotlines: Nino Valenti, Johnny Fontane's self-destructive childhood friend; Dr. Jules Segal, who identified Johnny's throat problem; all of Johnny's professional growth as an actor and producer; and virtually all of the events that occurred in Las Vegas. Johnny's character, so prominent in the book, was scaled back to four brief scenes.

Much of the Godfather himself was gone, too—his longer conversations, his beliefs about "destiny," and many of the incidents that characterized him as a master planner who saw his family's future in terms of events that might occur in decades to come.

Given Coppola's interest in Italian culture and the sharpened focus of the script as a study of power and crime, a surprising number of "Italian touches" were also eliminated. There are no references in the script to *Omerta* (the Sicilian Mafia code of silence), which is the foundation of crime families. Also cut were the often-used phrases *moustache pete* (to describe the older dons) or *90 calibre* (a term for a powerful person).

The word *pezzonovante* is used in the book to describe powerful men in politics, government, and religion ("the men who pull the strings"). It is perhaps the most important term in the book, because the Don has spent his life trying to build his family business outside the influence of the *pezzonovante*. This notion is just as important in the film (when the Don wishes that Michael could become "Senator Corleone or Governor Corleone," Michael brushes it off saying he would just be "another *pezzonovante*"). But use of the word *pezzonovante* is cut to only two references, its meaning only sketchily implied.

Also remaining in the script, and ultimately the final film, are an intriguing mix of Italian phrases that as expressed in the film needed no translation: After Sonny, the Don's eldest son, learns that Paulie Gatto, his father's bodyguard, has turned traitor, Sonny describes him as "that stronz" ("stronzo" translates roughly to "turd"). Likewise, translation is not needed when, during a fight between Connie Corleone, the youngest Corleone offspring, and Carlo, her slimy husband, they scream "vaffancul" at each other. ("Vaffanculo" means "go fuck yourself.")

A host of subtle touches—both Mafia and otherwise—were included, such as the memorable line, "Luca Brasi sleeps with the fishes"; the scene in which Calo, Michael's Italian bodyguard, mimicks his partner Fabrizio in an almost operatic style; and Clemenza, the Don's loyal *caporegime* (lieutenant), jovially giving cooking lessons to Michael, because "you might have to cook for twenty guys someday." Also added were large doses of Italian culture and flavor that only a writer with a director's eye could include: The rich detail of Connie's wedding reception; the cinematic orchestration of family meals; and the delicate nuance of old-world courtship between Michael and his Sicilian bride-to-be Apollonia, complete with formal family introductions and chaperons. (When Michael goes for a walk with Apollonia, she intentionally trips to give him a reason to touch her as chaperons look on and giggle.)

Much of the profanity from the book was deleted—both isolated swearing and colorful conversation—no doubt a concession to avoid additional problems with the ratings board of the Motion Picture Association of America, which would have plenty to critique, given the film's sex and violence.

Some script changes were made in the book's plot, but were then shifted back because of budget considerations. In the script, for instance, when Michael goes to meet with Virgil Sollozzo (the drug dealer connected to the Barzini family who orchestrates the attempted murder of Vito Corleone) and McCluskey (a corrupt police captain and Sollozzo's bodyguard), he is to wait for them in Times Square under the famous Camel Cigarettes' sign, for decades an actual New York advertising landmark that puffed real smoke. Because the sign would cost too much to create, the script was rewritten to have Michael wait in front of Jack Dempsey's, a brightly lit old-time sports bar—just as originally written in the book.

Some key dialogue was not written until after production began, including one of the film's most famous lines. In the original script, there is a scene early in the film in which Clemenza takes bodyguard traitor Paulie Gatto for a ride, and then has him killed. Clemenza's wife, with no knowledge of his imminent deed, asks him to pick up some cannoli. After Paulie is killed, Clemenza is simply to tell hit man Rocco Lampone to "leave the gun." In the rewrite, however, a line was added so Clemenza tells Rocco, "Leave the gun. Take the cannoli." With Paulie's body slumped over the steering wheel, his eyes staring lifelessly, it is a chilling cinematic moment.

Although the rewrite dispensed with some of Puzo's original dialogue, some elements of the book were just too popular to resist and made the final cut: the stand-up sex scene with Sonny and Lucy Mancini; the scene of movie studio chief Jack Woltz discovering a horse's head in his bed after refusing the Don's request to cast Johnny Fontane in a movie; even the campy historical reference to the horse's name, Khartoum, and the poetic justice of the horse's death by decapitation. (Charles Gordon, the British commander of Khartoum in the Sudan in 1885, was captured by Sudanese Muslims and beheaded, his head carried on a pole through the streets.)

Once production began, Coppola took some of the material cowritten with Puzo and transformed it into scenes more appropriate for the screen. For example, when Michael meets Apollonia's father, the original script called for him to speak entirely in Italian with subtitles. In the film, Michael speaks in English and Fabrizio translates sentence-by-sentence, which establishes a back-and-forth cadence for the scene, punctuated by the surprise conclusion:

MICHAEL

I am a stranger in this country. . . .

FABRIZIO

(*Translates*)

MICHAEL

And I meant no disrespect to you, or your daughter. . . .

FABRIZIO

(*Translates*)

MICHAEL

I'm an American—hiding in Sicily. . . .

FABRIZIO

(*Translates*)

MICHAEL

My name is Michael Corleone. . . .

FABRIZIO

(*Translates*)

MICHAEL

There are people who'd pay a lot of money for that information. . . .

FABRIZIO

(*Translates*)

MICHAEL

(*After Vitelli nods*)

But then your daughter would lose a father . . .

FABRIZIO

(*Translates*)

MICHAEL

. . . instead of gaining a husband.

Other elements that emerged from Coppola's involvement in writing the script came to light because he was a writer with years of training in cinema. In a vivid example of his expertise, after studio chief Jack Woltz wakes screaming when he discovers the horse's head in his bed, the scene fades back to an image of the Don in New York the next day. Coppola leaves unsaid how Luca Brasi, the Corleone family's chief killer, bypassed or bribed dozens of guards and stable-hands, decapitated a horse, entered a heavily guarded mansion, inserted the head and blood into a bed, and escaped undetected. Those details are for a book, not a film. The scene as filmed offers a far more powerful image and stands as a testament to the dramatic and frightening reach of Vito Corleone.

Another overlooked detail in the script is how Michael is able to return from his Sicilian exile after murdering Virgil Sollozzo and Captain McCluskey. In the book, readers learn that a convicted killer from another crime family implicates himself for the additional murders in exchange for financial support from the Corleones for his wife and children. In the film, the method of his return is left unexplained except in vague references, such as lawyer Tom Hagen's comment to the Don, "We're starting to work to bring him back now."

Coppola also clearly recognized that some events in the book could be condensed and juxtaposed to create masterful film moments. In the closing pages of the book, only enemy dons Barzini and Tattaglia are killed before Carlo, Connie's husband and a traitor within the family, is garroted (strangled with a cord or wire). In the film, Coppola created a grand massacre of casino owner Moe Greene and the heads of the opposing Mafia families—all in a bloody montage of violence set against the somber, religious scenes of Michael's godson being baptized.

"There was only one thing wrong, and that was that there was something missing at the end of the screenplay," Puzo recalled about a key moment in his work with Coppola. "I said to

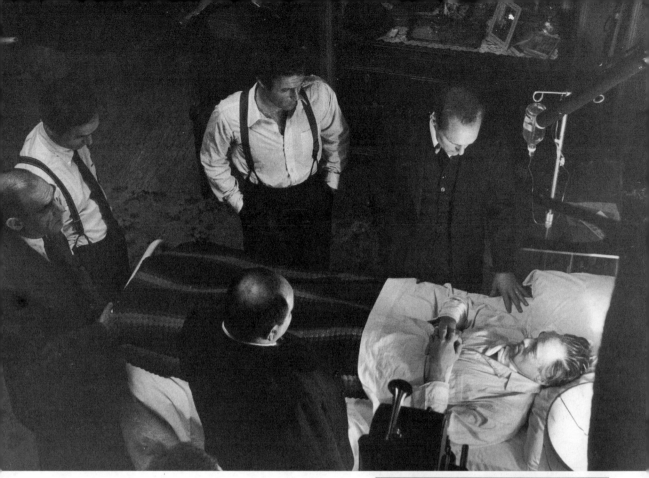

Francis, 'Look, there's something missing; I don't know what it is.' He took one look at it, and he said he knew what it was. He said, 'We'll have them all killed while the baby is being christened.' Oddly enough, that technique wouldn't have worked in the novel. It would have been absolutely awful in a novel. On film it was terrific. Francis saw that in two seconds."

As *The Godfather* production began, several major scenes that would be featured in the final film were still not included in the script—the reconciliation scene between Michael and his fiancée Kay Adams being one of them. If the "Third Draft" script dated March 29—the first scheduled day of production—had been filmed as written, viewers would not have seen Kay and Michael reunite. Instead, Kay and their children would have suddenly appeared in a scene when they take Michael to the airport for his trip to Las Vegas.

In the March 29 script there is, incredibly, no scene of the Don's death, a sequence that in the final film would become one of the movie's finest. Instead, in one scene, Michael and his father are talking about the future; in the next, the action cuts to a funeral procession. This funeral scene, which features Tom Hagen and Michael Corleone, was changed extensively. On the other hand, the March 29 script would have explained a key plot question that emerged in the final film: Why, in one scene, does Michael tell Tom that "he's out" of the family business (to protect him from intrigues to come), when only a few scenes later, he returns to become more involved than ever in the family's treacherous dealings? As the March 29 script explained, Tom was "brought back in" because the Don died too soon. Without his father, Michael needed to rely on Hagen more than ever before as he planned the violent episodes to come.

MICHAEL

Christ, Tom; I needed more time with him. I really needed him.

TOM

Did he give you his politicians?

MICHAEL

Not all . . . I needed another four months and I would have had them all.

(He looks at Tom)

I guess you've figured it all out?

TOM

How will they come at you?

MICHAEL

I know now.

(Hagen looks at him; understands)

While some scenes not written by the time production began would evolve quickly, the most important scene of *The Godfather*—the final meeting of the film between the Don and Michael—was still months from being written to Coppola's satisfaction. It was not until the film was midway through the production, with Marlon Brando's time commitment on the set only hours away from completion, that the critical scene that laced the plot together would finally be created.

A difference worth noting between the script and the final film had nothing to do with the dialogue or plot, but rather the written order of many key scenes. The "Third Draft" script was structured much like the book: The *results* of events are known before the events themselves are described. For example, in the book, Hagen receives a phone call from a hysterical Jack Woltz before Puzo reveals the scene with the horse's head. Correspondingly, in the March 29 script, Johnny sends flowers to the Don for helping him get a part in the Woltz production. That scene is followed by those in Hollywood, in which Woltz wakes up to the horse's head.

In both the book and the March 29 script, several other key scenes early in the film are structured in flashback—among others, the murders of Luca Brasi and Sonny Corleone. As a plot-fortifying book device, the flashback technique works well; in the motion picture, too much flashback sacrifices drama and impact. Fortunately, even though the script was initially conceived in flashback format, that approach was jettisoned during editing in favor of a linear plotline.

Structure aside, the most important issue that would emerge in the script was actually the fortuitous result of condensing hundreds of incidents from the book into the storyline that would pervade the film: the brutal, cold-blooded characterization of a Mafia family as embodied in the Corleones. In a film, a single line or brief conversation, backed by powerful performances and astute direction, can often tell a more powerful story than pages of exposition in a book. In the conversion of *The Godfather* story from book to script, plot points were honed to razor edges to characterize the fear, treachery, and endless suspicion that is the hallmark of life in the criminal underworld. To be sure, the script also brought out favorable points about family, loyalty, honor, and respect. But the scenes that coldly and calmly characterized the dark side of the Mafia offered the most important commentary on society and the human condition.

Page after page of the heartless scheming of the Mafia family that Puzo worked so hard to develop in his book were actually amplified considerably by distilling them into a few well-chosen scenes. For example, in one moment, Sonny kindly asks Paulie about his health. In the next, he methodically turns to Clemenza and orders the bodyguard's murder. Similarly, Clemenza jokes with Paulie about "extermination" only moments before he has him killed. Likewise, the script addresses the almost unconscious acceptance of a life of crime, as when Carlo sells out his own brother-in-law Sonny, only later to be ordered murdered by Michael; or when Michael lies to Kay about Carlo's execution; or in countless scenes when the family plots murders with the justification that they are "business, not personal."

Then there is perhaps the coldest line of all: At the Don's funeral, when Michael learns that Corleone family *caporegime* Sal Tessio is the family traitor who has arranged the attempt on Michael's life, Hagen leans to Michael and says, "I always thought it would have been Clemenza—not Tessio." It is a potent enough statement about criminal disloyalty to show that Tessio, part of the Corleone family for a quarter of a century, would without a moment's hesitation arrange the death of a young man he had known since birth. But more chilling is the fact that

Michael and Hagen are so immersed in a life of criminal deception that Tessio's sellout did not surprise either of them. Scenes such as these are a far more powerful indictment of the cold brutality of Mafia life than showing a hundred executions.

Later, amid a groundswell of acclaim, when *The Godfather* was also criticized for "glorifying" the Mafia, the critics would point to the captivating personalities behind the gunshots and strangulations as evidence of antihero worship. None of these critics would recognize that in the film's exploration of the Corleone family, behind the laughter, the bonding, and the dynamic personalities, every human encounter in *The Godfather* was a portrait of treachery.

The broad cinematic commentary about life in the Mafia would provide an ideal framework for the emergence of the character of Michael Corleone, who slowly and subtly evolves from a young idealist into a mature figure of enormous power and charisma. This transformation played an integral role in the book, but by stripping away hundreds of pages of material, Puzo and Coppola focused most of their attention on the growth of Michael's character: The idealistic college student and war hero, the protective son, the murderer, the scarred widower, and finally the unfeeling head of the crime family.

Ultimately, that transition between a character in a script and a personality on film takes place on the set, in a close collaboration between a director and an actor who create a thorough understanding of both character and motivation. What Coppola did not accomplish in his development of characters while cowriting with Puzo, he would later cultivate during the production of the film. The most critical juncture in the production of any great motion picture is the moment when the director takes over the script, and in one final rewrite, in rehearsal, or in front of the cameras, transforms the project into a personal vision of characters, intentions, and actions. Coppola would soon have that opportunity to create his own unique vision for the production.

The "M"
Word

WHILE **COPPOLA** and Puzo were busy rewriting each other's work, Al Ruddy faced the daily pressure of protests directed at *The Godfather* production. On many days in late 1970, Ruddy and his production team would arrive at their offices on the Paramount lot to find a gathering of protestors waiting for them on Melrose Avenue outside the gates. The protestors carried signs that read: INDIANS FOR INDIAN ROLES. MEXICANS FOR MEXICAN ROLES. ITALIANS FOR ITALIAN ROLES.

Another sign read:

MORE

ADVANTAGES

FOR

ITALIAN

ACTORS

Apparently concerns among Italians about "The 'M' Word" didn't extend to actors.

The conflict between Italian Americans and *The Godfather* began in Los Angeles with two seemingly contradictory problems: First, some protestors were worried that the movie would perpetuate stereotypes about Italians in the criminal underworld. At the same time, others were just as concerned that if Italians were going to be depicted in *The Godfather*, Italians should be cast to play them.

Echoing in Ruddy's ears was Evans's promise: *We are going to cast unknowns.*

Vincent Barbi, one of the protestors outside the Paramount gates, was described by a reporter as looking like he could play a "Mafioso type, tough as Italian salami."

"All along," Barbi complained, "they said they were going to cast unknown Italian actors, right? Some of us had three, four interviews. Then they said we weren't the right types to play one of the dons."

One Italian actor in Los Angeles pointed out an ironic conflict: The very protest about Italian stereotypes was making it increasingly difficult for Italian actors to get jobs.

"It's getting tougher all the time for us Italian heavies to get work," Joe Tornatore said. "If I go for an interview to work on *The FBI*, they say I can't work because the Anti-Defamation League says it casts aspersions on Italian Americans."

With a patient sigh, Ruddy said, "The casting is still going on. We'll be using the actors most talented and capable for the roles, and a large percentage will be Italians."

It was only a hint of the casting difficulties to come.

Although well intentioned, the critics ignored the fact that the cast was comprised primarily of Italians. As far as smaller roles were concerned, the problem with Italian-American actors in Hollywood was due to their location, not their ethnicity; most of the casting for brief speaking roles, bits, and extras was handled in New York. While the cast was large indeed, most appearances were brief—extras or bits had only a couple of lines.

Much larger concerns were coming. Obstacles were also popping up on the East Coast. Ruddy faced a real and growing problem—not from actors who wanted roles, but rather from one of the most influential new organizations in America.

• • •

It could certainly be said, long after Joe Colombo died in 1978 from complications from wounds he received in a gangland hit attempt seven years earlier, that his involvement in the Italian-American Civil Rights League was merely a smoke-screen to shield prying law enforcement eyes from his other more notorious activities. However, whether or not Colombo was indeed the head of a Mafia crime family could not discredit the beneficial community work conducted by the League, which in 1970 was the fastest growing Italian-American organization in America.

Politician Paul O'Dwyer, obviously not of Italian heritage himself, nevertheless spoke for many in the League in a speech at the 1970 United Day, a Colombo-sponsored program. "The Italians are damned well burnt up, and I think they're right. There are millions of Italians in the United States and just a dozen or two dozen or a hundred hoods, and yet these hoods have become symbolic of Italian Americans. This kind of thing affects their children."

On the other hand, New York State Senator John Marchi of Staten Island separated the feelings of honest Italian Americans from the actions of government officials against the real Mafia. Calling the League's actions a "futile exercise in ethnic paranoia," Marchi was a staunch supporter of federal and state investigations of the criminal underworld, no matter what nationality. "Lice are lice whether they bear Italian names or Russian or whatever origin," he said.

Criminal organizations have been a hallmark of every wave of immigrants to the United States. Gangs dominated by specific ethnic groups ran many of the criminal activities in New York as the city became a major metropolis—first the Irish in the late 1800s, then Eastern European Jews after the turn of the century. But throughout most of the twentieth century, organized crime families operated primarily by Italians had taken the spotlight and held it, particularly in New York City. Names with Italian origins like Gambino, Profaci, and Costello dominated FBI and congressional investigations, and terms like "Mafia" and "La Cosa Nostra" became near-generic terms to describe organized crime in America.

Honest Italian Americans defended their heritage, pressured government and entertainment to stop using these terms, and worked to defuse public characterizations of mobsters as olive-skinned and black-haired residents of Brooklyn. The League and other organizations marshaled political pressure, meeting with political leadership, sending letters of protest, and picketing the FBI and other government agencies.

The pressure worked.

The Justice Department under John Mitchell ordered that all official department documents would not use the words "Mafia" or "La Cosa Nostra." Some newspapers followed suit and stopped using the terms as well. The *New York Post* replaced these terms with "Mob" or "underworld." Likewise, by the late 1960s, most movies and television shows used "the Mob" or "the Syndicate." Even such hard-edged thrillers as Peter Yates's *Bullitt,* one of the toughest and most compelling police thrillers of the decade, described the bad guys as being from "the Organization." However, Paramount's own *The Brotherhood* did use the term "Mafia," a decision not lost on the Italian-American Civil Rights League.

In spite of successes for Italian-American organizations, *The Godfather* could have been the breaking point; clearly, the project was about the Mafia, and virtually all of the principal characters were Italian. Paramount may not have been sure the film would be a hit, but every Italian-American organization in America knew that at the very least, a film made from the most popular book of the day would raise the issue of Italians and the Mafia to a new level.

In July 1970, the League held a rally in Madison Square Garden that raised nearly $600,000 to stop production of *The Godfather.* Members sent form letters supplied by the League to every elected official in the federal government—and copies were sent to Paramount. In part, the letter read,

A book like *The Godfather* leaves one with the sickening feeling that a great deal of effort and labor to eliminate a false image concerning Americans of Italian descent and also an ethnic connotation to organized crime has been wasted. There are so many careers and biographies that could be made into constructive and intelligent movies, such as the life of Enrico Fermi, the great scientist; Mother Cabrini; Colonel Ceslona, a hero of the Civil War; Garibaldi, the great Italian who unified Italy; William Paca, a signer of the Declaration of Independence; Guglielmo Marconi; and many, many others.

The studio was told to expect a boycott of the film, protests, formal complaints to government civil rights organizations, and official requests that no civic aid be provided to the production. The League wasn't the only Italian-American organization involved in the protest; joining the protest were the Sons of Italy; Union National, a service club composed of business and professional leaders of Italian extraction; and several other groups. But it was the League, which claimed more than 40,000 members and signed another 500 to 700 a week, that was the force to be reckoned with.

Of course, not all of the protests brought to bear on *The Godfather* production and Gulf+ Western were as respectful as form letters and polite requests. Ruddy was threatened in anonymous phone calls; so were Evans, his then-wife actress Ali MacGraw, and their newborn son. Before *The Godfather* went into production, the Gulf+Western headquarters was evacuated twice because of bomb threats. While none of these threats were ever traced to the League or any other organization, they left behind a thick atmosphere of tension that couldn't help but permeate all of the production's dealings with Italian-American organizations.

Then, in the midst of this chaos, Ruddy was informed by the Los Angeles Police Department that he and his staff were being followed.

"One night my secretary was followed all the way home," Ruddy said. "Once she got inside the house she called the police, but the car that had been tailing her disappeared. I was notified by the LAPD that guys were trailing me. So every night, we'd swap cars around, so no one knew who was going where."

Ruddy, a self-admitted car nut, gave his secretary his Dual-Ghia, a low-slung sports car. The next morning she discovered the window had been shot out.

"I knew there were some problems," Ruddy said.

He became so concerned that he put a .45 automatic in his desk. "I was actually afraid that I might have to use this gun," he said. "I didn't know whether the calls were coming from the Mafia or not. But the calls threatened my life."

Ruddy's reference to the Mafia brought out a disturbing dilemma: It was becoming increasingly difficult to distinguish between the legitimate interests of Italian Americans and the criminal elements that were also involved in trying to hamper the film. However, even some protests known to be sponsored by the League turned ugly. The League had picketed a New York borough newspaper, the *Staten Island Advance*, which continued to use the term "Mafia" in stories (one crime reporter speculated that the picketing was really aimed at persuading the paper to stop printing stories about alleged Mafia members living on Staten Island).

In February 1971, violence broke out. An *Advance* delivery truck was burned and two drivers beaten. "They were forced to lie face down in the back of the truck," says Richard E. Diamond, the paper's associate publisher. "The hoodlums set the papers in the truck aflame with lighter fluid, closed the back of the truck, and said if the two [drivers] tried to get out, they'd shoot them."

Fortunately, the assailants left, and the drivers escaped. Police escorted *Advance* trucks until picketing ended in March.

The focal point of the League's public stance was Colombo. Hardly the aging Mafia don, at forty-eight, Colombo, who described himself as a "real estate salesman from Bensonhurst," was a well-liked, public man about town—a less flashy version of another underworld figure of a generation to come, John Gotti.

In addition to his legitimate goals for the League, Colombo had plenty of legal problems to contend with. He was under indictment on charges of controlling a $10 million-a-year gambling syndicate, income-tax evasion, and larceny and conspiracy in a $700,000 diamond robbery in 1968. Assistant District Attorney John Fine alleged that Colombo directed "criminal usury operations and loan-sharking in New York" and "gambling operations" in parts of New York and Nassau County.

Hardly a secretive figure, Colombo often publicly discussed allegations of his underworld connections and described the accusation that he is a Mafia chief as "ridiculous."

"Mafia, what is the Mafia?" he asked a reporter. "There is not a Mafia. Am I head of a family? Yes, my wife and four sons and a daughter. That's my family." When asked why he didn't sue his accusers, Colombo replied, "What's the use? They'll subpoena all my friends, and I don't want to put them through that."

Ironically, the very nature of the actions against *The Godfather* production—legitimate or otherwise—did nothing but give the impression that there *was* a Mafia behind the attacks against the production. The actions of thousands of honest people in the League would be tainted by the actions of a few real criminals.

Regardless of who was responsible, in early 1971 it became clear that preproduction for *The Godfather* was beginning to suffer. In February 1971, negotiations for a location site in Manhasset, Long Island, for the Corleone family compound stalled when local residents began to reject the production team and make impossible demands. The Manhasset location soon fell through, and another suitable site had to be found on Staten Island. The cost of the alteration: $100,000.

The Manhasset incident was quite real, but even the suggestion of other problems was nightmarish; if problems with location scouting could occur so easily, could more serious issues be far behind? What would happen to *The Godfather* production if trucks stopped rolling, food quit arriving, union members started striking? The quite legitimate concerns about the characterization of Italians on-screen could have easily translated into production delays or the forced cancellation of *The Godfather* project—especially in New York. By February, Ruddy must have longed for the relative calm of St. Louis or Kansas City.

Time was beginning to run out. The production, originally slated to begin shooting in November, had been postponed until January when the director's search was delayed. It had been changed again to accommodate casting and the move to New York; yet another delay would begin to cause significant dents in the budget.

Ruddy was caught in a rapidly closing vise with two powerful jaws—on one side, the legions of Italian Americans who were protesting the film; on the other, the uncertain specter of the Mafia and its yet-to-be-revealed potential role in subverting the production. The vise was beginning to tighten.

I**N LATE** 1970, even while Coppola and Puzo continued their revisions, casting for *The Godfather* had to begin. First on the list was casting Don Vito Corleone—a part that was, without question, one of the most desirable roles in Hollywood history. Coppola and Ruddy knew that the success of the film would be determined largely by the credibility of the actor chosen to play the Godfather. The part called for a rare blend of talent: An actor who could convey a quiet authority with an undercurrent of power and violence, who could portray a loving father with the command of a president and the humility of a peasant, and who could also project an unforgettable presence on the screen.

Every actor in Hollywood wanted to play the Don.

Hundreds of performers who were middle-aged—or thought they could play a middle-aged role—put in bids for the part. TV stars David Janssen and Vince Edwards, as well as 1930s singing heartthrob Rudy Vallee, all asked for auditions. Anthony Quinn's name was tossed around briefly at Paramount, and some rumors floated through the studio that Frank Sinatra wanted to play the Don—an interesting prospect, given Sinatra's reaction to Puzo at Chasen's. The FBI reported from its wiretaps of organized crime figures that among real Mafia dons, the preferred choice to play Vito Corleone was Ernest Borgnine.

Trial lawyer Melvin Belli, who had appeared on television in the 1960s, pestered Ruddy regularly for an audition. Belli told James Bacon, the film columnist for the *Los Angeles Herald Examiner*, that when he went to Paramount to meet with Ruddy, the producer's secretary asked if she could leave him a pass at the studio gate. Belli told her, "I drive a pink Rolls Royce. I don't even need a pass at Fort Knox." The same story was told to a reporter at the *Los Angeles Times*, except he was told that Belli drove a Cadillac.

San Francisco Chronicle columnist Herb Caen told Bacon that in San Francisco he spotted a billboard painted in large letters: ALIOTO IS THE GODFATHER. Some critics of the San Francisco mayor would later say that the reference had nothing to do with casting a movie.

Then there were the vast legions of amateur actors who thought they'd be perfect to play a Mafia don.

"We got hundreds of letters from pizza makers, Italian waiters, and just about anyone who had ever eaten spaghetti," Ruddy said.

Ruddy and the studio executives had already begun to consider actors before Coppola came to the production, but they had little success—"the studio simply wasn't sure who it wanted," Ruddy remembered. Late in 1970, after Coppola arrived, two veteran actors were being seriously considered: John Marley, who would be nominated for an Academy Award in 1971 for his supporting role as Ali MacGraw's father in Paramount's *Love Story*; and Richard Conte, a versatile leading man and character actor who had starred as gangsters and tough guys in more than forty films. Both were judged unsuitable for the lead role, but were later hired for other pivotal parts in the film.

The need for a formidable acting talent was obvious, but the right actor was not. To bring Vito Corleone to the screen with the impact that the part required would demand the "world's greatest movie actor to pull it off," Ruddy said.

Coppola, as always, had strong feelings about who he wanted for the role.

"It became obvious," said Coppola, "that the role had to go to an actor with incontestable magnetism, an actor who could create a stir simply by walking into a room."

Among studio executives at Paramount, no actor generated much enthusiasm for the part of Vito Corleone, but Coppola, Puzo, and Ruddy knew who they wanted—the actor was known simultaneously as "the greatest actor in motion pictures" and "the biggest pain-in-the-ass in Hollywood."

Paramount may have been befuddled about casting *The Godfather*, but long before the book became a movie project, Mario Puzo knew who he wanted to play Vito Corleone. He had only one man in mind to play the Don on screen: Marlon Brando.

Through more than twenty years in motion pictures, Brando had developed a screen personality of superstar proportions that was admired by fans and served as the model for an entire generation of American actors. But in the late 1960s, Brando had developed another kind of reputation—as unbankable. Brando's films had achieved only marginal success throughout the 1960s, and the actor had earned—he claimed unfairly—a reputation for off-screen antics, conflicts with directors, and on-set fussing that delayed production and produced only average performances.

While Brando often commented that his declining screen popularity should really be attributed to the films themselves—and rightfully so—he failed to note that his recent roles were odd at best. His most recent picture at that point was *Burn!*, a sweaty and unsuccessful political drama set in the Caribbean. While to Brando, some of his characters may have seemed like interesting acting experiments, to producers they were quirky, offbeat characterizations that didn't capitalize on his screen appeal or ticket-selling power.

"To mention the name Brando in those days did not exactly elicit enthusiasm with anyone," said Bart. "He had just finished *Burn!*, and he was popularly known in Hollywood as 'burned-out Brando.'"

Paramount executives may also have remembered the financial sting of Brando's first and only directing effort, *One-Eyed Jacks*, which was produced for the studio in 1961—a project whose cost and production time doubled over the course of the filming. "Naturally, this didn't please Paramount," Brando observed.

But there remained no question that, in the proper vehicle, Brando was in command of screen acting skills beyond anyone else in the business. Even more important, Brando had an unparalleled screen presence that endowed him with a star appeal that remained robust—bankable or not.

Through a mutual friend, Puzo had sent Brando the book, but the actor wasn't interested.

"I had never played an Italian before," Brando recalled, "and I didn't think I could do it successfully."

However, Alice Marshak, Brando's assistant, read the book, thought otherwise, and encouraged the actor to consider the part if it was available. Puzo kept after him as well.

When Puzo and Coppola began to work together on *The Godfather*, Coppola quickly came to agree with the author's opinion about Brando as a candidate for the lead. Once Coppola bought the idea of Brando as the Don, he was, as with all important ideas that struck him, possessed to the point that no other alternative was possible—or, as Ruddy put it, "when Francis wants something, the guy will think of fifty fucking angles to get it."

Coppola wanted Brando. He halfheartedly tested dozens of other veteran actors, but none of them had the performing firepower he sought and knew Brando could deliver.

"The Don is in the movie no more than 30 percent of the time," explained Ruddy. "But we had to have an actor with the power and mystique to permeate those scenes in which he didn't appear. Brando has that blunt power."

Everyone on *The Godfather* production team was enthusiastic about Brando as the Don—except the executives who had to make the decision to hire him. In spite of a succession of pleas from Coppola and Ruddy, the studio stood firm.

Paramount President Stanley Jaffe put it bluntly when, after repeated attempts, Coppola again asked for Brando. Coppola remembers Jaffe saying, "As long as I'm president of the studio, Marlon Brando will not be in this picture, and I will no longer allow you to discuss it." (Coppola would also remember another version of the Jaffe declaration: "If Marlon Brando is in this picture, it will gross $5 million less than if no one is in it.")

Coppola did continue to discuss it. Evans squeezed five minutes out of Jaffe for one final Coppola attempt.

"I got up, as if I were about to defend a man condemned to death, and I listed the reasons that made Brando irreplaceable, one of them being that he had an aura about him when he was surrounded by other actors, similar to that of Don Corleone with his people," Coppola said.

Jaffe, finally worn down, agreed to at least consider Brando, with three conditions that he hoped would be deal killers: First, Brando would appear in the movie for a salary far below the actor's usual minimum; second, he would take personal financial responsibility for any production delays he caused; and third, he would consent to a screen test—a previously unheard-of concession for the actor.

Coppola agreed. So, like Dorothy pursuing the witch's broomstick in *The Wizard of Oz*, Coppola went in search of a screen test of Brando.

While Coppola was pleading Brando's case, the actor was blissfully ignorant of the high-level studio dramatics that were determining the future of what would become the most famous role of his career. Although he knew that Puzo and Coppola wanted him to play the Don (he had told the director that he thought the part was "delicious"), he had not been formally approached.

But Brando *had* considered how he might develop the role. He had played with the character in front of the mirror and tinkered with his hair and face to see how he might look as a Mafia chieftain twenty years his senior.

And although Brando didn't yet know it, he had a remarkably similar view of the Don as that of Coppola and Puzo.

"I saw him as a man of substance, tradition, dignity, refinement, a man of unerring instinct who just happened to live in a violent world and who had to protect himself and his family in this environment," Brando said. "I saw him as a decent person regardless of what he had to do, as a man who believed in family values and was shaped by events just like the rest of us."

So by the time Coppola showed up at Brando's house, the actor was ready.

Coppola was, by his own admission, "scared shitless" of Brando and afraid that the actor would reject the idea of a screen test. Coppola arrived at Brando's house with a portable video-tape recorder and found the actor wearing a kimono (the "inevitable kimono," a friend once called it), with his hair tied back in a queue—hardly the outfit to project the image of a Mafia don. In one version of the story, Coppola and a friend came in silently, "like ninjas," and set up and shot the test without comment. In another version, Coppola and Brando discussed the role first; instead of calling it a screen test, Coppola suggested they "try out some things" on tape.

Coppola, Brando, and others tell countless versions of the story of the famous screen test. The exact story may be lost to the ages, but one thing is certain: In all versions of the story, Brando slowly transformed himself from a vigorous forty-seven-year-old actor into the aging don. He blackened his hair—supposedly with shoe polish—dabbed on a small moustache, and pushed Kleenex into his lower cheeks ("I want to look like a bulldog," Brando said). He slumped slightly, half-closed his eyes, and puffed on a small Italian cigar that Coppola had brought along, all without saying a word—just mumbling quietly. Suddenly, Coppola was watching Vito Corleone. Even in this early test, the screen aura that made Brando a legend was evident.

The original videotape shot of Brando by Coppola is, sadly, long gone. However, other footage of Brando that still exists from makeup and costume tests early in *The Godfather* production reveals the same astonishing transformation: One moment, a viewer is watching Marlon Brando—smiling, charming, and lively. The next, he *is* the Godfather—dynamic, powerful, and marvelously understated. In his costume tests, Brando was thoroughly immersed in the character as he would appear on the screen, but instead of dialogue, he again muttered nonwords as he held a thin Italian cigar and quietly mumbled in an effort to build a sense of his character.

Coppola had all the footage he needed. He galloped back to Paramount and showed Ruddy the test.

"It was just amazing," Ruddy remembered. "We couldn't even recognize him. That piece of no-dialogue tape is a classic."

Ruddy and Coppola showed the tape to Evans and Jaffe, burying the Brando segment in between other tests. "They flipped out," Ruddy said. "They didn't even know it was Brando until the end." (Ruddy, like Coppola, tells various versions of Brando casting stories. He also reported that the studio brass reacted to the test "like World War III had just broken out.")

Evans agreed enthusiastically with Ruddy and Coppola; Jaffe grudgingly said that he was convinced. Then, as with the decision to hire Ruddy, the final determination rested with Charles Bluhdorn.

"When we showed Charlie the tape with all the tests on it, and Brando came on-screen, he said, '*Who are ve vatching? Who is dis old guinea?*'" Ruddy said. "We told him it was Brando."

Coppola remembered: "Bluhdorn said, 'That's incredible. That's incredible.' He was so enthusiastic about the screen test that the money and the bond were just a matter of working it out."

Once Paramount signed Brando, the studio embraced the choice, put on a happy public face, and made a grand public announcement about it on January 27, 1971.

After all of the talk from Paramount about casting unknowns, the trade papers couldn't resist a barb or two. In a story headlined, NO STARS FOR GODFATHER CAST—JUST SOMEONE NAMED BRANDO, *Variety* described Paramount's enthusiasm over its selection.

"Paramount Senior VP for worldwide production Robert Evans, who said in September, 'We're going to cast real faces in *The Godfather,* people who are not names, nor are we going to have Hollywood Italians,' yesterday confirmed Marlon Brando has the title role," *Variety* reported.

"What makes this casting all the more gratifying and exciting," Evans said, "is the fact that in writing the novel and first-draft screenplay, Mr. Puzo had always envisioned Mr. Brando as the Godfather."

Brando was signed with a clause that would penalize him severely if he delayed the production—just as Brando received guarantees that would pay him generously if production delays that were *not* his fault would force him to extend his work on the production.

In Brando, Coppola had found his Don Vito Corleone. Now the production would have to find a cast that would not be overwhelmed by his talents.

IN EARLY September 1970, Ruddy had predicted that filming of *The Godfather* would begin in the middle of November, even though at the time he had not yet hired a director, a production team, or any of the actors. Once Coppola came aboard at the end of the month, casting could begin, but with work just started on the script and the production moving forward at a fever pitch, screen tests and cast selection would not start until November—a process that would then drag out over four months.

"Four Corned-Beef Sand-wiches"

Meanwhile, *The Godfather* production staff was quickly learning just how poor a choice of words Evans used when he said they would be casting unknowns. In October, Coppola tried to clarify what Evans had meant, emphasizing that while he planned to use unknowns, that meant unknowns with acting experience. Later, Ruddy explained that "we are not going to use amateurs, just unknown faces. There's a big difference."

None of this stemmed the tide of applicants; the *Los Angeles Times* reported that during casting, "all hell had broken loose" in Mario Puzo's office in Los Angeles. Letters poured in by the hundreds from would-be actors, amateur performers, and anyone who felt qualified to appear in *The Godfather* simply because they had read the book. Every "applicant" had a good reason for appearing:

"I'm an unknown."

"I've read *The Godfather.*"

"I'm dark-haired."

"I weigh 235 pounds."

"I'm starving, but I've always wanted to come to Hollywood, and this would be my last chance."

"My father, who was second-generation Italian, was slightly connected with the Mafia."

"I've read that you may be filming the picture in Cleveland. My father is the Godfather in Cleveland, and he can make things easy for you."

"If you are looking for an unknown who has never done any acting, I might fill the bill. Granted I'm no Ali MacGraw, but what do you expect for an Italian?"

Ruddy was unimpressed by the unknowns who applied for parts. "Somebody else sent a picture of themselves holding a pizza saying they would be perfect for a part." One eager candidate, Ruddy said, went to such extremes to appear in the picture that he spent $2,000 for an audition tape featuring his friends as costars.

Unfortunately, warnings from Coppola and Ruddy failed to stop the unscrupulous from taking advantage of the eager. Casting had generated such intense interest in *The Godfather* that several "talent schools" in Los Angeles and New York recruited students by using portable videotape equipment to record a "test." For $100, the schools assured students that Ruddy's office would review the test.

"Our legal department has already issued restraining orders against these people, both in New York and Los Angeles," Ruddy said at the time. "They are not affiliated with us in any way, and I'm not looking at any of their 'tests.' It's all a fraud, and I want to warn everyone."

Ruddy would eventually explain to prospective applicants the real story: While the production would test dozens of actors for each part, they would come through the traditional channels.

"We're going to do more screen-testing for this picture than any other film since *Gone With the Wind*," said Ruddy. "Casting will begin in two weeks, and there will be no general interviews. Agents I've talked to have specific people in mind who will be considered. Every major part will be screen-tested before the final casting, and nobody—I repeat—nobody has been approached by my office. A couple of people know they are going to be tested, but that's it."

By early November, the start date had been moved to January 15, but it would be pushed back if necessary, Ruddy said, to make casting "absolutely perfect."

"We tested so many people, it got insane," Ruddy said. "We worked through Thanksgiving on golden time testing actors."

By Thanksgiving, the question was not whether Coppola would have an "absolutely perfect" cast, but rather if he would have a cast at all. Even then, Ruddy and Coppola had plenty of people to consider, but no one had signed; as 1971 began, none of the principals—at that point not even Brando—were set. After two months of screen tests in Los Angeles, interviews with actors continued in New York as production moved east in early 1971. When Brando was eventually signed at the end of January, he was the first principal player to be cast. Even after the start date was postponed again—this time until early March—auditions continued through January and February in New York for featured roles. The start date was by then only a few weeks away.

Meanwhile, Coppola knew which actors he wanted to hire for two of his most important costarring roles. In particular, he wanted two performers who had worked for him before: To step into the role of Sonny Corleone, the volatile eldest son, Coppola sought his old buddy from Hofstra and the star of *The Rain People*. For Tom Hagen, the young lawyer and consiglieri (counselor) to the Don, Coppola wanted Robert Duvall, a veteran performer who had also appeared in *The Rain People* and starred in *THX-1138* for George Lucas.

Coppola shot tests and improvisational scenes of Caan and Duvall early in production. "That cost him four corned-beef sandwiches," Caan remembered.

But Paramount had yet to be convinced of any performer for the principal roles. Coppola would have to fight for the performers he wanted and go through the time and expense of testing dozens of actors to justify his choices to the studio.

Coppola, along with casting directors Fred Roos and Andrea Eastman, tested using a variety of improvised shots and several key sequences. The tests of Sonny featured the character's dialogue after Michael declares that he will kill Sollozzo and McCluskey (the "you blow their brains all over your nice Ivy League suit" scene). For the tests of Michael, they relied on the point early in the script in which Michael explains to Kay how the Don used Luca Brasi to threaten a bandleader to release Johnny Fontane from a deal (". . . either his brains or his signature would be on the contract").

The casting extravaganza peaked on February 11, in one mammoth day of testing. Coppola reviewed dozens of semifinal candidates, both to get one last look at the contenders and to appease the studio before he demanded the players he really wanted. Some actors who arrived early in the morning waited until past midnight for a chance to test.

In tests for the role of Michael, sitting opposite many of the candidates was a twenty-five-year-old actress named Diane Keaton, already the top contender to play Kay Adams, Michael's

love interest. Keaton was well known to television audiences in the late 1960s as the whimsical housewife in a television commercial who, clad in a track suit, ran around inside her home declaring that deodorant kept her dry "hour after hour." She also appeared occasionally on *The Tonight Show* with Johnny Carson as part of Johnny's stock company, perfecting her role as an on-screen "kook."

Keaton had played in leading roles on Broadway in *Hair* and *Play It Again, Sam* (she would also appear in the film version of that Woody Allen–written production that reached America's theaters at the same time as *The Godfather*). Coppola saw Keaton in the film version of *Lovers and Other Strangers* and brought her to *The Godfather* production to see if she could inject some of her innate quirkiness into a straight-arrow role. "I thought maybe Diane could bring some eccentricity to it," Coppola said.

In the tests to cast Michael, Keaton would eventually repeat the bandleader scene hundreds of times during the final tests—looking at each coperformer with the same starry-eyed interest that she would later show in the film's real scene.

Although several actors were tested for the role of Tom Hagen, Duvall never had any true

competition. A versatile, highly regarded actor who had appeared in films since 1962, Duvall's screen credits included *M*A*S*H*, *True Grit*, and *To Kill a Mockingbird*. He was the ideal choice to play Hagen, cool-headed counselor to the Don.

Casting Sonny's part was more of an open field, at least as far as Paramount was concerned. The role of Sonny—sensitive, explosive, and ultimately self-destructive—was almost as sought-after as the role of Michael. Both parts were sure to be star-making appearances.

Several up-and-coming actors were strong contenders for Sonny, including two who would later appear in other Coppola projects. Carmine Caridi, a character actor who more closely resembled the big, physically threatening Sonny of the book, was seriously considered. (Caridi would later have separate roles in each of *The Godfather* sequels—in *Part II* as Carmine Rosato and in *Part III* as Don Albert Volpe.) Another candidate who tested for Sonny was a young actor who had already appeared in several minor film roles but was also struggling to break into major features. Robert De Niro's test for Sonny was a powerhouse performance; mild-mannered and jovial off-camera, De Niro would transform before the cameras—in an eerie foreshadowing of his role in *Taxi Driver*—into an explosive psychotic killer.

THE FAMILY BUSINESS
MEETS WITH DRUG DEALER
SOLLOZZO (AL LETTIERI).
THE PRODUCTION DESIGN
BY DEAN TAVOULARIS
CALLED FOR METICULOUS
SET DETAIL, RIGHT DOWN
TO PERIOD CHRISTMAS
CARDS AND A DAILY
CALENDAR (BACK LEFT)
FOR TOTELLINI BERTAGNI
PASTA.

With his hair pinned back under a hat, De Niro performed the scene between Sonny and Michael improvising the written lines in a test that Coppola remembered as "electrifying."

You gonna take both of them—you take them? You know what they gonna do to you? You know what you do when you knock somebody off? You take a gun and shoot 'em right up against his fuckin' head—that's what you do. You get his brains all over your nice new Ivy League suit, Michael—that's what happens. Prove it to me—go on, prove it to me.

"It was spectacular," Coppola said, "but it was Sonny as a killer, nothing I could ever sell."

Of course, two years later, Coppola would hire De Niro for a character with an entirely different personality—the young and supremely self-assured Vito Corleone.

By the second week of February, casting was completed for most of the key roles. Diane Keaton and Robert Duvall were signed February 15 and, in the third week of February, two actors were signed for supporting parts: Richard Castellano as Peter Clemenza, the portly *caporegime* to the Don, and John Marley as Jack Woltz, the lecherous movie studio boss who wound up in bed with his horse's head. Both Castellano and Marley had just been nominated for Academy Awards for Best Supporting Actor —Castellano for *Lovers and Other Strangers* and Marley for *Love Story.* Also signed soon after were Abe Vigoda to appear as Sal Tessio, the Don's other *caporegime,* and Alex Rocco, to play Moe Greene, the family-backed owner of a Las Vegas hotel. (Later, when outsiders visited the set, they would often assume that Vigoda—tall, dour, and gravel-voiced—was a Mafiosi assigned to observe the production. The real "wiseguys" hanging around the set usually went unnoticed.)

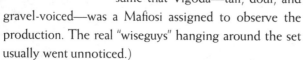

ALEX ROCCO AS CASINO OWNER MOE GREENE.

TERE LIVRANO, WHO CAME OUT OF PARAMOUNT'S TELEVISION MUSIC DEPARTMENT TO PLAY THERESA HAGEN, TOM'S WIFE.

The parts of family wives went to Julie Gregg, a Tony Award nominee for her performance in *The Happy Time,* who was cast as Sonny's wife, Sandra; and Tere Livrano, an assistant music editor at Paramount's Television Music Department, who was chosen for the role of Theresa Hagen, Tom's wife, after a friend submitted her photograph to Coppola.

The part of Don Barzini, the Corleones's most dangerous nemesis, went to Richard Conte. Conte would appear in only four scenes—three of them without lines—yet he would prove a worthy adversary for the Don.

Vic Damone was first cast as singer Johnny Fontane, only to be replaced by Al Martino (Damone dropped out of the production, saying "as an American of Italian descent, I could not in good conscience continue in the role." Damone later admitted that he dropped out because the part was much smaller in the script than in the book). Al Lettieri was signed as the treacherous drug dealer Virgil Sollozzo, and Morgana King as Mama Corleone. King, who was appearing in her first film role, was well known as an accomplished jazz singer who the *New York Times* described as performing "an outstanding melange of humming, singing and vocalizing that slithers sinuously around a melody." Sterling Hayden, a veteran leading man and character actor of the 1940s and 1950s who by the 1970s had chosen to devote more time to writing and sailing than films, was signed to play Captain McCluskey.

For Fredo, the weak-spirited middle Corleone brother, Coppola cast John Cazale, a superbly talented performer who had won two Obies (Off-Broadway theatrical awards). *The Godfather* marked Cazale's first film appearance, but before his untimely death from cancer in 1978, he would appear in five motion pictures: *The Godfather, The Conversation, The Godfather Part II, Dog Day Afternoon,* and *The Deer Hunter*—a quintet of signature films of the 1970s.

Also signed in mid-February was Talia Shire, Coppola's own sister, to play Connie, the youngest Corleone child and only daughter (the name Shire came from her marriage to composer David Shire). Shire had started her performing career as a dancer and choreographer, but later switched to acting. At twenty-five, Shire was yet another Corman colleague; in 1970, she had appeared in his youth-oriented film, *Gas-s-s-s! Or It Became Necessary to Destroy the World in Order to Save It.* (The publicity slogan for the film was "Lay a Little Fun on Yourself!")

Long after *The Godfather* had become a success, Coppola would say that Shire had not been his choice for the role; he had envisioned Connie as a "homely Italian girl."

Ruddy remembered the casting decision differently.

"Francis made it very clear to everybody that he would love Talia to get the part, but he told us that as the director, he couldn't take that position because she was his sister. So he deferred to the rest of the group. He was very aboveboard about it, and he didn't push at all because it was his sister. He was very honorable that way. And as it turned out, she was, of course, perfect for the part."

Even though Coppola wasn't responsible for casting Shire, the presence of the director's sister on the set did not endear the director to his production crew. Once filming began, the perception of nepotism spurred some of the early grumbling on the set that would later contribute to the ongoing friction that would torment Coppola during the production.

LENNY MONTANA AS LUCA BRASI. "FRANCIS'S EYE-BALLS POPPED OUT," SAID RUDDY. "HE FELL IN LOVE WITH HIM."

Other small but memorable roles would wait until after shooting started. The role of Luca Brasi, the family's loyal hit man who would be the first to die in the film, would not be cast until Ruddy spotted a giant body and a mammoth head—those of Lenny Montana—off-camera during a scene shot in Little Italy.

"Lenny was working as a bodyguard for one of 'the boys' visiting the set—a friend of the production," Ruddy said with a smile.

"I told Francis, 'I've got someone here you've got to meet.' Francis's eyeballs popped out; he fell in love with him."

Of all the minor roles, by far the wackiest casting adventure involved the role of Carlo Rizzi, Connie's no-good husband and eventual traitor to the Corleone family. The part went to a true unknown with no acting experience but plenty of chutzpah: Gianni Russo, a native of Las Vegas who had created his own local television show called *Welcome to My Lifestyle*, had indeed read Evans's comments about casting unknowns and became determined to appear in *The Godfather*. Far more persistent than the other would-be actors who annoyed the production company, it was Russo who had created the aforementioned $2,000 screen test and sent it to Ruddy. Russo somehow charmed his way into Ruddy's good graces and, after weeks of pestering, earned a shot at the part.

To test for the role, Ruddy asked Russo to play the scene in which Carlo beats up his wife. The producer recruited the secretary of Paramount president Stanley Jaffe to read Connie's lines. In a meeting at Gulf+Western headquarters—and with an audience of Ruddy, Evans, Bluhdorn, Jaffe, and Roos—Russo played the scene so realistically as he screamed and thrashed at the secretary that she was terrified. "Russo got the part," Ruddy said.

Russo, overflowing with confidence, was a perfect pick for the brash, crude, scheming Carlo.

"When Gianni went to work," Ruddy remembered, "his first scene was with Brando. I was worried that he might freeze up, so I gave him the usual bit about working with a huge star—you know, Brando puts on one shoe at a time like everybody else, that kind of stuff. Russo says, 'What, are you kidding? Who do you think they're gonna be looking at when they see me and this fat guy on the screen?' There was nothing I could say, except, 'Go with God—you're in good shape.' Ignorance is bliss."

• • •

In mid-February, Coppola headed to London for consultations with Brando, then on to Italy to cast the scenes in Sicily. On that trip, Coppola cast Simonetta Stefanelli as Apollonia, Michael's short-lived Sicilian wife; Corrado Gaipa as Don Tommasino, Michael's protector; and Angelo Infanti and Franco Citti as bodyguards Fabrizio and Calo. In America, he left behind the lone remaining principal casting decision unresolved. Even though the new production start date—now March 29—was scarcely a month away, the part of Michael was still not cast.

Paramount clearly recognized the importance of the role of Michael as a potential launching pad to popularity for a young talent or a plum part for an established performer. Both Warren Beatty and Jack Nicholson were considered, even though both looked many years older than the character as written. Dustin Hoffman expressed interest, but an audition never materialized. Paramount lobbied for a "Robert Redford type" such as Ryan O'Neal, who had leaped into stardom with his appearance in Paramount's blockbuster of 1970,

SIMONETTA STEFANELLI AS APOLLONIA, ON THE MORNING AFTER HER WEDDING TO MICHAEL IN SICILY (DELETED FROM THE FILM).

Love Story. The studio rationalized that a young blondish star could portray Michael as a Northern Italian, even though the Corleone family was from Sicily—as far south in Italy as one can get.

The studio's suggestions fell on deaf ears. Coppola knew who he wanted to play Michael, and he was ready to fight to get him. To get the actor he wanted, he would have to battle as tirelessly as he had for Brando.

Of all the actors who appeared in *The Godfather*, Al Pacino had suffered through the longest professional trial, had achieved the least success, and had the most to lose. For Pacino, a high school dropout who had always wanted to act, the fourteen years that followed school would be a constant struggle to succeed—acting for low or no pay, working at menial jobs to survive and often winding up fired, and achieving little recognition or progress in his career. Like thousands of other actors in New York, Pacino dangled on the fringes for years, working hard, scraping by, and hoping for a big break.

"Ever since I did shows in junior high school, all I cared to do was act," Pacino said. "If I

AL PACINO AS MICHAEL
(IN THE SAME SCENE IL-
LUSTRATED ON PAGE 61).
THE ACTOR WHO HAD SUF-
FERED THROUGH THE
LONGEST PROFESSIONAL
TRIAL, HAD ACHIEVED
THE LEAST SUCCESS, AND
HAD THE MOST TO LOSE.

couldn't do that, I'd read. At work I'd go into the men's room with a book, lost in some dream world. But I didn't really know what I was aiming for . . . then there was a time when I appeared in a Strindberg play and something happened. I realized I was an artist. I realized I loved to observe people, follow them, watch their responses."

Most of his odd jobs ended in disaster. Pacino was routinely fired for loafing on the job: He preened in front of a mirror in his usher's outfit; he once led patrons into a non-existent waiting line across the street from a theater. The only job he regretted losing was one at Carnegie Hall. "The music was wonderful, but I kept putting people in the wrong seats."

Years later, when he was earning seven-figure salaries, Pacino could afford to joke about his early years as an usher. Back then, many days it was a struggle just to earn enough to eat. Pacino passed out handbills and moved furniture; he would often wind up sleeping on the couches of friends for weeks at a time when money ran short. Once, after nearly a decade of struggling in theater, he became so emotionally distraught that he called friends and told them he wanted to commit himself to a mental hospital. Instead, he became involved in the Actors Studio, the training center directed by Lee Strasberg.

Finally, in the late 1960s, Pacino began to make progress. He won an Obie in 1968 as Best Actor of the Year for his appearance in *The Indian Wants the Bronx*, and the next year he received a Tony Award for his role as a psychotic killer in *Does a Tiger Wear a Necktie?* Both Coppola and Ruddy saw him in the role and would remember him when casting for Michael. To Ruddy, "it was a scary performance."

Pacino's new stage success attracted moviemakers; he appeared in a bit part in *Me, Natalie* starring Patty Duke and, in 1970, he played his starring film role as a junkie in *Panic in Needle Park*, a role that won him notoriety when the motion picture was presented at the Cannes Film Festival. But one film role does not make a career, and by the time casting began for *The Godfather*, Pacino, nearly thirty-one, was still looking for a breakthrough role.

To Ruddy and Coppola, Pacino was a deep, brooding performer capable of a screen intensity that would captivate audiences—even in scenes with Brando. But to Paramount, Pacino had nothing to offer; to anyone who had not seen him in performance, he was too short, "too Italian," and so low-key that on first appearance he seemed listless. Even after his appearance in *Panic in Needle Park*, no one at any of the Hollywood studios recognized the potential star quality that Pacino was capable of delivering—that dark and intense screen persona that would mark so many of his performances. The well-regarded character he created for *Panic in Needle Park* was that of a nervous junkie, not the calm, ruthless leader of a powerful crime family so necessary for *The Godfather*.

"He wasn't a star, which was not pleasing to the executives at that time," said casting director Fred Roos. "He didn't look like a star looked at the time in the business."

Those who watched Pacino in other performances were thoroughly convinced of the actor's capabilities. After seeing *Does a Tiger Wear a Necktie?* Coppola was possessed by the image of Pacino as Michael.

"When I read *The Godfather*," the director remembered, "whenever I would see the character of Michael, I saw Al's face."

Ruddy was equally impressed and laughed off comments that Pacino was too short to play Michael.

"I met him after the play, and I couldn't believe he was short," Ruddy said. "When I watched him in *Does a Tiger Wear a Necktie?* he looked about seven feet tall onstage."

However, unlike Brando, who sold everyone on the strength of his screen test, Pacino was thoroughly underwhelming in his film tryout. Knowing that only Coppola was backing him and the studio stood firmly in opposition, Pacino could muster little enthusiasm to test for a role he felt he had no chance to win. Coppola understood the actor's frustration, but to a director who believed he could win every argument, Pacino's attitude was mystifying; after struggling through a test with the actor, Coppola called Pacino "a self-destructive bastard."

"Francis knew I could do the part, and so did I, but he kept asking me to test again and again," Pacino said. "I didn't want to go . . . I don't go where I'm not wanted. If someone doesn't want me for a part that's OK, I understand. I don't even get mad—they just tell me, and I don't come around again. But when they don't want me and keep telling me to come back, well, under those circumstances, I'm not learning lines. If that's being self-destructive, then OK, call me self-destructive."

Pacino's potential was also hindered by the principal scene used for his tests. The bandleader scene was a simple storytelling—hardly the stuff of bravura performances.

Still, Coppola knew that Pacino was right for the part. He tried to wear down Evans by testing Pacino again and again, mixing in his test footage with that of other actors.

Despite Coppola's continuing enthusiasm for Pacino, Evans would not be convinced. He met with Ruddy over lunch to discuss the role, and when the subject came around to Pacino and the unending barrage of tests, the studio chief got hot. Pounding his fist on the table, he wound up yelling at Ruddy, "Why the hell are you testing Pacino again? The man's a midget." Later, at a meeting with Coppola, Evans once again tried to persuade him to use another actor. "Francis," Evans told the director, "I must say that you're alone in this."

Watching Pacino's early screen tests for *The Godfather* reveals a portrait in frustration. Tired, unsure, and overly sensitive, Pacino was clearly discouraged by the seemingly unending ordeal of testing. Paramount's concerns extended beyond Pacino's acting ability. Under the harsh lights of the test set and without the benefit of appropriate makeup, Pacino looked pale and uncertain— not at all the image of the cool and powerful Mafia don.

The tests also reveal—to those who were willing to see it—a sense of explosive under-statement, a trait Brando called "an intense, brooding quality." Others agreed with Coppola; Marcia Lucas, wife of George Lucas, edited together the tests and told Coppola that Pacino should play Michael "because he undresses you with his eyes." When Coppola asked Keaton who she thought should play Michael, she, too, supported Pacino.

Coppola either had to draw out enough of the actor's abilities in tests to convince Paramount or, as he usually did, simply wear down those who disagreed with him. Coppola's eventual success required a combination of both strategies—plus the director's guarantee that Pacino would produce when he wanted him to deliver.

Not surprisingly, both Evans and Ruddy take credit for clearing the path for Pacino. Evans said that after talking to Brando about Pacino, the studio chief approved him for the role on the spot. Ruddy recalled hashing out the deal with Charlie Bluhdorn. "I was up in Charlie's office drinking one night, and we were talking about casting Michael," Ruddy recalled. "I said, 'Charlie, no one can agree who should play Michael Corleone. Let's say we compromise. At least if you go with Al Pacino, you compromise with quality. He's one of the brightest actors on Broadway. He's Italian, he's as-written.' Charlie agreed. I called Francis and told him."

Coppola would emerge victorious yet again. On March 4, 1971, the studio announced that Pacino would play Michael—for $35,000. It would be the last time he would command less than a high-six-figure paycheck to appear in a film. Still, Pacino continued to be a problem—a legal, not artistic problem. After years of struggle, Pacino was now wanted by two studios at once and came close to losing the most important role of his career. Only days before Coppola won approval for him to appear in *The Godfather*, his agent signed him for a supporting role in *The Gang That Couldn't Shoot Straight*, a humorous gangster picture based on the book by columnist Jimmy Breslin. On March 10, little more than two weeks before *The Godfather* was scheduled to go before the cameras, Paramount was legally enjoined by MGM from using Pacino at any time after April 15, which would have made his appearance in *The Godfather* impossible. The two studios wrangled over the problem for nearly a week before finally reaching an out-of-court settlement that would permit Pacino to proceed with his work on *The Godfather*. In exchange, Coppola released Robert De Niro, whom he had cast in a small role as Paulie Gatto, the Don's turncoat bodyguard, to replace Pacino in *The Gang That Couldn't Shoot Straight*.

"We finally got Al," Ruddy said with relief.

Pacino may have been short, he may have been unknown, and he may not have been the big star the studio wanted. But in Pacino, the production got a young "newcomer" who could hold his ground on-screen with Brando.

After five months of casting, the production had come full circle to the four performers that Coppola had wanted all along: Brando for the lead, plus Pacino, Caan, and Duvall in the key supporting roles. "They spent $400,000 on tests," Caan sighed, "and still wound up with four corned-beef sandwiches."

Coppola, who had already convinced the unenthusiastic studio that he and Puzo should create a script that transcended the traditional gangster picture, had finally won his three toughest battles: Getting the green light to shoot in New York, persuading Paramount that Brando was right for the lead, and casting Pacino as Michael. But the director would pay a formidable price for his victories: The concessions made Paramount more concerned than ever about the fate of the production, and the studio watchdogs would question decisions large and small, second-guessing the director every step of the way. The intensified pressure of added studio scrutiny over the filming would become a near-constant battle, creating a pressure-cooker environment for Coppola as he struggled to make his film.

The Look of a Bulldog

IN LATE 1970, as Ruddy and Coppola waded through the morass of casting, the director began to assemble his production team. Ruddy and Coppola were already spending their money wisely; because Brando was hired cheaply and other performers commanded relatively low salaries, costs for the entire cast comprised only 25 percent of the budget.

The torment of casting would not be repeated in assembling the off-camera talent. Ruddy and Coppola brought together a veritable all-star team of moviemaking: cinematographer Gordon Willis, production designer Dean

Tavoularis, makeup designer Dick Smith, costume designer Anna Hill Johnstone, and special effects supervisor A. D. Flowers.

Gordon Willis had been working as a motion picture cinematographer for only two years when he was brought into *The Godfather* production,
but he had already begun to establish a reputation among his peers as the best theatrical film photographer in the business. Willis had been involved with film—either picture photography or
motion pictures—most of his life. He worked as a still photographer before the Korean War, and
when he enlisted in the Air Force, he worked in a motion picture unit. Later Willis made docu-
mentaries, commercials, and served as an assistant cameraman until 1969. In the two years before
The Godfather, he worked as cinematographer on six films.

With his vast experience in filmmaking for a variety of media, Willis was known as a top-
flight cinematographer with vast technical skills and an artist's eye. He had also gained a reputation as iron-willed, stubborn, and forceful, with no patience for young directors and a reputation
for intolerance with actors. While the reputation may not have been entirely justified, Willis was
indeed known throughout the industry as a cinematographer who got things to happen *his* way.

"Everything happens on the set the way Willis wants it to happen," confided one cinematographer. "That's power."

In contrast to Willis's style was that of Dean Tavoularis, who as production designer of *The Godfather* was responsible for creating the visual quality of the project—set design, locations, costumes, and props. Mild-mannered and calm, Tavoularis was, like Ruddy, a lapsed architect. He entered filmmaking in animation for Disney Studios and moved to live-action productions at Colombia and Warner Bros. before debuting as production designer for Arthur Penn's *Bonnie and Clyde*. After work on *Candy*, *Zabriskie Point*, and *Little Big Man*, he came to *The Godfather* through his association with the film's associate producer Gray Frederickson, who had been one of the production managers on *Candy*.

In Tavoularis, Coppola would have a production designer with a broad sense of visual design, depth, and an exceptional eye for detail.

"Period films are interesting, and the research is fascinating," said Tavoularis. "When you do the research and look at the faces in books and photographs, you see that these people lived in another world. In a period film, every detail is important. You can't, for example, just put a can of soup on a shelf—it has to be the right can of soup."

The Godfather was Tavoularis's first picture with Coppola, the beginning of a creative relationship that would span both of their careers. He would design all three *Godfather* pictures, as well as, among other collaborations, *Apocalypse Now, Rumble Fish, The Outsiders,* and *Tucker.*

For makeup, Ruddy and Coppola hired Dick Smith, one of the pioneers of advanced makeup in television and motion pictures. At the time of *The Godfather,* Smith had worked in makeup for nearly twenty-five years, after stumbling upon a book on stage makeup while a pre-dental student at Yale.

"Actually, it was one of the worst books ever written on makeup, but to me it was wonderful," said Smith. "I started to do makeup on myself. Every weekend when I had time, I would make myself up as one of the famous Universal characters like Frankenstein or Dracula and go to the movies dressed that way."

Smith left dentistry behind and at NBC became one of the first staff makeup artists in the industry. In the late 1950s, he made the jump to film; by the time he joined *The Godfather* team, he had earned a reputation for innovation in creating theatrical makeup that was capped by his work on *Little Big Man* in 1970, in which he transformed a thirty-three-year-old Dustin Hoffman into an unrecognizable 121-year-old man.

For costumes, Coppola chose Anna Hill Johnstone, a New York–based costume designer. As most of her work was on East Coast projects, Johnstone was not as well known in film circles as some of her Hollywood-based colleagues. In New York, she was recognized for her twenty-five years of work in theater costumes, for work in period projects, and for her designs for twenty-nine films before *The Godfather,* including *Portrait of Jenny, The Pawnbroker, Fail Safe,* and *The Group.* Johnstone had designed costumes for several of Elia Kazan's films, including the wardrobes for Brando and others in *On the Waterfront.*

For a film awash in blood and violence, the production needed a top-flight special effects coordinator, and A. D. Flowers was the best. Flowers broke into studio work as a greenskeeper at MGM in the 1940s and moved into props, then special effects. He developed an unsurpassed expertise for special effects explosives and other violence effects, but was equally skilled in devising all kinds of effects. The year before he began work on *The Godfather,* he won an Academy Award for *Tora! Tora! Tora!,* the Pearl Harbor spectacle, and in 1972 won another Oscar for *The Poseidon Adventure.* He and colleague Joe Lombardi would tackle the veritable smorgasbord of simulated violence for *The Godfather.*

As Coppola assembled his creative team, he held extensive and exhaustive meetings with his two principals, Willis and Tavoularis, to review the script from start to finish, discuss the visual elements, and begin to develop a look to the production and how it would be shot.

"Francis, Gordon, and I went over the entire production scene by scene, which probably took about eight hours," Tavoularis said. "We walked through the whole script with a court stenographer taking notes, so Francis would have a record of everything we wanted to accomplish."

Coppola included excerpts from those notes in a packed binder that was his constant companion, both in preproduction and on the set. The notebook was the director's personal guide to the project—it contained notes and memos about every scene, highlighted pages from the book, and scatterings of references to other films, other directors, and his own work that could be used as a visual guide when plotting camera positions (note, for example, the overhead shot of the Don being wounded—a trademark Hitchcock technique for a scene of high drama). Coppola could often be seen in deep conversation with an actor or member of the production crew, clutching the notebook to his chest like a teddy bear.

As the production developed, Coppola went over his detailed needs for the various elements of production, particularly with Willis. All visual elements of a film spring from the visualization of director and cinematographer working closely with the production designer; early in preproduction, Coppola and Willis developed a cinematic plan and an overall look for the film that was, recalled Willis, "a kind of forties New York grit"—with the exception of the Sicilian scenes. Willis underexposed his film and also strived for a color balance that he called a "yellow tone"—actually a soft amber.

The key to Willis creating his look for the film was to shoot the entire picture in a "tableau format"—literally setting the shot as if it was viewed as a painting in a frame and using primarily a stable camera, with minimal movement, zooms, or pans.

"Before *The Godfather* started shooting, Francis and I discussed what the film was going to look like," Willis said. "We agreed never to use zoom lenses, for instance; we agreed that it was a tableau form of moviemaking, and that contemporary mechanical items were not to be used. And that's basically how the film was executed."

It was a simple agreement in principle that would become much more difficult to manage in practice. The lengthy discussions between pragmatic cinematographer and enthusiastic director would often be lost in Coppola's ever-expanding vision for the film, becoming one of the principal sources of conflict on the set.

To supplement his tableau format, Willis relied on low light levels for interiors to provide a visual contrast to the psychological developments emerging on-screen.

"The technique or the approach to the movie visually just came out of a thought process— and the process, in my mind, was based on evil; it was based on the soul of the picture," Willis said. "I guess the best example of it was the wedding, where outside in the garden there was a very sunny, almost Kodachromey, 1942 feel to it. Then we cut inside the house with Brando; it was very down and very ominous. So while one thing was happening out here, another thing, in fact, was happening inside. And so it was a very simple philosophy."

Willis may have created a happy accident in his attempt to bring his vision of evil to the screen; in addition to portraying evil, most viewers would recognize his cinematic plan as a successful conveyor of the images of power—the sumptuous tones of influence, strength, and

JAMES CAAN AS SONNY AND JULIE GREGG AS SANDRA CORLEONE. "I WANT TO STRIVE FOR DEPTH TO THE DESIGN," TAVOULARIS SAID. "I'VE NEVER LIKED 'THE WALL'—I LIKE THE IDEA OF LAYERS."

RUDY BOND (LEFT) AS
CUNEO AND VICTOR
RENDINA AS PHILLIP
TATTAGLIA. WITH AN
EVER-PRESENT
ORANGE.

wealth. And Willis's cinematic tableaus—each delicately lit and meticulously framed—would indeed look like beautiful paintings, still lifes, or family portraits. Even scenes of violence would contain a kind of tragic beauty in their artful composition.

Shooting a period film in Willis's tableau style provided an ideal palette for a designer with Tavoularis's interest in research, historical settings, and rich detail—especially with a director like Coppola, who insisted on meticulous attention to realism in every element of the design.

"I want to strive for depth to the design," Tavoularis said. "I've never liked 'the wall'—I like the idea of layers. I always want to put a door in the wall, and see the wall of the next room, and maybe put a window in it, then show a little bit of a tree, and add a light in the neighboring house. In this case, I was always thinking like that—like in stage design, where you're very limited, yet you're trying to get a sense of depth."

Tavoularis's ideas about historical detail and set depth would involve the production in an extraordinary recreation of mid-century New York streets and homes. Even the simplest room settings contained elements to add depth: carefully placed windows, attached rooms, or intriguing decorations. In Sonny's house, for example, as he learns of his father's shooting, his wife Sandra can be seen through a doorway in the background washing dishes.

One element of Tavoularis's design in particular would be remembered as a symbol for horrors to come. The use of oranges as set decorations was viewed by some academics and film historians as an intentional foreshadowing motif of the death or violence to come. Oranges do appear throughout the film, often in moments before violence occurs (of course, few film theorists seem to notice that most scenes in the movie are precursors to violence): The Don buys oranges before he is shot, and the fruit is scattered across Mott Street as he falls; they also appear in, among other places, the table setting in Jack Woltz's dinning room, in front of Corleone enemies Barzini and Tattaglia at the meeting of the dons, and in the garden when the Don dies.

But for Tavoularis, oranges were simply another carefully chosen complement to otherwise somberly dressed sets. "We knew this film wasn't going to be about bright colors, and oranges make a nice contrast," said Tavoularis. "I don't remember anybody saying, 'Hey, I like oranges as a symbolic message.' Oranges just look nice in low lighting and in Gordon's photography."

Actually creating a film is, of course, a far different process from lunchtime discussions or a review of creative goals for a project. For *The Godfather*, that translation to screen would prove to be a major challenge.

After weeks housed in temporary quarters in the Gulf+Western building, in mid-February *The Godfather* production staff moved to its permanent offices on the Filmways Studio lot. By now, the production had a start date that would stick: March 29. Preproduction rolled forward in a rush to create the major settings and handle the myriad details. After the Manhasset location fell through, the goal was identifying a new site for the Corleone family compound—referred to in the book and the script as "The Mall"—a location that would require several out-of-the-way houses that could be encircled by a "stone" wall constructed out of painted Styrofoam, with interior sets on the Filmways lot and dozens of exterior locations in New York, New Jersey, Brooklyn, and the Bronx.

Soon after the move, the production acquired two items that would appeal to a gadget-hungry Coppola. The first shot of the film at Best & Co. would require a snow machine to re-create a Christmas mood, assuming that real snow didn't cooperate with the production schedule. As crew members arrived at Filmways for Brando's makeup and costume tests on March 10, they trudged through a man-made snowstorm as the machine was tested in front of the studio. (To function effectively, the machine required a temperature no higher than 28 degrees—an optimistic hope at best for a shoot in late March.) In addition, the production obtained a cinemobile bus—a complete portable film studio that would considerably simplify the setups for location shooting.

The Godfather offices were at once a portrait of frenetic confusion and tightly coordinated logistics. The offices were strewn with production schedules in a constant state of addition and revision. Prop masters, set designers, and location scouts maintained a frantic and nonstop hunt for props and sites. Yet the shooting itself would have to be managed as carefully as a military campaign. With all costs included, each production day would cost about $40,000—or $5,000 an

hour. Overtime charges and penalties could easily add half that amount to the daily cost.

Even though the film was set in a period that was only twenty-six years earlier, it was indeed, as Tavoularis said, a different world. Beyond identifying specific locations for filming, the highest priority of the production staff was identifying and obtaining specific props and set dressings that would be necessary for every scene. Tavoularis, art director Warren Clymer, set decorator Philip Smith, and their staff of designers and prop masters would have to re-create not just one period, but the span of a decade. A film that opens in August 1945 and closes in the early autumn of 1955, *The Godfather* would demand vintage cars from several different years, subtle changes in clothes, and hints of new technology (such as the addition of a television to the Don's office for scenes late in the film).

In *The Godfather* production files were historical photographs of life in midcentury Manhattan from the broadest view to the most minute detail: shots of Little Italy, business furniture from Rockefeller Center, Bakelite radios, purses, and on and on. Even the Don's cemetery monument plaque had to be re-created in the style of the era. The Don's age at his death, as established in

THE DON'S CEMETERY MON-
UMENT, WHICH APPEARS
FOR ONLY A MOMENT IN
THE FILM, INCLUDES HIS
DATE OF BIRTH AND DEATH
AS ESTABLISHED FOR *THE
GODFATHER.* HIS BIRTHDAY
WOULD CHANGE FOR *PART
II* TO DECEMBER 7—
THE DAY MICHAEL
ENLISTED IN THE MARINES.

CORLEONE

VITO
APRIL 28, 1887
JULY 29, 1955

the first *Godfather* film, was sixty-eight. The plaque on the family monument, which appears in only a brief cut, reads:

CORLEONE
VITO
APRIL 28, 1887
JULY 29, 1955

In *The Godfather Part II*, the Don's birthday would be changed to December 7, for the closing scene of the film, to coincide with Michael's enlistment in the Marines on the day the Japanese attacked Pearl Harbor.

Fortunately, clothing could be re-created from patterns of the time, and under Johnstone's direction literally hundreds of suits, dresses, and uniforms would be produced or acquired from New York vendors. Items that couldn't be reproduced, such as automobiles, trucks, and items too expensive or time-consuming to fabricate, had to be found. Literally thousands of twenty-five-year-old items would have to be purchased, rented, or borrowed—a fleet of more than eighty vehicles including cars, trucks, taxis, limousines, and police cars; plus books, lipsticks, combs,

PROP NEWSPAPERS, CIRCA 1945.

hospital equipment, record players, weapons, FBI identification cards, cameras, furniture, kitchen utensils, telephones, magazines, and religious icons—the list was endless.

Research also continued throughout preproduction to identify items that could be created but needed to be studied carefully to ensure that Coppola's demands for authenticity were met. Creating hairstyles of the 1940s and 1950s was handled by Phil Leto and his staff—a formidable task in the shaggy-haired, sideburned early 1970s. The production would also need massive floral arrangements in the style of the forties and fifties for Connie's wedding and the Don's funeral.

Even highly unusual items from the 1940s that would be used to "sweeten" the background of a scene had to be located or fabricated. For example, during World War II, with vital materials scarce and scrap drives in full swing, parts of automobiles that were not necessary to operate the car, such as bumpers, were often sacrificed to the war effort; owners would replace the chrome bumpers with wooden substitutes. After the war, as the automobile industry geared up for peacetime production, chrome was still in short supply, and the first new cars off the line were shipped with wooden bumpers. In a scene cut from the film, Clemenza complains to Rocco Lampone about how "stupid Dee-troit" delivered his new car with wooden bumpers, and the chrome bumpers would be shipped in a few months.

To meet the needs of the scene, the production staff either had to find a postwar era automobile already equipped with wooden bumpers or create realistic wooden substitutes for an otherwise perfectly restored car. Although the scene of Clemenza complaining about Detroit was cut (it later turns up in *The Godfather Trilogy*, Coppola's melding of all three films), a car with wooden bumpers actually does make an appearance in *The Godfather*; it is parked inside the Corleone compound behind Clemenza and Michael as they return to the house after Michael's jaw is broken.

Beyond individual props, the logistics of transforming sections of New York City into a midcentury look were difficult. Many buildings, of course, remained from that era, but every location had to be "sanitized" of all evidence of 1971—advertisements, modern fixtures, television antennas—and replaced with the visual elements that suggested the forties and fifties. Naturally, it was a time-consuming, expensive effort. One specific change

THE FRONT OF THE
GENCO OLIVE OIL
COMPANY, READY
FOR THE SHOOTING
OF THE DON.

alone was a budget-buster: When a New York City maintenance crew removed a modern concrete streetlight, it cost $250; to install an original "shepherd's crook" light of the earlier era cost another $250. At the end of a shoot, the shepherd's crook light would be removed ($250) and the ugly concrete modern light replaced for another $250. Thus, to make the complete switch for each streetlight cost a minimum of $1,000. Multiplied by dozens of streetlights and weeks of location shooting, this meant tens of thousands of dollars in unavoidable costs—"just for the damn streetlights," as Ruddy put it.

Despite the challenges, *The Godfather* production team got plenty of help with its location shooting. The film was produced in close cooperation with the New York City Film Commission, an office created by Mayor John Lindsay to facilitate the needs of production companies who wanted to shoot in the city. Given the vast amounts of cash that a motion picture production can pump into the economy, the office was willing to do nearly anything during the filming to ease the process: reroute traffic, close streets, and provide security and barriers in cooperation with the police to manage the onlookers a production would inevitably attract.

The first New York location scene shown in the film provides ample illustration of the challenges to the production staff. The first day of shooting, outside of the closed Best & Co. department store on Fifth Avenue, required 143 extras, all dressed in postwar clothes—soldiers, sailors, WACs, Christmas shoppers, a Santa, mothers and children, nuns, and taxi drivers. Each extra carried appropriate props of the period, such as purses, wrapped presents, shopping bags, toys, and umbrellas. All of the streetlights around Best & Co. were replaced, and cars, taxis, and trucks of the period were either parked or driven around the location. In the store's windows, mannequins were dressed in "New Look" clothing—costumes carefully re-created from the postwar fashion rage. The snow machine provided a wintry atmosphere, and boxes of fake snow were used to touch up the scene and serve as emergency snow as the weather warmed and the snow machine stopped operating.

All of this for a three-second establishing shot of the department store, plus one brief shot of Kay and Michael, laden with packages, walking in front of its windows.

However, even the most meticulous re-creations of midcentury Manhattan, and the complete cooperation from the city, were not enough for two scenes in *The Godfather.* In a period before computer technology and digital film enhancement, a film crew could re-create a street or section of a neighborhood, but not main thoroughfares and skyscrapers of a bygone era. To create the shots needed for the drive-through of New York as Clemenza, Paulie, and Rocco look for locations to "go to the mattresses" (house a team of Mob soldiers), *The Godfather* production staff turned to storehouses of color stock footage actually shot in the late 1940s. The script called for two shots of a sedan driving in New York: one on a broad avenue, the other under a section of an elevated commuter train. When the shots were found, the staff then needed to find a car that matched the model in the footage and create a duplicate of its license plate. Paulie Gatto's car was thus "cast" for the film as a duplicate of the vehicle shot twenty-five years before.

Clothing was reproduced under Johnstone's direction, working with men's wardrobe supervisor George Newman and women's wardrobe supervisor Marilyn Putnam, who used patterns and photographs of the 1940s (although original personal items—watches, rings, brooches, hatpins, necklaces—were needed by the bushel). Costumes for the men were primarily expertly tailored business clothes, tuxedos for Connie's wedding, some casual apparel for movie studio chief Jack Woltz at home and for Michael as he practices shooting in Clemenza's basement, and for Carlo's "slick bookie" outfit that he wears in the scene when Sonny beats him up.

Clothes for the women were carefully chosen in-fashion dresses for the younger women and more traditional matronly outfits for mothers and grandmothers. In the freewheeling early 1970s, the transformation of the female actors was especially pronounced as they dressed for their roles. Eleanor Coppola remembers watching Diane Keaton arrive on the set in her "big boots and kooky clothes" and emerge "all flattened and straightened into Kay Corleone."

Michael's clothes provided visual evidence of the changes in his character: bland brown suits of the college student and returning war veteran early in the film; lower-class Italian suits and "Mafia casual" slacks, vest, and cap for his hideout in Sicily; and well-cut suits in deep gray tones and black for his emergence as the young Don.

For Don Vito, Johnstone created clothing designs to complement a character with immense power but who cared nothing about clothes. The Don wore what was required for a given situation: For a wedding, a traditional tuxedo; for scenes during his later years and death scene, old familiar clothes for work in his beloved garden; for the office, straightforward yet simple business clothes typical for an aging businessman seemingly from the lower-middle-class—a shirt with a too-large collar, a tie knotted backward so the label was exposed, and his belt worn below the loops; and for a meeting with the five families, a dynamic "power suit" of the finest cut.

All of the film's clothes required the same meticulous accuracy as other props and sets. For example, Michael's military uniform, which he wears in the wedding scene, was simply the standard issue business dress uniform of a U.S. Marine circa 1945. To get his hat right, Johnstone had to have it stitched with a brocade across the top—a design no longer used by the Marines. Even though the hat appears on-screen for only a few seconds, it was still an important detail for a director constantly driven by the demands of accuracy.

In addition to realism in his settings, Coppola also wanted realistic violence. For a motion picture filled with crime and murder—although the actual body count is relatively low and the most graphic depictions of violence are photographs of real-life Mob hits—Coppola wanted the results of violence to be accurate and graphic. He called on Dick Smith, A. D. Flowers, and effects technician Joe Lombardi to combine makeup and effects to produce the realistic violence the film demanded.

The production would require gunshot wounds through clothing, flesh, and sets, including two extraordinary effects: an intricate makeup wound for McCluskey's forehead and Sonny's assassination, with more simulated bullet hits than had ever before been attempted on one person. To show the effects of violence on inanimate objects, Flowers would also need to rig cars for bullet holes and bombs, windows to shatter as shots were fired, and many other unusual and carefully timed effects. For the murder of Moe Greene—a scene Coppola described as "disgusting"—Flowers would have to prepare a pair of glasses to shatter as a bullet enters Greene's eye and blood flows.

Blood would indeed flow in large quantities during *The Godfather* production—often by the gallon. Smith's own formulation for film blood, which had become an industry standard, was a remarkably simple combination of ingredients: Karo syrup and powdered red food coloring, with just a touch of yellow to compensate for the bluish cast the red coloring would display on film. The Karo blood recipe worked perfectly in pools or smeared on nonporous objects, but it would bead up on clothes or skin, so Smith added a wetting agent called Photo-Flo 200 that would make the Karo blood flow and soak into fabric, just like the real thing.

Smith's Karo blood recipe was an ideal filmmaking prop: Simple to clean, the liquid was, of course, sweet and easy on the tastebuds when an actor had to hold it in his mouth and let it pour out as James Caan would be required to do during Sonny's assassination.

In spite of Smith's proven success with Karo blood, Coppola wanted to be sure that the formulation was indeed the best simulation for his production. He and Smith examined and test-filmed virtually every possible substitute for blood—including animal blood—before the director was convinced that the Karo recipe was the most effective.

Beyond supplying blood, Smith played far more important roles in *The Godfather*'s planning, including one that would produce the most closely guarded secret of the production. As a well-regarded makeup artist, Smith would direct his staff in handling the daily makeup needs of all of the players in the film, including the subtle aging of several characters over the course of ten years. However, as perhaps the industry's leading innovator in makeup illusions, Smith was also responsible for creating appliances for Michael that would realistically display the effects of a broken jaw and—most important of all—handling Brando's makeup, which would transform the virile forty-seven-year-old superstar into a tired, yet still powerful, old man.

For most of the performers in the production, a need for makeup was limited: For women, basic makeup (1940s-style); for men, little or no makeup, thanks to Willis's underexposed film and carefully planned overhead lighting. For Duvall, who was nearly bald, Smith supplied a modest hairpiece for the 1940s and a slightly thinner version for the 1950s scenes.

For Michael, Smith designed a subtle makeup plan that would mature him slightly over the course of the film—an almost unnoticeable progression—except when comparing scenes from the beginning and the end of the film. (The effect is even more pronounced at the end of *The Godfather Part II*, when Michael reflects back eighteen years to his enlistment in the Marines. Viewers can compare Michael made up to look a young twenty-one to Michael at a weary forty.)

For scenes that follow McCluskey breaking Michael's jaw, Smith produced a makeup effect that created the illusion of a severely traumatized face. Smith constructed a foam appliance that, when carefully fitted to Pacino's face and matched to his skin with makeup, would simulate the outward appearance of a swollen and distorted cheek.

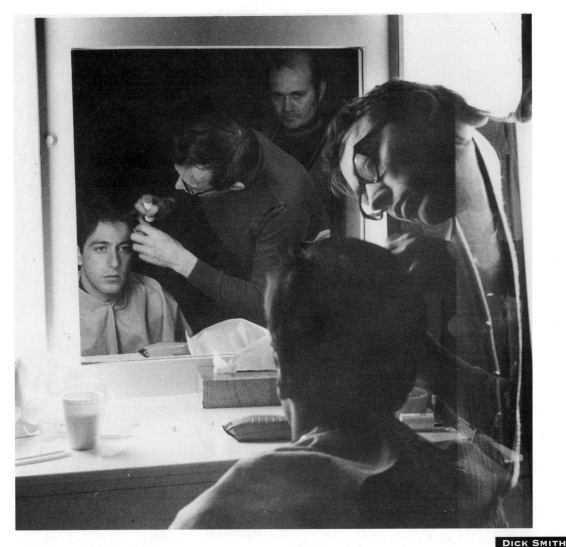

Smith also collaborated with dentist Henry Dwork, who developed effects at Coppola's request that were designed to create menacing physical characteristics for two of his actors. For Al Lettieri, who played Sollozzo, Coppola wanted a more sinister appearance. Lettieri already wore a dental bridge as a replacement for two teeth, so Dwork, a frequent consultant on film productions, replaced the original false teeth with a new bridge that contained a full gold crown on one tooth and an open-faced gold shell for the other. Coppola also wanted a more rugged look for Sonny's character, so Dwork simply built out the front of each of Caan's cuspids (the third tooth on each side of the top row). "In this case," Dwork said, "we proceeded on the theory that in humans, just as in wild animals, well-formed cuspids tend to give the impression of both strength and ferocity."

(1)

(2)

(3)

(4)

While the dental work for both Lettieri and Caan was flawless, it is visible briefly in only a few frames of the film, and then one has to look carefully to catch a glimpse. However, the appliances no doubt accomplished what Coppola wanted: A supplement to the more subtle character builders that the director tried to nurture in every actor, in a process that would soon become an integral part of rehearsal and performance.

The top priority for Smith was creating the critically important realistic aging for one of the world's most famous faces. Fortunately, nothing as complex as Smith's work for *Little Big Man* would be required for Brando; and, to suit the actor's temperament, Smith's work had to be relatively quick to apply.

"Marlon was willing to sit in the chair as long as needed—but no longer," Smith said. "We created makeup that wouldn't require three hours of his time."

Smith relied on a carefully designed and applied combination makeup effects. Most of the Don's aged appearance was created with applications of "old-age stipple," also known as liquid latex compound. When applied, stretched, dried, and released, old-age stipple creates the illusion of old and wrinkled skin. Smith began the application of old-age stipple around Brando's eyes, moved out across the face.

"At the eyes, for example, we would apply the latex to Marlon, and then pull up the skin above his eyebrows as high as it would go," Smith said. "With the latex applied, the skin can't return to its original shape, so it buckles and forms wrinkles of varying thicknesses, depending on the amount of latex."

The process of application, stretching, and releasing would continue across Brando's face and down to his neck—a daily ritual in facial exercise for Brando.

Two coats of stipple were used for Brando in his early scenes; to accentuate the illusion of aging, four coats were applied for the scenes of the Don in semiretirement and as a dying man.

A thin layer of oil mixture would eliminate the makeup look. Then Smith touched up the job with the addition of age spots and the mixed pigmentation of age, finally adding delicate lines to deepen wrinkles on Brando's forehead.

In the daily makeup sessions, Smith would need to do little to age Brando's hair. The actor's natural hair color at the time was blonde going to gray, and he dyed most of his hair a dark brownish-black, leaving some front strands untreated and naturally gray. With his hair combed back, Brando appeared to be balding; a few gray streaks applied by Smith to his hair and moustache heightened considerably the illusion of age.

To complete the job, Smith discolored Brando's teeth with a slight yellowish tint, which became more pronounced as the Don aged.

In his original test for *The Godfather*, Brando had stuffed Kleenex in his cheeks to give him the "look of a bulldog." To create the illusion of sagging jowls for production,

MARLON BRANDO IN MAKEUP BY DICK SMITH: (1) THE DON IN HIS EARLIEST SCENES SHOT ON THE PICTURE (NOTE THE SLIGHT EXTRA JOWL CAUSED BY THE UNTRIMMED DENTAL PLUMPERS); (2) READY FOR THE WEDDING SCENES (WITH SLIGHTLY LESS SAG TO HIS CHEEKS, AFTER THE PLUMPERS WERE SLIMMED; (3) WEARING THE MAKEUP FOR HIS CHARACTER'S OLDEST STAGE; AND (4) A VIGOROUS FORTY-SEVEN-YEAR-OLD, FINISHED WITH HIS WORK ON *THE GODFATHER*.

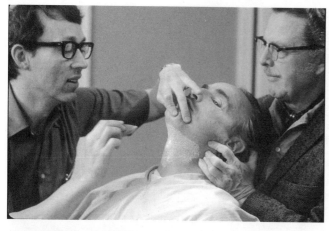

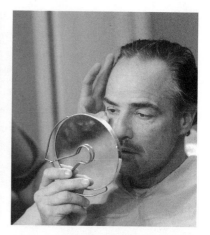

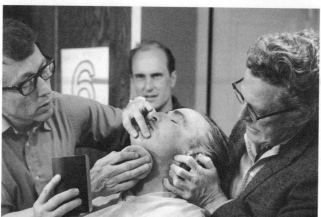

Dwork created "dental plumpers," flesh-colored blobs of acrylic that fit into the sides of Brando's mouth and flush up against his teeth. To hold the appliances in place, a metal band attached to the plumpers was wrapped around the base of Brando's teeth, with the ends wrapped around his molars like a piece of bridgework. (In spite of many reports since, the plumpers had no effect on Brando's speech; all of the actor's hoarseness and the strained voice of old age were intentional aspects of his performance.) The plumpers also succeeded in pushing out Brando's lower lip the slightest fraction of an inch, further distinguishing Brando the Superstar from Vito the Mafia Don.

The entire process of makeup for Brando in his early scenes of the Don required one and a half hours to complete, plus another fifteen to twenty minutes for the scenes of Vito Corleone as an older man. Stretch latex makeup cannot be reused, so each day's work required the same painstaking application; at the end of the day, Brando simply tore it off. "Getting out of that makeup was like peeling huge sheets of sunburned skin," said Smith.

Over the course of the production, Smith fine-tuned Brando's makeup. Brando was seldom available for costume fittings and makeup checks during preproduction, so when he arrived for rehearsal with the plumpers, they did not fit properly. Smith sculpted the plumpers just before shooting began, and continued to modify the appliance as Brando's scenes proceeded. Smith carefully shaved the appliance to perfect the sag they produced. The result was the slightest difference in Brando's appearance between his early shots (the wounding of the Don and the meeting with Sollozzo) and scenes filmed later (such as the wedding and meetings in his office).

In early March, Brando arrived in New York for rehearsals and makeup tests, and Smith completed his first makeup application for Coppola's approval. On March 10, Brando wore the makeup for the first time, along with a double-breasted gray suit and the other accessories that would complete the transformation: A false stomach, pads to round his shoulders and shorten his neck, and weights in his shoes to slow his gait. The combination of makeup and character immersion was truly startling, and Smith's efforts achieved precisely the effect that Coppola sought. Even face-to-face conversations with Brando or the unyielding eye of a close-up lens would fail to reveal the illusion of makeup.

Few performers were at Filmways on March 10, but to those at the studio who knew Brando as Johnny in *The Wild One,* Terry in *On the Waterfront,* Mr. Christian in *Mutiny on the Bounty,* or the charming, charismatic forty-seven-year-old who had disappeared into the makeup room only a short time before, the vision of the actor as the very essence of the war-weary Mafia Don provided a vivid first impression of the moviemaking magic they hoped to capture.

Brando's appearance—or rather, rumors about his appearance—would become the talk of New York during production. Ruddy and the Paramount publicity staff capitalized on Brando's appearance by wisely choosing to keep his makeup a closely guarded secret, shielding the actor from photographers while in his makeup. Speculations about how Brando would look only intensified interest in *The Godfather* while the production was in New York.

In mid-March, Coppola was able to gather his actors for his first rehearsals. The performers were all contracted for two weeks of rehearsal. Of course, Coppola would have preferred more.

"I always get what they give me, which is two weeks," Coppola said. "I always ask for three. I think more spatially, less linear, so I need to see the whole thing in order to be motivated to go on. I want all of it at once, to bring it up, like the way a Polaroid comes out, and that's very different."

On March 17, Brando arrived on the set for his first rehearsal.

"I remember the first day Brando showed up to rehearse," Ruddy said. "Everyone was sitting around telling jokes and entertaining each other. Fucking Brando walked in and no one could say a word. It was like Christ had come down from the cross. The greatest living actor in the world. So Brando started telling jokes. He was fantastic. He could not have been more gracious to everyone on the set."

Coppola began the rehearsal with the opening scene of the movie. Frank Puglia, the first actor cast to play Bonasera the undertaker, began the scene alone with Brando. Other principals would soon arrive, reading their lines and discussing the development of their characters with the director.

The rehearsal was much like any other run-through: The patient combination of readings, discussions, guidance, and interpretation. But Coppola, like a few other directors who are particularly interested in deep interpretations of character and personality, would take his readings a step further by expanding his rehearsals into broad exchanges and meetings about intricate details of character, motivation, and personal history—issues that would never appear on screen. For a production as rich in relationships as *The Godfather*, a key to Coppola's direction and rehearsal was the creation of "acting memories"—the background, problems, and likes and dislikes of each character, which the actors remembered and imbedded either consciously or subconsciously in their performance.

In rehearsals, Coppola supplemented the actual text from the script with a variety of additional improvised sequences.

"I add scenes in rehearsals—not in the shooting script—to give the actors memories," Coppola recalled. "One thing I often do is have a scene where two characters meet for the first time, even though in the story they've already known each other for a while. I find that giving the cast sensual memories always helps them. As artists, they're playing a scene, just the fact that they share a memory—it becomes like a little emotional deposit in their bank account that enables them to better know each other."

Much of the work in early rehearsals revolved around group settings such as meetings and meals, so the rehearsal stages at Filmways were strewn with character-reinforcing tools the actors could use to supplement their work: thin Italian cigars (which would later be puffed off camera by several in the cast), prop pistols, Italian wine and food, cooking utensils, silverware, newspapers, and other personal items.

For a film with meals and family gatherings as a plot cornerstone, discussing character development over dinner was ideal. The back room at Patsy's Restaurant, at the time in East Harlem on 116th Street, became the site of several informal rehearsal meals, including the first one with the full Corleone family cast on March 17.

To create the atmosphere of the Corleone household and inspire the spark of character development, Coppola had arranged the evening to represent a real family dinner. The evening thus became not only an opportunity to explore the characters, but to actually *assume* characters in a natural setting and without the distractions of a production on-set.

"It was the first time they had all met, and all I did was have them improvise for two or three hours, over a meal, that they were a family," Coppola said. "They'd never met before really, and it was like playing at a family, a kind of sensual opportunity for them to relate to each other. It was very, very valuable."

One can only imagine this powerhouse assemblage of actors, improvising in character for an evening: Brando at the head of the table; Talia Shire setting the table and serving the spaghetti; and Duvall, Caan, Pacino, and Cazale holding normal dinnertime conversations as they slowly submerged into their characters.

"We were all new to each other," said John Cazale. "We stood there not knowing what to do. It was Brando who broke the ice. He just went over, opened a bottle of wine and started the festivities. I think we all realized then that he was acting with us the way the Don would have acted with his own family."

"Everyone was doing what their roles were," said Pacino. "We were doing it, and you knew you were doing it in a crazy kind of way. You couldn't help it. I thought, what else are we here for? We would never have been there if it wasn't for the movie."

Coppola's technique of developing acting memories in rehearsal, combined with infusions of his Italian heritage, would help create the bonds, the family, the loyalty, and the "Italian-ness" of the production. While these textures were not integrated into the written material, virtually every scene in *The Godfather* would be touched by acting memories in countless bits of nuance. When Michael offers to murder Sollozzo and McCluskey, Sonny toys with his brother, gently slapping at him like an affectionate older brother would while Michael, the youngest son, wards off the pretend blows with open palms, just like a defenseless little brother. Early in the movie, when Michael, still feeling like the outsider of the family, greets Tom at the wedding, he first offers his hand. Tom pulls him into a hug, and Michael hesitates for a split second before returning the embrace—but he still keeps a chair between them. In a later scene, as Michael leaves to kill Sollozzo and McCluskey, he hugs Tom warmly and grabs his neck in an affectionate gesture of intimacy as the psychological wall he has built between himself and the family begins to crumble.

These rehearsals—both the traditional rehearsing of the script and the improvised development of acting memories—continued throughout the early stages of the production. As the third week of March drew to a close, Coppola worked closely in discussions with his performers, and the characters began to take form.

With only a few days left before shooting began, few in the cast or crew yet knew that the insular world of their work was about to be thrust into the national spotlight. Outside the confines of the studio, the project was still in jeopardy as Ruddy dealt with the Italian-American Civil Rights League and its founder, Joe Colombo, in a struggle to keep the production from falling apart.

"Do We Trust This Guy or Not?"

MOST OF the mail and political heat from the League about *The Godfather* was directed at Robert Evans at Paramount or Charles Bluhdorn at Gulf+Western, not at the production itself. In early March, only weeks before production was scheduled to begin, Evans wisely delegated responsibility for dealing with the problem to Ruddy.

"Evans told me, 'You've got to get together with this guy Joe Colombo,'" Ruddy recalled. "'He's putting pressure on the studio about *The Godfather*. I told him you are the producer—you meet with him.'"

Ruddy—tall, good-natured, gravel-voiced, straightforward in his dealings with everyone—would have been the ideal peacemaker to meet with the League even if he had not been associated with *The Godfather.* So Ruddy arranged for a meeting with Colombo at the League office to explain his position about *The Godfather.*

"I said, 'Joe, this is not a Hollywood attempt to defame Italian Americans—it's a much better film than that,'" Ruddy recalled. "'As a matter of fact, the film takes quite a skeptical look at Irish cops and Jewish movie producers and a lot of other people.'

"At this point, no one outside the production had seen the script. So I told him, 'Why don't you come to my office and I'll show you the screenplay?'

"Colombo came to my office the next day with two of his boys. I give him a 155-page script. He said, 'These glasses, these glasses don't work too good.' He gave the script to his boys, and soon they were passing the script around—none of them wanted to read a 155-page script.

"So after a little more conversation about the picture, we had built up a rapport. Colombo looks at his two pals and says, 'Hey, do we trust this guy or not?' They would have said yes to Hitler at this point. So we cut a deal."

Ruddy ironed out the details of an agreement at La Scala Restaurant with Nat Marcone, president of the League, and Anthony Colombo, Joe's son and vice president of the League. A few days later, Ruddy met with a large group of League members.

"I told Anthony Colombo I just wanted to sit around and talk about the movie," Ruddy said. "So we met at the Park-Sheraton Hotel, about 600 members of the League and me. I told them that it was my intent, and I believe the book's also, not to defame any ethnic group. I was not going to make a schlock gangster movie—and I told them so. They reacted favorably."

Later, at least one reporter would characterize the meeting as a quasi audition for roles in the film; others called it an attempt to bribe the League. Ruddy says no. "They didn't get one fucking nickel out of us. Not one nickel, and they never asked for one, either."

While members of the League and their friends were later cast as extras in the film or used as production assistants to help with crowd control in Italian-American neighborhoods, there were no deals cut for work that night, said Ruddy—only discussions about the tone of the film, the use of the words "Mafia" and *"La Cosa Nostra,"* the offer of proceeds from the premiere to go to a charity of the league's choice, and assurances that the film would not defame Italian Americans in general.

The League could have asked for other concessions, such as moderation in the use of ethnic stereotypes, accents, and nasty slurs. As the final film turned out, slurs against Italians were included—like Woltz's rapid-fire tirade to Hagen about "dago guinea wop greaseball gumbahs." But there were no cultural stereotypes, such as overdone campy Italian accents. A fine line exists between portraying a culture and painting stereotypes with a broad brush, and Coppola didn't cross it.

In fact, James Caan recalled literally dozens of actors who were rejected for parts large and small who fit the stereotypes for Italian tough guys in manner, dress, and speech—"they talked in *deeze* and *doze*," Caan remembered. The toughest characters in the movie—the Don, Barzini, Sollozzo, and Tattaglia—had no trace at all of Italian accents. Only Salvatore Corsitto as Bonasera the undertaker speaks with the typical Italian movie accent and then only once ("her nose was a'broken, her jaw was a'shattered. . . ."), because that was Corsitto's natural way of speaking. In a singsongy voice, Clemenza uses the same accent when he kids Michael about telling Kay that he loves her ("I love you with all-a my heart! If I don't see you again soon, I'm a-gonna die!"), but only as a joke.

In the final film, Coppola injected plenty of authentic Italian culture, color, and family bonding, which merged seamlessly with scenes of violence and sociopathic behavior—precisely the dichotomy Coppola wanted to demonstrate. Rather than insulting Italian Americans, *The Godfather* as directed by Coppola would help viewers appreciate the distinction between Italians portrayed as murderers, and murderers who happen to be Italian.

"That contrast was the whole point to Francis's approach to the film," said Tavoularis. "He wanted the audience to see that these guys were in many ways like us—that's the paradox of it. Like Hitler holding a party. These people had their kids and their wives, and that all had a place in their lives. You can't relate to a guy blowing someone's brains out, but you can relate to a guy making spaghetti. And then when you see that same guy sit in the back of a car and kill somebody—I think that was one of the great strengths of the way Francis made the film. Not that it had never been done before, but Francis did it in a very strong way that captivated people."

In sealing his deal with the League, Ruddy was acting on his own. Although Evans had asked him to meet with Joe Colombo, Ruddy had not been authorized to make a deal promising script changes or offering the proceeds from the premiere to a specific charity. And, while Bluhdorn was in New York, most of the senior Paramount management was out of the country.

But Ruddy had run out of time. Production was scheduled to begin in ten days, and the producer had to ensure that work would proceed, if not with cooperation from the League, then at least without the group's interference. When Ruddy's deal with the League was made public on March 19, the announcement created national news, caused substantial corporate embarrassment on both coasts, and nearly cost the producer his job on the production.

On Friday, March 19, flanked by Anthony Colombo and Nat Marcone at a press conference, Ruddy announced the deal: In exchange for League cooperation in the making of *The Godfather*, Ruddy assured Colombo that the words "Mafia" and "*La Cosa Nostra*" would not be spoken in *The Godfather*. In addition, the proceeds from the film's world premiere would be donated to the League's hospital fund.

Afterward, Ruddy would acknowledge privately that he had been asked to concede much more. The League members had suggested substituting generic American names for Italian names, a not-so-veiled suggestion to remove the Italian-American emphasis in the film. But Ruddy drew the line.

"Even after I made the deal, some League members wanted us to drop Italian surnames and use names like Smith and Jones and Johnson. But I made it clear that we weren't going to change the quality of the book."

The concession was minimal. Only early drafts of the script contained the word "Mafia," and then only twice. The phrase "La Cosa Nostra" was included through all drafts, including the March 29 version that contained the conversations between Michael and the Don as an old man—a scene that was entirely rewritten midway through production.

Almost immediately, some critics of Ruddy's deal—and later some film historians—hinted that the producer had somehow hoodwinked the League by persuading them to cut a deal even though the objectionable terms weren't in the script to begin with. But all parties involved in the press conference—including the League—acknowledged that only three references were removed from the script.

What the League did receive was much more important than changes to the script: First, they received Ruddy's good faith assurances that the word "Mafia" would not mysteriously reappear in the film, and second, that The Godfather would not make Italian Americans ashamed of their heritage. The producer was true to his word.

Ruddy's problems with the League were over. But his troubles with the studio were just beginning.

After all of the delays in production, the unofficial start of shooting for The Godfather began a week earlier than expected. To take advantage of a forecast for snow at the Best & Co. location, the production started with a one-day shoot on March 23. The first shots of the production were the exterior scenes of Kay and Michael leaving the department store after their Christmas shopping.

The production was poised to begin an eighteen-hour first day in three principal locations, but a bigger drama was unfolding a few blocks away at the Gulf+Western headquarters.

The crew had awakened to a media broadside over Ruddy's deal with the League: An article and an editorial in the New York Times (which followed the paper's page-one coverage of the deal on March 20) carried reactions from New York state legislators and an angry backlash from the studio denouncing Ruddy's actions.

"So we were there shooting—the first day—and the next thing I know it's all over the papers," Ruddy said. "I get back to the hotel and I get a call from a friend in publicity at Paramount: 'Whatever you do, don't answer the phone. Charlie's trying to fire you tonight. But come in early in the morning and talk to him.'"

Judging by the reaction in the media and the halls of the state legislature in Albany, onlookers might have assumed that Ruddy had signed a pact with the Mafia itself. Already the lines of distinction between the League and the Mafia were being blurred by the press and a rapid-fire succession of stories appeared in the New York Times and the Wall Street Journal, relating the story of Ruddy's deal with the Italian-American Civil Rights League and offering many details linking

Colombo to the underworld. *Newsweek* called the making of the film "Shooting the Unmentionable."

After reading about Ruddy's concessions to the League, State Senator John Marchi wrote him a letter that said, in part, "Apparently you are a ready market for the League's preposterous theory that we can exorcise devils by writing them out of the English language.

"Mr. Ruddy, there just might be a Mafia, and if you have been reached I have only the feeling that the Italian Americans as well as the larger community have been had. Your action amounts to a monstrous insult to millions upon millions of loyal Americans of Italian extraction who must deeply resent this assault on the right of free expression at their expense.

"Thanks for nothing."

But the worst publicity—as far as Paramount was concerned—came on the editorial page of the *New York Times*.

Under the headline, YES, MR. RUDDY, THERE IS A . . . , the editorial blistered Ruddy for his agreement with the League.

To imply that any ethnic, national or racial group is particularly prone to criminal or antisocial deeds is despicable. It is also—as the melting pot of crime in America shows—simply not supportable by facts.

It is one thing, however, to oppose such irrational smears but quite another to deny that some illegal associations or rings are led or dominated by members of certain ethnic or nationality groups. This is why the efforts of the Italian-American Civil Rights League in fighting not the Mafia but all references to its existence are so deplorably misguided. The latest chapter in that incredible campaign to make the Mafia disappear by expunging the term from the American language is the League's success in persuading Al Ruddy, producer of the motion picture *The Godfather*, to censor the forbidden word.

The League could render its most constructive service if it were to join with Americans of all nationalities and races in opposing the Mafia, instead of trying to render it invisible by making it unmentionable.

The situation would worsen later in the week with the publication of a *Wall Street Journal* story, a crusher for those at Paramount and Gulf+Western who paid attention to the publication's vast audience in the investment community. The article appeared under the headline, COLOMBO'S CRUSADE: ALLEGED MAFIA CHIEF RUNS AGGRESSIVE DRIVE AGAINST SAYING "MAFIA." The story went on to talk about Joe Colombo and his alleged ties to the underworld.

"The founder of the League is Joseph Colombo, a Brooklyn real estate salesman who also happens to be, according to federal authorities, boss of one of five Mafia 'families' in New York and a member of the Mafia's national council," the *Journal* reported. "Joe Colombo greets such accusations good-naturedly. 'If I'm the head of an organized-crime family,' he challenges, 'let them prove it.'"

The story also mentioned the earnest efforts by the League to conduct charitable work to maintain accurate and positive images of Italian Americans, but the bulk of the story focused on Colombo and his background.

Of all the coverage, the line that no doubt riled Bluhdorn the most was a *New York Times* lead that described the proceeds from the premiere as "going to the League," and not a more accurate statement indicating that the money would be used for a hospital fund. Intentional or not, the line suggested that Paramount was bribing the League; even more indirectly, the *Times's* report and other coverage implied that the company was working in cooperation with the Mafia.

Paramount, initially caught flat-footed by the national publicity over the announcement of Ruddy's deal, fired back with a statement on March 21. The studio announced that it was taking "great umbrage" at the publicity about the deal and called the agreement "completely unauthorized." The studio reneged on the deal to give the premiere's proceeds to a League charity; however, the studio executives also said that they "will go along with eliminating 'Mafia' and 'La Cosa Nostra' from the screenplay, per U.S. Attorney General John M. Mitchell's directive on government reference to organized crime."

Neither the studio nor Gulf+Western could have been happy when Ruddy, three days after the deal was announced, attended a dinner for the League—a $125-a-plate testimonial dinner that honored Colombo as "man of the year" for his humanitarian services. Especially embarrassing to Gulf+Western was the *Times's* follow-up coverage of the squabble that appeared on March 23. Under the headline, CORPORATE RIFT IN GODFATHER FILMING, the *Times* suggested that Gulf+Western's Leisure Time subsidiary was acting without the parent company's consent.

"An executive of Gulf+Western said that Mr. Ruddy had no authorization to set up the press conference at which the agreement was announced, nor the right to give away the opening night proceeds," the *Times* reported. "A Paramount executive said, however, that although it was true that Mr. Ruddy had acted on his own, 'it was in line with Al Ruddy's efforts in getting help with the production here.'

"The Gulf+Western and Paramount executives differed sharply on the announcement that the opening night proceeds would go to the League's hospital fund. The parent company's spokesman indicated strongly that his organization greatly disapproved of the arrangement while the Paramount executive was not unhappy with the plan.

"The Gulf executive, without elaboration, said that Mr. Ruddy's performance as producer of the film will be examined closely."

All of this hubbub over proceeds of a premiere and three words in a script.

Ruddy had no patience with the critics. "When I made the deal with the League it looked as if we had knuckled under and would emasculate the film," Ruddy said angrily. "I felt at that point that I was taking a beating from the press and some of my friends. But ultimately I had to stand or fall with what turned out on the screen.

"What annoyed me at the time was that the press made a big thing out of our dropping the terms 'Mafia' and 'La Cosa Nostra' from the picture. But Attorney General John Mitchell had already issued a directive that his department would no longer use those words. And ABC had agreed not to use the words in its FBI television series. But those agreements just barely made the news."

Ruddy was upset, but Bluhdorn was even more so. His company had been publicly embarrassed, it appeared that one of its struggling subsidiaries was thumbing its nose at the corporate headquarters, and there were those close to the company who had real concerns that the Mafia was infiltrating its operations. As a result, Ruddy came within a whisker of retreating to Los Angeles unemployed.

The next day, when Ruddy was ushered into Charles Bluhdorn's office at Gulf+Western's headquarters, the chief executive was boiling.

"I went in that morning, and Charlie was holding the *New York Times* from the day before," said Ruddy. "He was screaming at me about the price of the company's stock. I told him, 'Charlie, what can I say? I'm not a shareholder in G+W. I don't own one share in this company. My job is to get this movie made. I think I made a very good deal to allow us to shoot in New York and get some overt and covert cooperation.'

"Bluhdorn was still yelling about firing my ass. I said, 'No hard feelings. I got my deal, my money, it's your company, see you around.' What really drove him crazy is that he always offered me cigars when I was there. When I left, I went to his desk, opened his humidor, took about five cigars, and walked out. I swear to God he wanted to murder me.

"I went back to the hotel to pack, and Bob Evans calls from the Bahamas. He said, 'What did you do? Charlie said you didn't apologize—he said you just took some cigars and left.'

"I said, 'Bob, what do I have to apologize for? I told Charlie the truth. I made the deal to get the movie made.'"

Bluhdorn stopped the production (although with six days until the next shooting day, there was little to stop) to consider how to handle the problem. It was Coppola, who had been defended so often by Ruddy over his decisions about the casting and the script, who rescued his producer.

"Charlie told Francis he was firing me," Ruddy said. "Francis said to him, 'You're making a big mistake. He's the only guy who can keep this thing going in New York.' Given our problems with the League, Charlie realized that was probably true. He reluctantly changed his mind and put me back on the picture. He called me in again and said, 'If you talk to one press guy again, I will murder you myself.' So I was back on the movie."

Regardless of media and corporate denunciation of Ruddy's deal with the League, no one could gripe with the result. As soon as Ruddy reached a deal with Colombo, the production's problems evaporated. Prospects of union troubles disappeared. Threats of picketing were called off. Concerns about location shooting vanished.

Paramount withdrew Ruddy's offer to donate the premiere's proceeds to the League, but it didn't matter. Ruddy had dealt in good faith with the League, and Colombo wouldn't forget it.

"Colombo called and said, 'You didn't bullshit us, you've been straight up with us,'" Ruddy remembered. "'Anything I can do to help you, I'm gonna help you.' And they helped us on a number of occasions."

As Ruddy had discovered, there were distinct differences between Italian Americans, the Italian-American Civil Rights League, and the Mafia. But in the preproduction fuss over the filming of *The Godfather*, the differences were often obscured, unfortunately, for the tens of thousands of responsible members of the League and millions of Italian Americans who had no association with the underworld.

The media was responsible for much of the blurring between the League and the Mob. Then and later, the press often characterized Ruddy's deal with the League by reporting that *the Mafia* stopped interfering with the production, thus stating outright that the League and the Mob were one and the same. Ruddy more accurately described his deal and the near-instantaneous cooperation the production received in New York: "The League urged New Yorkers of Italian descent whom we'd be working with to cooperate with us."

However, Ruddy is clear about his distinction.

"I know there is a Mafia," Ruddy said, "but people use the word indiscriminately. The Mafia is just a small part of organized crime—the Italian part. Other ethnic groups are just as deeply involved. Maybe they aren't as colorful.

"Certainly some of the League members belonged to the Mafia. But I met with thousands of hard-working, honest Italian Americans who know nothing about organized crime."

But the question remains: Did the Mafia really help make *The Godfather?*

"Without the Mafia's help, it would have been impossible to make the picture," Ruddy said. "There would have been pickets, breakdowns, labor problems, cut cables, all kinds of things. I don't think anyone would have been physically hurt. But the picture simply could not have been made without their approval and if the boys hadn't helped us."

Later, the differences between the League and the Mafia became simpler to identify. Once the deal was struck with the League, the organization maintained a discreet distance from the production. Colombo and "the boys" not only helped smooth the rough waters, they also aided directly in acquiring locations and serving as regular, paid production aides for traffic and location support. Colombo was particularly helpful in arranging for the Staten Island location for the Corleone Mall after the Manhasset site fell through.

"Most of the homeowners in the area were ready to cooperate, except for one man," said Ruddy. "We did everything we could—we literally offered to send his child to college if he would let us use his house. This guy was an Italian American, and I told some of the boys about our problem. They sat down with him and said, 'Hey, this movie is going to be good for our people, why don't you help them?' It wasn't overt intimidation, but the message was clear. I felt like a lowlife being there."

Once the movie got under way, an affable relationship began to develop among the production staff, cast, and "the boys" as Ruddy, Frederickson, and—especially—Caan frequently joined them for meals or drinks.

"They've got incredible moves," Caan said. "I watched them with each other and with their girls and wives. It's incredible how affectionate they are to each other. There's tremendous interplay. They toast each other—'centa'nni,' 'salute a nostra'—all of this marvelous old-world stuff from guys who were born here and don't even speak Italian."

"All the guys on the movie wanted to meet the real boys," Ruddy recounted. "Everyone got to be very friendly. Jimmy Caan would come back in another life as one of the boys. The guys were great to us. Hey, they love show business, too."

Others involved in the production had already had experience dealing with the Mob. When Brando starred in *On the Waterfront*, the actor recalled that to shoot film of cargo operations, director Elia Kazan needed permission from organized crime leaders—a particular irony, given that the film was *about* corruption on the docks. Brando said he even accompanied Kazan to a lunch meeting with the head of the Jersey waterfront.

In his book, Brando recalled that when *The Godfather* was shooting on Mott Street in Little Italy, the production was visited by Joe Bufalino who asked to be introduced to Brando. The actor remembers giving him a tour of the Corleones' olive oil company set in a Little Italy warehouse.

Ruddy spotted Carlo Gambino watching the filming from a window on Mott Street. "It wasn't like there were three hundred wiseguys hanging around every day, but they were there," Ruddy said. "We could hear them talking—'You think Brando looks good in those clothes? Nah, the boss shouldn't dress that way'—that sort of thing."

For Caan, associating with Mob figures was like a little leaguer running around with the Yankees. The *New York Times's* Nicholas Pileggi wrote, "Caan was, in fact, seen in the company of Carmine (The Snake) Persico and other federally certified Mafiosi so often and had absorbed so many of their mannerisms that undercover agents thought for a while that he was just another rising young button in the Mob."

Gianni Russo claimed several friends in the Mafia—in particular on Staten Island. The Mob, Russo noted, "is like the Boy Scouts or Girl Scouts. Everyone should have an organization."

Of course, Boy Scouts don't execute members of other troops. Several in *The Godfather* knew to keep the relationship between the Mob and the movie in perspective. Said Duvall, "A guy from Harlem, a friend of mine, gave me some tips, and I went out with a few hoods to get a little flavor. They admit they're hoods, they joke about it, but there's a viciousness underneath it with every one of them."

Singer Al Martino had more experience dealing with the boys than anyone would ever want. Martino had actually been one of Puzo's models for Johnny Fontane—in particular for an incident involving Martino's early years working in a Mob-run nightclub. When Martino wanted to move on, the boys weren't happy. Martino was beaten severely in the parking lot and soon after left for Europe, where he performed for eight years. He came back when he felt "the heat was off."

Despite all the rumors, good-natured bonding, a few roles as extras, and some on-set fashion commentary, the Mafia had no direct influence on the production itself.

"Some of the boys asked us to get a particular musical group into the wedding scene, but we wouldn't do it," Ruddy said. "We didn't give them a fucking thing. But they were great to me."

As the production evolved, the relationship between *The Godfather* production and the Mafia developed into an intriguing mutual admiration society; the cast and crew enjoyed the superficial romance of the Mob, and the boys liked the production because they wished their lives were really like those of Puzo's fictional characters.

"I think down deep it was the book that hooked them," Ruddy said. "Later they liked the movie—they just didn't want to see a schlock movie made. Everyone's always depicting Italians like 1930s Hollywood mobsters, flipping coins in the air and killing kids. Enough of the boys came by the show every now and then, that I think at a certain point they fell in love with the whole thing—Brando, and Jimmy Caan, and the others. It started to turn into a happening for them. All they got out of it was a few parts as extras—but that doesn't mean shit when we hired three hundred extras and a few of the boys were hanging around at the right time. They never got a part they didn't deserve, then never got any money, they had no control over the picture—zip.

"I always said I would rather deal with one of the boys than a Hollywood lawyer. Because when they shake your hand, and you know what the deal is, you have a contract.

"They got a lot of friends," continued Ruddy, "and a lot of laughs, and we all enjoyed having them around, and they loved coming down to see the movie made. It turned out to be a good experience for them and for us. I don't have any regrets about the boys I did business with."

Once Ruddy's deal with the League was settled, the issue would quickly die away as all Hollywood blowups do. But even through the chaos, executives at Paramount could see that the deal with the League had become a publicity windfall.

In the saga of *The Godfather* and the Mafia, there were lessons to be learned by all. For the studio: *There's no such thing as bad publicity.* For Ruddy and company: *When you want to shoot a movie about the Mafia in New York, be careful what you wish for.*

For the Mafia, the lesson would come decades later: *Listen to Don Vito Corleone.* Precisely twenty-five years after *The Godfather* was filmed in New York, in an extraordinary case of life imitating art, members of the last of the New York crime families that had remained relatively unscathed in federal investigations of organized crime were brought to justice. In April 1996, seventeen members of the Genovese crime family were arrested on charges that included illegal gambling and the murder of a mentally ill member who spilled family secrets. News reports said that while investigations had dealt crippling blows to the city's four other major crime families, the Genovese had remained intact, *"partly by sticking to construction and labor racketeering schemes and avoiding drug dealing."* One can almost hear the echoes of Vito Corleone in his meeting with the other Mafia dons: "I believe this drug business is going to destroy us in the years to come. . . ."

"It's Only a Gangster Picture"

AFTER MORE than a year of planning and five months after the original start date, Coppola was ready to go: He had the most talented creative staff available, a handpicked cast, and a script he had cowritten. However, from the studio's perspective, the production no doubt looked like a nervous band of filmmaking novices: a young director with no track record for major productions, a producer with more success saving money than making it, an erratic star, and an insecure second lead—all working on developing a property that was potentially the most valuable in cinema history.

Coppola's production team was prepared to shoot in dozens of locations around Manhattan, New Jersey, Long Island, Sicily, Las Vegas, and Los Angeles. On Staten Island, a side street and several houses were quickly being transformed into a walled fortress for the Corleone Mall while the Genco Olive Oil Company offices were being fitted into an upstairs floor of an old building in Little Italy. On a Filmways soundstage, the main set for the ground floor of the Corleone residence was under construction, as were several other smaller sets to be used as other rooms and isolated areas, such as the door and walls used for the sex scene between Sonny and Lucy. (Because of the pressure of completing many other production details, the house interiors would not be completed until late April.)

Coppola was ready for his most important test as director. He would be a constant figure on the set—first to arrive and last to leave, always in motion. Usually clad in loose pants and a bright shirt in warm weather or a long leather coat and a knit cap in the cold, he was perennially rumpled and consistently shaggy; the passage of time on the production could be measured by the length of his hair and beard until hairstylist Phil Leto corralled him for a quick trim.

On March 23, while Ruddy was busy pacifying the brass in the aftermath of the League

deal, the production crew prepared for a single-day shoot, orchestrated to take advantage of the possibility of snow for the Best & Co.
scene. The shoot used two other locations in a grueling eighteen-hour
marathon of setup, shooting, and moves around midtown New York
and lower Manhattan.

That day, cast and crew got their first taste of the excitement the
production would generate among New Yorkers. Even though the
shoot started in early morning on a cold spring day, hundreds of spec-
tators gathered to watch the production set up; later other locations would draw thousands. Television crews and print reporters covered the shoot as a news story. To manage the spectators, the
production was supported by New York Tactical Patrol officers, who had the formidable task of
clearing avenues and side streets during the morning rush hour. The traffic control, combined
with the spillover crowds, would create driving nightmares at virtually every location used for *The
Godfather*, but New Yorkers struggled on in spite of the confusion.

As setup began for the Best & Co. scene, it soon became clear that snow would not fall. The
snow machine worked early in the day, spreading a small blizzard of white across the sidewalk

and part of the street. Fake snow was needed to "dress" the location, and the plastic flakes were also blown around during each take of Pacino and Keaton (in the shot used in the film, Pacino appears to get a flake in his eye that he quickly brushes away).

The work moved along quickly through the morning and was completed by noon, so the crew moved on to the second location of the day, Polk's Hobby Shop on Fifth Avenue at 31st Street, for an exterior shot of Tom Hagen's abduction—a simple shot that was handled quickly. Late in the evening, the production moved back to midtown to the front of Radio City Music Hall, for shots of Michael and Kay exiting the theater and learning of the attempt on the Don's life.

The outside of the theater had been dressed for a Christmas 1945 showing of the film, *The Bells of St. Mary's*, starring Bing Crosby and Ingrid Bergman (hence Kay's query to Michael, "Would you like me better if I were Ingrid Bergman?"). The distinctive curved facade of Radio City displayed the title, LEO MCCAREY'S THE BELLS OF ST. MARY'S, and the large display windows were fitted with reproductions of posters from the film (a Paramount picture, naturally). In real life, Radio City Music Hall was featuring *A New Leaf*, starring Walter Matthau and Elaine May. To avoid customer confusion, ushers walked the aisles to announce the actual program for the evening.

Filming of the simple scene of Michael and Kay walking, then discovering the shocking news about the Don, moved slowly. Coppola asked for numerous takes and offered many suggestions to his actors. The day's work finally concluded after 2 A.M., and still Coppola was not satisfied; the shots would continue on another day. Fortunately, the rest of the production would revert to its original schedule and not pick up again until March 29.

This first day of production provided an indication of the pressurized atmosphere the cast and crew would face for the next three and a half months. While few days would be as intense as March 23, many would involve quick moves between two or more locations to maintain the steady pace needed to produce a three-hour movie in eighty-two shooting days in New York and Sicily.

Although Coppola settled many of his major disagreements with Paramount before production began, *The Godfather* provided far more than the routine creative pressure that accompanies every motion picture. The unique creative and financial setting Coppola had created for himself at American Zoetrope was on the line, and Warner Bros. was already planning to grab the first of his earnings from the profit of *The Godfather*—assuming, of course, there would be profits to grab.

If Coppola failed on *The Godfather*, he would lose everything, including Zoetrope. Certainly he would be able to find work as a writer, but that would mean going back to the Hollywood mill, struggling again to find a foothold for rebuilding his shattered dream.

"My history with *The Godfather* was very much the history of someone in trouble," Coppola said. "I found the first movie very tough to do and very tough to finally pull off. I was a young director, I hadn't really done a lot of work, and I had this opportunity to do this novel. I knew that as the book became more popular and more successful, I realized that in a sense it was beginning to outclass me.

"I had to hang in. Everything was at stake."

Of course, even under the best of circumstances, directing a major production was, in Coppola's words, "like running in front of a moving locomotive. If you stop, if you trip, if you make a mistake, you get killed. And *Godfather* was worse than most."

Like Coppola, Pacino was worried about his tenure on the project. Early in the production, Pacino's creative growth was hampered by negative muttering about his work, and he believed he was perilously close to getting fired. The week that passed between the first and second days of shooting didn't help; it gave the studio a chance to study his first day's work and the actor too much time to think.

"They kept saying, 'When is he going to do something? He seems so dull,'" remembered Pacino. "While we were shooting, there were hints coming back to me that I wasn't wanted. It was more than hints—people were actually giggling when I went on camera."

Today it seems quite understandable why the studio was unimpressed with Pacino's first work on *The Godfather*. The takes of Pacino from the March 23 shoot in front of Best & Co. are cute, goofy-in-love scenes—hardly the actor's milieu. In these scenes, Michael smiles at Kay; he squints, wipes snow from his eyes, looks

PACINO EARLY IN PRODUCTION— MORE LIKE A SCARED RABBIT THAN A PROSPECTIVE MAFIA DON.

distracted, and kisses her awkwardly as they walk. The day's later scenes shot in front of Radio City Music Hall were no more impressive; viewed in isolation and without benefit of earlier scenes from the film, the scenes showcase Pacino looking more like a scared rabbit than a prospective Mafia don. (In both scenes, Pacino also looks noticeably shorter than Keaton. He wore lifts in other scenes, such as that of their arrival to Connie's wedding and the final scene of the film. He returned to a shorter-than-Keaton stature during their reconciliation scene set in New Hampshire, which was filmed after principal photography was completed.) Neither early scene shows any of the actor's potential for dynamic performance that would soon become so apparent. In the broad framework of the final film, both sequences would appear perfectly acceptable, but in a cold, isolated appraisal, they seemed evidence of a casting decision that had potentially gone very wrong.

"I was out," Pacino was convinced, until the murder scene in Louis Restaurant shot on March 31.

"They kept me after that scene," Pacino recalled. "That looked pretty good I guess, when you shoot a guy. They wanted me to assert myself, so there's a kind of assertion."

Actually, Pacino had already begun to show the form that would shape the backbone of his character. Two days earlier, Coppola filmed Michael's drive with Sollozzo and McCluskey to dinner, a scene shot at Filmways in a real car with a simulated background of a night street created by passing lights and screens in front of and behind the actors. Despite the visual distractions, Pacino's suppressed anger over the shooting of his father, combined with the terror of preparing to commit his first murders, were more than convincing.

Although Pacino may have felt like he was about to get a pink slip, he wasn't ever really in danger of losing his shot at stardom.

"Once the movie started—never," said Al Ruddy. "Shooting a movie in New York is tough enough—you never want to fire an actor, unless he is so horrendous that you're willing to stop and restart the whole production. No one at the studio wanted to do that, and pretty soon they began to see rushes that showed Al's real talents."

The stories about Pacino's possible firing were probably only the product of the off-camera rumor mill that can be especially unkind to novice film actors.

And if Pacino's job had truly been in question, firing him would have only produced logistical and financial problems. Several key scenes involving Pacino scheduled for early in the production were shot on location and involved several actors whose contracted time on the project was limited. Replacing Pacino, even within a few days, would have required rescheduling expensive on-location shooting and extending the contracts of, at the very least, Sterling Hayden and Al Lettieri. Besides all these considerations, Coppola would never have allowed a new actor to assume the role of so pivotal a character without days of discussions, readings, and rehearsals.

None of this, of course, was obvious to Pacino—a young, apprehensive actor working desperately to capitalize on his first big break. What never occurred to Pacino was that in the harsh light of studio decision-making, firing him would not have been worth the time, trouble, or money.

As Pacino began to settle into the role, the creative experience he would face was by far the most artistically challenging in the production, as his character evolved from the young idealist to family protector to Mafia don.

"Playing Michael was a hellish experience," Pacino said. "I used to get up at five in the morning thinking about where I was in the film, what the transition was. That's why I have to block out a part, to figure out the transition from one block to another. I had to be sure I was building up to the point where Michael takes over from the Don."

It is a rare motion picture that is shot in sequence, and the filming of *The Godfather* was far more disjointed than most. Pacino was thus not only required to develop a screen persona in one of the most complex film characterizations ever attempted, but to do so in a production schedule that shifted at whim throughout. It remains an extraordinary visual and emotional experience to watch Pacino build Michael's character across the span of the film—a feat made even more extraordinary when one considers how the process occurred in scenes often shot months apart.

The March 23 shoot, for example, focused on an early scene of Michael and Kay buying

Christmas presents. As previously mentioned, the next scene Pacino shot was the sequence of Michael, Sollozzo, and McCluskey driving to dinner, a scene that occurs much later in the movie, after Michael has seriously reevaluated his role in the family. Later that same week, Pacino filmed the Sollozzo and McCluskey murder scene, followed by the hospital sequence with Brando, which takes place before the murders. Later in the production, over the course of a few days, Pacino shot scenes of Michael as the leader of the family in 1955, and *then* scenes at Connie's wedding, his earliest appearances in the film.

On July 2, the last shot of principal photography was the scene of Michael's pickup in front of Jack Dempsey's restaurant. In the final film, this shot was followed immediately by the scenes filmed inside the car on March 29; thus one of the first and the last scenes of Pacino's work in principal photography, shot more than three months apart, wound up one after the other in the final film.

On March 31, the production moved to the Bronx for Michael's murders of Sollozzo and McCluskey. Word had spread fast throughout Manhattan about *The Godfather* production; even though the shot was indoors, a huge crowd gathered.

PACINO NAPS DURING PREPARATION FOR THE MURDER SCENE OF SOLLOZZO AND MCCLUSKEY.

"When we filmed up in the Bronx, the windows of the restaurant were gelled to control the light, so no one could see anything," Ruddy said. "Five thousand people stood around just watching the cinemobile bus."

To save costs and simplify on-location logistics, the production did not travel with portable dressing rooms to the site; a neighborhood beauty parlor subbed for the makeup trailer, and a bar on the same street served as an on-site dressing room.

In the sequence, after McCluskey is wounded in the throat, he is killed with a shot to the forehead, as blood slowly and dramatically drips down his face. To satisfy Coppola's insistence on realistic violence, Smith created an unforgettable special makeup effect.

"At that time, the only thing that could make a bullet hit appear on flesh was a blood gun, which shoots a wax cylinder filled with a few drops of Karo blood," Smith said. "With a wax shot, the blood diffuses and goes in all directions."

STERLING HAYDEN IS RIGGED FOR THE SECOND TAKE OF MCCLUSKEY'S MURDER.

For McCluskey's injury, Smith created a combination of latex, Karo blood, and a squib (a miniature explosive charge used to simulate a bullet hit by blowing a hole in clothing or a prop). Smith mounted a low-power squib on a thin round metal plate curved to fit Hayden's forehead. To cover the squib, he then glued a latex appliance to the actor's forehead, leaving a small gap unglued. Smith filled a hypodermic needle with a half-teaspoon of Karo blood and squirted it into the gap, and then carefully camouflaged the delicate appliance with wrinkles and powder to match Hayden's skin tone. Finally, Smith ran a wire through Hayden's hair to a switch that fired the squib on cue.

Smith first tested the makeup effect on an extra with no ill effect; it worked just as well on Hayden. As Pacino fired a blank shot, the mini-squib burst through the appliance and the blood flowed down Hayden's face in perfect unison with the crack of the window behind McCluskey's head.

The rigging and makeup for this single shot required more than an hour of preparation. "Thankfully it required only two takes," Smith said.

The latex appliances were only used for the one gunshot scene and not in other scenes of Hayden in the restaurant, so Smith's work had to be virtually undetectable. His work was successful; even a close-up inspection of the scene does not reveal the setup.

While Hayden was being rigged with a new development in makeup effects technology, Al Lettieri was being set up for his death scene. To simulate the bullet hit on his forehead—which, unlike McCluskey's wound, would be visible for only a fraction of a second—A. D. Flowers and Joe Lombardi used the Hollywood standard for this sort of effect.

But Coppola wanted more. In the book, Puzo had described Sollozzo's brains being blown out, "a huge gout of blood and skull fragments." Coppola wanted that same image on film—a fine mist of blood that would balloon out in a wide pattern and linger on-screen for a horrible moment. To achieve this effect was nearly impossible with liquid; drops shot through a tube were too big and gushed out, and an aerosol rig behind Lettieri would not produce a blast of mist that would remain suspended in midair long enough to be visible on film. Consequently, Smith and Flowers combined forces to produce a grisly and memorable effect.

"We decided to use red powder—simple red face powder that was packed in an air tube," Smith said. "We filled a tube with the powder, ran it up behind Lettieri's head, and blasted the powder out as the shot was fired."

It was a complicated arrangement. To shoot a wax bullet to a precise target requires a keen marksman—especially for a head shot, since a wax cylinder can seriously damage an eye. Flowers and his team, expert marksmen all, handled the sequence of events perfectly in a gory choreography of Pacino standing, Lettieri turning his head, the shot being fired, the wax bullet hitting Lettieri's forehead, and the billowing mist of blood bursting out behind him. Only a frame-by-frame examination of the scene can reveal any flaws in the scene's realism: The blood appears on Lettieri's forehead a microsecond before the sound of Pacino's blank shot, and a tiny speck of wax is visible for a single frame.

The complicated effects, along with the extensive dialogue filmed in the scene, extended the shoot to a second day. After nightfall, the sequence was completed with a shot of Michael's exit from the restaurant and leap to the running board of Clemenza's car.

Unfortunately, Pacino misjudged his jump and twisted his ankle, severely straining a ligament. While not shooting, Pacino used a wheelchair, crutches, and a cane to stay mobile. (In the scene in the Don's study, when Michael declares his intention to shoot his father's would-be assassins, Caan can be seen holding a cane, which viewers assume belongs to Brando's character but is actually Pacino's.)

As luck would have it, Pacino's bumper hopping—and resulting injury—was wasted. As he ran out of the restaurant, he veered around a car and to the left of the screen, so his jump was nearly off-camera. Viewers can only see the car drive by and, in reflection in the restaurant's windows, roll away.

Key scenes were rescheduled to accommodate Pacino's injury, but fortunately he was not needed for a shot that required walking or running for nearly two weeks.

Brando's first day on *The Godfather* production was scheduled for April 12 at the New York Eye and Ear Hospital. He didn't make it. Scheduled to arrive on an overnight flight from Los Angeles, he missed the plane; although not his fault, the gaff cost the production an entire day's work, to the tune of $40,000. The scene was rescheduled for the next day, after the production first shot on the loading dock at Lincoln Hospital. Coppola filmed the loading of

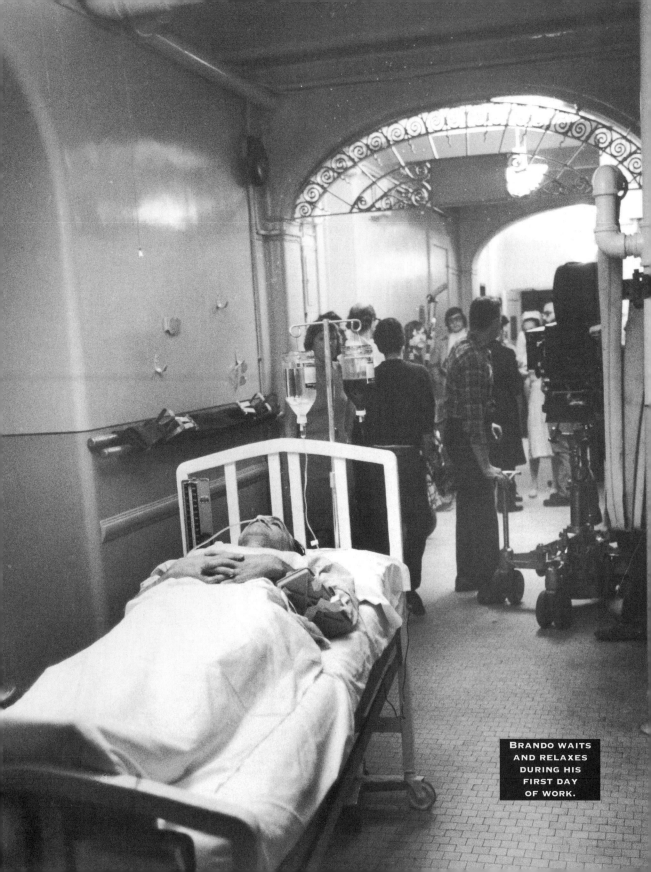

BRANDO WAITS
AND RELAXES
DURING HIS
FIRST DAY
OF WORK.

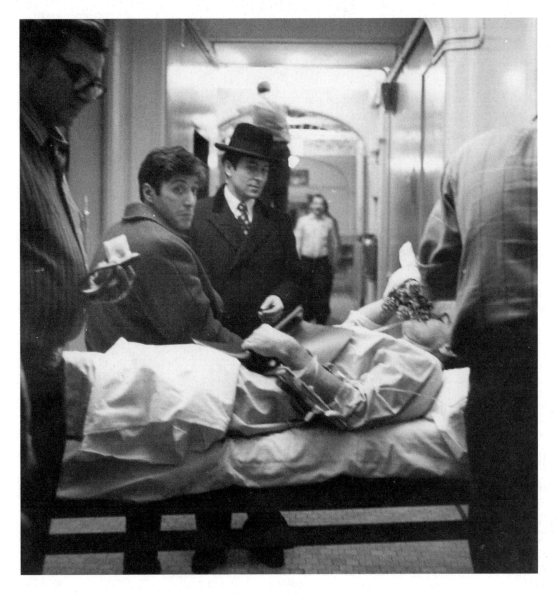

the Don into an ambulance for his return to the family compound (a body double substituted for Brando).

Brando's first filmed sequence for *The Godfather* must have been the most relaxing of the actor's career: For the scenes in the hospital, Brando was scheduled to lie in the bed, feigning a semicoma while Pacino played out Michael's entrance into family affairs ("I'll take care of you. I'm with you now.").

Even in such a relaxed state, Brando wasn't particularly comfortable in his makeup; no one would be, wearing layer upon layer of latex, powder, and plastic blobs on a metal band in his mouth. On most days, when the actor knew his work in makeup was done, he would shed the carefully applied work with Smith's help in mere minutes—"The faster the better," remembered Smith.

However, for the sake of another actor's work, Brando would leave on the makeup, even if he himself was off-camera.

"For the shots at the hospital, Brando was filmed first," Smith said. "When it came time to film Pacino, Brando's on-screen appearances in the scene were finished. I asked him if he wanted to get out of his makeup. 'Oh, no,' he said. 'I have to stay like this for Al.'"

The next day's work would require more exertion from Brando. On Mott Street in Little Italy, the crew prepared to shoot the first scenes in the Corleone family offices of Genco Olive Oil Company. The office set was built into an old building in the heart of the Italian-American district of Manhattan on a street that had changed little from the 1940s, with old brownstones, family stores, and narrow streets. (A trivia note: Although the office was shot on Mott Street, its address in the movie is 128 Mulberry Street, one block away. The company's address is on an advertising sign printed over the doorway, but isn't visible in the film.)

The set itself is a perfect example of Tavoularis's designs translated into a setting for Willis's low-light tableau photography. Although the office is old and worn, the walls are richly colored, the desks are realistically strewn with office equipment and stationery of the 1940s (including Christmas cards of the period), and the rafters are piled high with boxes of Genco goods.

"I had talked with Dean Tavoularis both before and during production about lighting, or color," said Willis. "I knew what he was doing, and he knew what I was doing. There were no opposing forces in that area, and the result holds together. Actually, his work is so good and always looks so nice that it was never necessary to discuss things at great length."

On April 15, 1971, the 45th Academy Awards was held in Los Angeles. Richard Castellano and John Marley, both members of *The Godfather* production, were each nominated for Best Supporting Actor in other films. Neither Marley nor Castellano won the Oscar; the award went to Ben Johnson for *The Last Picture Show.*

Coppola did, however, win the Academy Award for Best Screenplay for his work on *Patton* (he shared the award with Edmund North, the other credited screenwriter on the film). Though Coppola did not go to Hollywood to receive his Oscar, the award was a welcome relief. Even a month into filming, Coppola still feared that he might be fired from *The Godfather;* he viewed winning the Academy Award for *Patton* as an insurance policy that encouraged the studio to keep him on the production.

On April 19, the Don was scheduled to be gunned down on Mott Street. For the first time, Brando's top-secret appearance would be on public display.

For the two days of filming, Mott Street was re-created as the Little Italy of a quarter century earlier. An art deco facade had been built for the building, along with a large sign (not visible in the film) for the Genco Olive Oil Company. The prop masters had brought in cars and trucks of the 1940s and earlier, along with rolling fruit and vegetable carts.

In most location shots, Tavoularis would include a selection of period items for background placement to add additional touches of realism. For example, in the scenes of the Don buying fruit, viewers can spy a small poster advertising a Jake LaMotta boxing match, just barely visible in the background. (In later scenes, for Sonny's beating of Carlo, Tavoularis covered a wall with "Thomas Dewey for President" posters, some carefully obliterated by signs for Camel cigarettes that had been plastered over them.)

Although Brando would be visible to passersby, in a master stroke of publicity, Ruddy and the Paramount public relations staff declared Brando off-limits for photographs. Paramount also worked out an agreement with *Life* magazine that gave the publication exclusive cover rights to Brando photos, provided they were among the first to appear. To shield the scene from photographers, the production put up a virtual human wall around the outdoor set, using police, New York Tactical Patrol officers, production assistants, and members of the League.

"All photos of Brando in makeup were locked up," said publicist Marilyn Stewart. "The result was intense widespread interest about how Brando would look. I was sitting at Elaine's with Al Ruddy and the reporter from the *New York Times Magazine* during production. Author Gay Talese came over and asked, 'Hey, what's Marlon Brando really look like as the Godfather?' I don't think any of us realized that such curiosity about Brando's physical appearance in the role had been created by closing off the set."

With crowds constantly following the production and the press regularly covering the filming, the nervous executives at Paramount and Gulf+Western were getting a small earful of the film's increasingly loud buzz; the infighting about Ruddy's deal with the League quickly died away. In one of the first published accounts of the production, the June 28 issue of *Newsweek* reported that "with a sure-fire seller, about all Paramount can do is try to create some publicity tension by keeping star Marlon Brando under strict wraps. No pictures. No interviews."

Newsweek ran no photos of Brando in its early look at *The Godfather* production, but it did offer a vivid description of the most closely guarded secret of the film: what Brando looked like in "a role that signals an immense change in his career—from rebel and sex symbol to autocratic crime figure."

"The makeup men have given Brando a bay window under the boiled shirt front and jowls Churchill would envy," reporter S. K. Oberbeck wrote. "The hair is graying, greasy, slicked back as though waiting for the band of a white fedora; the eyebrows are a hard, cruel line, the eyes sinisterly hooded. They haven't touched the Brando nose, but the tight little Brando smile has a new kind of lip-curling menace. He looks sixty-five, a sleek Miami sixty-five. 'God, you should see him,' one teenage observer attested. 'He comes off the set and just peels off his face like a rubber mask.'"

For the fateful hit sequence, Coppola also wanted plenty of blood to flow once Brando hit the pavement.

"On the morning of the scene, Coppola declared, 'We'll need a lot of blood for the gutter—probably two or three gallons,'" Smith recalled. "I said, 'Francis, why didn't you tell me *yesterday?*' We sent assistants scouting everywhere for Karo syrup, and we made it on the spot for the gutter."

In dramatic portrayals of death and wounding, Brando had no peer: His death scene in *Viva Zapata!*—taking a fusillade of bullets from a mass squad of executioners as he lies crouched on the ground, his feet twitching—and his beating in *The Chase*, with his unbearably slow fall from a table, are vivid screen moments. Likewise, the near-fatal attack on the Don—with his sprawl across the hood of the car, his agonizingly slow collapse to the pavement, and his final slump against the bumper—would produce the most memorable performance-in-pain of Brando's career.

Even though the shooting was supposed to take place in late afternoon, it was shot in the morning so Willis could take advantage of the soft even light; a giant tarp crossing Mott Street was unfurled to keep the sun off the street. Coppola, Brando, and John Cazale—who as Fredo would slowly slide into shock after watching his father gunned down—carefully reviewed the choreography of the scene before they attempted the first take. Brando was in his element. He ran across the street, fell in a hail of bullets, and leaped to his feet as the onlooking crowd roared its approval.

"When he fell to the street, there were gasps from the crowds and a horrified silence," Ruddy said. "When Marlon stood up after Coppola yelled 'cut!' the crowd cheered, and Brando made a low, sweeping bow. He loved the people on Mott Street, and they loved him."

In spite of his showmanship, Brando maintained an actor's discipline. Much of the morning was filled with other scenes related to the attack, such as shots of

WILLIS'S TARP BLOCKED THE MIDMORNING SUN ON MOTT STREET DURING THE SHOOTING OF THE DON.

BRANDO TAKES A
bow as LITTLE
ITALY APPLAUDS.

Fredo descending into hysteria while the Don lies unconscious in the gutter and a crowd gathers. To maintain continuity, Brando had to lie in the gutter motionless in precisely the position he had fallen for as long as forty-five minutes at a time as work proceeded around him.

"After one of those takes, I had to touch up Marlon's makeup," Smith said. "One of the assistant directors leaned to me and whispered, 'Be careful—he's asleep.' It was incredible, but with all the work going on around him, he could tune it all out."

• • •

BRANDO, RIGGED WITH EXPLOSIVE SQUIBS TO BLOW OUT THE BACK OF HIS COAT AS BLANK SHOTS ARE FIRED, WAITS FOR THE TECHNICIANS TO WIRE HIM TO A FIRING BOX.

After the street sequence was completed, the production moved upstairs to the Genco office set for reshooting of scenes between Sollozzo and the family. The first shots had produced flat, rushed performances that did not meet expectations.

For Coppola, the second takes of the Sollozzo meeting would be a crucial moment in the production. The studio was still nervous about Coppola's vision for the project and all the concessions it had granted him. Between the first-day shots of Pacino and dissatisfaction with Brando in the previous Sollozzo meeting takes, the rumors that Coppola might be fired began to be taken seriously. According to Peter Bart, "the early weeks of *The Godfather* were nothing short of disastrous."

The studio's concerns about the footage quickly spread to the production staff. Although Coppola had more than a decade of experience in the film business, many on the crew considered him a virtual novice. Given his emotional profile, his perfectionism, and his seemingly endless bickering with the studio, the director quickly alienated some on his crew. Years later, Coppola told family and friends that during the shooting of *The Godfather*, he was sitting on the toilet in a stall at the studio, and two crew members walked into the bathroom. "They were talking about how the film was a load of shit and the asshole director didn't know what he was doing," said Eleanor Coppola. "Francis said he lifted up his feet so they wouldn't recognize his shoes."

"Making the first *Godfather* film was like nonstop anxiety, and wondering when I was going to get fired," Coppola said.

The grumbling and rumors were hard on Coppola. Even before production began, studio gossips whispered the word that Coppola would be replaced by Elia Kazan, Brando's director for *On the Waterfront* and other films and reputedly the only director who could handle the actor. As early as February, it was rumored that a copy of the script had been sent to the director.

Coppola's friends and Zoetrope associates urged the director to keep going, even if his job really was on the line. One colleague left him a note that read, "Don't quit—make them fire you," so Coppola would be ensured of getting paid and keeping his San Francisco enterprise afloat.

Even if Kazan wasn't being considered a possible replacement, others in the production did believe Coppola might be at risk. Robert Duvall even thought there might be a second director on staff, just waiting for Coppola to fail. "In case Francis was fired," Duvall said, "he goes right in." Duvall was likely thinking about Aram Avakian, the supervising editor who worked closely with Coppola on the project during preproduction.

As long as doubt haunted him, Coppola remained possessed by the fear of being replaced without warning. He even dreamed about Kazan coming up to him on the set and taking over the reins—a director's equivalent of the student's nightmare about missing final exams.

The rumor mill ground on—about Coppola's work, about Pacino's acting, about the possibility that Ruddy and Frederickson would be fired over the deal with the League, and on and on nonstop throughout the production. Some rumors were particularly brutal and did nothing but create jittery nerves for everyone. For example, in May, after filming the scenes with Jack Woltz and the horse's head, word began to spread that the horse had died of encephalitis, a potentially lethal virus that can cause paralysis and death. In fact, the horse was dying of terminal *emphysema* (which is not contagious at all) when it was humanely destroyed at a slaughterhouse. In any case, encephalitis cannot be passed directly from animal flesh to humans. Still, no one who passed along the rumor questioned its validity until Smith asked Gray Frederickson about it, and the shocked associate director reassured him that the story was false.

In the early weeks of the production, in what to Coppola seemed like his darkest hour, Brando came to his support with just the emotional first aid the director needed. The actor said that if Coppola was fired, he would walk off the picture.

"Brando saved my neck," Coppola said.

After the second round of takes from the Sollozzo meeting, however, Coppola began to pull the production together. Pacino's character had already begun to take form, and Brando came to life in sequences that called for more challenging acting than just lying in bed. As with the notion that Al Pacino might be replaced, Ruddy asserts no changes were in the offing.

"I think there was a moment in the first day or two of filming Brando when there was concern about the footage," Ruddy said. "Brando was, after all, giving this rather exotic portrayal of a gangster. So it was a momentary concern about the quality of the footage and Francis. But there was *never* a time when anyone from the studio suggested we make some changes. The truth was that when this kind of production starts, it's a disaster to stop it. Had we gone into this movie for a month, and we started losing time and money and the footage was bad—sure, they would have pulled Francis off so fast your head would spin. But the quality became apparent very quickly, and for the most part we were on-schedule and on-budget."

Ruddy had stood by Coppola from the start, and when the production began, he backed his director unequivocally—especially after Coppola's support through the public fiasco with the League.

"I was just as protective of Francis," Ruddy said, "as he was of me."

In the end, the only people fired from the production Coppola fired himself. He removed two assistants for their role in what Coppola would call a conspiracy against him, and for supposedly bad-mouthing him to the studio.

A quarter century after the production, with nearly a billion in revenue from the three *Godfather* films and nearly all associated with the production elevated to the ranks of creative superstars, it is easy to dismiss the concerns of Coppola, Pacino, and others as unfounded. But with so many careers at stake, it's no wonder the individuals felt the weight of great responsibility on their shoulders.

"There was a lot of pressure on everybody," Ruddy said. "We were all very tired. You can't shoot in New York at our pace and not feel the pressure. There's an old adage in the business: 'Unhappy sets make great movies.'"

• • •

BRANDO TALKS WITH
COPPOLA ABOUT MOURNING
HIS SON. "LOOK HOW THEY
MASSACRED MY BOY."

The most credible aspect of the Elia Kazan rumor was that Marlon Brando had a reputation as a difficult star. Despite this fact, however, Brando created virtually no problems during the filming of *The Godfather* and was often one of the more calming influences on the set.

"In spite of his reputation, he was always on time—except for one morning," Smith said. "Marlon came in forty-five minutes late, and he was upset about not arriving on time. I was working on him for about twenty minutes, and he said, 'I think that's going to be OK.' I said, 'Bu-bu-but Marlon. . . .' He gave me a sly wink and said, 'I just wanted to see how you'd react.'"

Brando's discussions with local mob figures gave him an up-close view of the real Mafia, and he gained an intimate appreciation of life in the criminal underworld by listening to wiretap tapes of several Mafia bosses the FBI gave Ruddy, among them a tape of Frank Costello, a hoarse-voiced don whose voice served as one of Brando's models for his performance.

"They were great characters," Bart said. "Brando enjoyed talking to them and hearing them talk, and he began to become a brilliant mimic and assimilate some of their characteristics."

Coppola and Brando worked well together, and both would remember their work together on *The Godfather* as a warm creative experience (they would work together again four years later on *Apocalypse Now*).

"He's the easiest actor there is to work with," said Coppola. "You just kind of point him in the right direction, have some good props, and he'll do something wonderful."

Coppola learned quickly that gentle coaching and specific directions were the best route to success with Brando.

"I was smart enough to know that you shouldn't give him a lot of acting double-talk," Coppola said. "Marlon likes to be directed like 'more angry or less angry'; 'more sleepy or less sleepy.' He just wants quick shorthand to give him a little guideline."

Off-camera and out of costume and makeup, Brando was at his superstar cool best, lounging in one of his cashmere sweaters and chatting with friends and crew. Fully fitted as the Don, however, Brando was a model of Method acting—on or off camera. He often stayed in character between scenes, mumbling and shuffling as he walked and, during rehearsals, often not responding because of the earplugs he wore. He used the earplugs to eliminate background noise and keep himself focused on other actors' lines. (Although Brando did wear earplugs in some actual filmed shots, they were usually removed for close-ups. The actor's earplugs can, however, be seen in the cover photo of *Life* magazine that hit the newsstands when the film was released.)

Brando was a veritable poster boy for film acting gadgetry: heavy makeup, body pads, mouth plumpers, earplugs, and weights in his shoes to slow his walk. He carried his own personal air conditioner invented by Smith—a requirement for his makeup because the latex could turn white in warm weather and could be affected by perspiration, thus requiring constant touch-ups for outdoor shots, especially for important scenes filmed in balmy late May and June. Smith constructed a "personal cooler"—a portable hair dryer connected to a Styrofoam container filled

with ice. "It was hardly ever used," Smith said. "Brando had such self-control, he could almost keep himself from sweating. He would keep himself calm and not move a muscle in between scenes."

Then there were Brando's cue cards.

As early as his appearance in *The Young Lions* in 1958, Brando had used cue cards for his lines—an aid, the actor believed, that increased his spontaneity. Brando's cue cards were usually oversized cardboard sheets covered with block letters held in his line-of-sight. (When he appeared in a long scene in *Superman* in 1978, Brando walked around the circular set preceded by a rolling camera with an assistant walking backward holding cue cards next to the lens.) Depending on the set and the camera angles, Brando would find places for smaller notes as needed, taping them on walls, hiding them behind props, or actually attaching them to other actors. For the scenes of Hagen, Sonny, and the Don talking about their plans to meet with Sollozzo, Robert Duvall held Brando's cue cards in front of his shirt.

Some would attribute the need for cue cards to Brando's allegedly bad memory, others to his innate laziness. None disputed, however, their effectiveness in helping the actor achieve the performance he desired.

On April 29, the crew filmed Luca Brasi's murder in the bar of Bruno Tattaglia's nightclub, a scene that would include the pinning of Luca's hand to the bar with a knife while he is garroted. Shot in the Edison Hotel, the bar featured a decoration that foreshadowed the events to come: As Luca enters the bar, the camera pauses a moment on a glass panel engraved with tropical fish. The symbol is a not-so-veiled reference to Luca's imminent death, the disposal of his body at sea, and the return of his bulletproof vest to the Corleones wrapped around a fish—a Sicilian message that "Luca Brasi sleeps with the fishes."

To prepare Lenny Montana, the actor who played Luca Brasi, for the scene, Smith used a prop knife welded upright to a thin plate. Smith applied the knife to

SET UP FOR THE MURDER OF LUCA BRASI.

MONTANA AS LUCA, RIGGED FOR THE STABBING. "WHAT MADE THAT SCENE SO EFFECTIVE WAS THE EDITING," DICK SMITH SAID. "I'VE TALKED TO MANY PEOPLE WHO SWEAR THEY SAW THE KNIFE GO INTO THE HAND."

Montana's hand with a thin tape and covered the base with makeup and blood. From that point on, Montana simply had to pretend he was pinned down while being assassinated. The illusion he created is powerful—aided in part by Al Lettieri as Sollozzo and Tony Giorgio as Bruno Tattaglia, who held down Montana's hands while the assassin did his work.

The illusion of the knife in the hand is gruesome and effective—a combination of makeup, editing, and sound effects. As Sollozzo swings a real knife down toward the bar, the viewer hears the clunk of the blade passing through Luca's hand and hitting the bar as the shot cuts to Sollozzo holding the knife that is already penetrating Luca's hand.

"What made that scene so effective was the editing," Smith said. "I've talked to many people who swear they saw the knife go into the hand."

The credibility of the garroting scene was aided by Montana himself, who used muscle-tensing tricks learned in his days as a wrestler to make his face purple and his veins swell.

With the completion of the Corleone house set at Filmways in late April, *The Godfather* crew could move to more traditional—and less public—filmmaking surroundings. The set featured the ground floor of the residence: The Don's study, a small living room (where Hagen, Sonny, and the Don discuss the Sollozzo meeting), the kitchen with a breakfast nook, the dining room, an entrance area, and the staircase, which led just to the second floor landing. Tavoularis and crew had re-created a somber yet homey set, complete with comfortable furnishings of a middle-class 1940s home, including dark wooden accessories, intentionally mediocre artwork, and religious icons.

While a large set, it was not the complete Corleone home; a doorway (used for the site of Sonny and Lucy's stand-up sex scene) and the Don's bedroom were built on other stages. When Hagen visits Woltz at his studio, the actors are actually standing on the stage used for the house set. In *The Godfather Trilogy*, the back of the flats that comprised the house set can be seen behind the birthday party, heavily stenciled with WOLTZ INTERNATIONAL PICTURES.

The first day of shooting in the Corleone house involved the first shot of the film, in which the undertaker Bonasera asks the Don for vengeance after the beating of his daughter. Salvatore Corsitto, who was cast as Bonasera to replace the ailing Frank Puglia, shot his first scene on April 30. Gordon Willis used a computer-timed lens, designed to take carefully controlled shots, to film Bonasera as the camera slowly zooms back to show the side of the Don's head. (Ironically, in this very first scene of the film, Coppola violated his vow not to use a zoom lens. The shot does, however, end in a tableau.)

In the opening scenes of the film, subtle changes can be heard in dialogue as a result of on-set editing, actors' improvisations, and Coppola's suggestions. There are slight but distinct differences between the script for the Don as written in the March 29 shooting script, for example, and the dialogue as filmed.

As written in the script:

Bonasera, we have known each other for years, but this is the first time you come to me for help. I don't remember the last time you invited me to your house for coffee . . . even though our wives are friends.

As spoken in the film:

We've known each other many years, but this is the first time you came to me for counsel, for help. I can't remember the last time that you invited me to your house for a cup of coffee, even though my wife is godmother to your only child. But let's be frank here: You never wanted my friendship. And, uh, you were afraid to be in my debt.

As written in the script:

Then take the justice from the judge, the bitter with the sweet, Bonasera. But if you come to me with your friendship, your loyalty, then your enemies become my enemies, and then, believe me, they would fear you.

As spoken in the film:

Bonasera . . . Bonasera . . . what have I ever done to make you treat me so disrespect-fully? If you had come to me in friendship, then this scum that ruined your daughter would be suffering this very day. And then by chance if an honest man like yourself should make enemies, then they would become my enemies. And then they would fear you.

As written in the script:

Some day, and that day may never come, I would like to call upon you to do me a ser-vice in return.

As spoken in the film:

Some day, and that day may never come, I'll call upon you to do a service for me. But until that day—accept this justice as a gift on my daughter's wedding day.

Whether these changes were due to Coppola's tinkering, Brando's improvising, or a bit of both, the seemingly simple dialogue in this opening scene was clearly invested with thought, subtlety, and emotion. Many other script alterations that were—unlike this one—outright edits. A few minutes after the scene between the Don and Bonasera, for example, Michael and Kay are shown eating lunch at the wedding reception. In the original script, Kay is eating spaghetti, not lasagna as in the final film; spaghetti was deemed too messy for close-ups.

In this scene, with dialogue that relies heavily on text from the book, Michael explains Luca Brasi's role in the family business:

MICHAEL

Once upon a time, about fifteen years ago, some people wanted to take over my father's olive oil business. They had Al Capone send some men in from Chicago to kill my father, and they almost did.

KAY

Al Capone!

MICHAEL

My father sent Luca Brasi after them. He tied the two Capone men hand and foot and stuffed small bath towels into their mouths. Then he took an ax, and chopped one man's feet off. . . .

KAY

Michael . . .

MICHAEL

Then the legs at the knees . . .

KAY

Michael, you're trying to scare me. . . .

MICHAEL

Then the thighs where they joined the torso.

KAY

Michael, I don't want to hear anymore. . . .

MICHAEL

Then Luca turned to the other man . . .

KAY

Michael, I love you.

MICHAEL

. . . who out of sheer terror had swallowed the bath towel in his mouth and suffocated.

KAY

I never know when you're telling me the truth.

MICHAEL

I told you you wouldn't like him.

In contrast, the scene in the final film was much briefer—and much more potent an explanation of why Michael was alienated both from the family business and his father:

MICHAEL

Well, when Johnny [Fontane] was first starting out, he was signed to this personal service contract with a big bandleader. And as his career got better and better, he wanted to get out of it. Now, Johnny is my father's godson. And my father went to see this bandleader, and he offered him $10,000 to let Johnny go. But the bandleader said no. So the next day, my father went to see him, only this time with Luca Brasi. And within an hour, he signed a release for a certified check of $1,000.

Kay prompts Michael to continue, and he explains how his father was able to "negotiate" so shrewd a business deal.

MICHAEL

Luca Brasi held a gun to his head, and my father assured him that either his brains or his signature would be on the contract.

(*Kay stares*)

That's a true story.

(*Pause*)

That's my family, Kay. It's not me.

One memorable scene actually evolved out of necessity to accommodate Lenny Montana's stage fright during his first scenes with Brando. Montana and Brando eventually became pals on the set, but in his first professional encounter with Brando—in the scene in which Luca Brasi presents a bridal gift to the Don with the wish that Connie and Carlo's first child be "a masculine child"—Montana was terrified. Coppola shot more than a dozen takes of Montana trying to deliver his simple lines, and each time the big wrestler would, in Ruddy's words, "clutch up."

Finally, Coppola added a new short scene to the wedding sequence, in which Kay first notices Luca as he is practicing his speech to the Don. The final film includes one of Montana's blown takes, in which he stumbled over the word "daughter," repeats part of a line, and then says, "I pledge my *ever*-ending loyalty." So in the end, because of his repeated mistakes, Montana actually wound up with an extra scene in the film.

On the other hand, other characters' roles were reduced substantially. The part of Johnny Fontane, already much reduced from the book, was cut to its barest essence. In the original shooting script, Johnny explains his problems to the Don at length.

JOHNNY

I kept trying to call you after my divorce, and Tom always said you
were busy. When I got the wedding invitation, I knew you weren't
sore at me anymore, Godfather.

VITO CORLEONE

Can I do something for you still? You're not too rich, or too famous that I can't help
you?

JOHNNY

I'm not rich anymore, Godfather, and . . . my career, I'm almost washed up.

In the final film, this unnecessary conversation is replaced by the scene in which the Don
greets Johnny. After Johnny whispers in his ear, the Don replies, "I'll handle it."

It was at about this point in the script that the Don would have delivered what Puzo thought would be the movie's most famous line:

VITO CORLEONE

Remember my new consigliere. A lawyer with his briefcase can steal more than a hundred men with guns.

Puzo adored the line, and during production asked both Coppola and Evans if the line would be included. But no one else had the same enthusiasm for it; Brando considered it preachy, and Coppola didn't think it contributed much to the scene or the atmosphere. But another phrase captured the public's attention and became the signature line from *The Godfather:*

VITO CORLEONE

I'm gonna make him an offer he can't refuse.

Changes, additions, improvisations, and deletions were constant as the dialogue evolved throughout much of the production to become cleaner and tighter. One key scene still remained to be fixed, but that would have to wait until the waning days of Brando's commitment on the picture, with his time literally running out.

On May 12, Coppola filmed the scene of Sonny and Lucy having sex against a door of one of the smaller sets. Most of the production staff happened to drop by the set for the shot of James Caan and Jeannie Linero, who played bridesmaid Lucy. "People always come around the killings and sex scenes," Willis snorted. Coppola asked the visitors to leave, shooting the scene with only Willis and his team on the set.

At the same time, Eleanor Coppola was about to give birth. When the shots of the sex scene were completed, Coppola picked up Eleanor (and his video camera) to go to the hospital. His daughter, Sofia, was born the next day.

Coppola's family—including Sofia—featured prominently as extras in *The Godfather.* His mother Italia played the switchboard operator at Genco Olive Oil Company (the scene was cut). In *The Godfather Part II,* Italia would have the briefest of appearances as the dead Mama Corleone in her coffin; Morgana King declined to appear in a casket. His father Carmine appeared as the musically inclined mobster playing the piano during the montage scenes that follow the killing of Sollozzo and McCluskey; and all of Coppola's children appeared in the baptism scene. His boys, Gio and Roman, were among the spectators, and the newborn Sofia appeared as Michael Francis Rizzi, the child being baptized. (Sofia would become one of the few actors other than principals to appear in all three *Godfather* films. She would, of course, have a starring role in *The Godfather Part III,* and in *Part II* she and her brothers appeared as immigrants on the ship that carried the young Vito Corleone to America. As Oreste Baldini, the eleven-year-old who played Vito, rises to walk the deck and look at the Statue of Liberty, Sofia, a three-year-old, can be seen in the background with her on-camera mother.)

Others associated with the production would also have their shot at cinematic immortality. On May 19, during the shooting of the birthday party sequence at the Woltz studio, Coppola recruited associate producer Gray Frederickson for a bit part in the scene. Frederickson was outfitted as a 1940s

COPPOLA, HIS FATHER CARMINE, AND JOE SPINELL AS WILLIE CICCI PREPARE TO FILM THE CORE FOOTAGE OF THE MONTAGE SEQUENCE.

THE BIRTHDAY PARTY FOR STARLET JANIE AT WOLTZ INTERNATIONAL PICTURES. ASSOCIATE PRODUCER GRAY FREDERICKSON IS THE COWBOY WITH THE PONY. THE WOOD FLATS IN THE BACKGROUND ARE THE WALLS OF THE SET FOR THE CORLEONE HOME.

cowboy star, complete with a jaunty hat, western scarf, and studio-style cowboy shirt. Frederickson would present a pony to Janie, the starlet who would later wind up as a Woltz concubine (the scene was eventually deleted from the film, but restored for *The Godfather Epic*, Coppola's chronological marriage of *The Godfather* and *The Godfather Part II*.)

Viewers curious about what producer Al Ruddy looked like will find him in two scenes. When Hagen arrives at the Woltz studio (actually the Filmways entrance) and exits his taxi, Ruddy is the guard at the gate who gives him directions. In that scene, Ruddy is visible from behind, and then for only a second; he is more prominent in the montage sequence that follows Michael's murders of Sollozzo and McCluskey. Ruddy can be seen on the front page of the *Daily Mirror* under the headline, MOBSTER BARZINI QUESTIONED IN UNDERWORLD FEUD. Ruddy appears as the tall police officer shown on Barzini's left. On Barzini's right in the photograph is his lawyer, who is played by Ruddy's real attorney at the time, Bruce Ramer.

• • •

On May 21, production moved to Long Island for two days of shooting that included the film's most notorious and grisly scene: the discovery by studio boss Jack Woltz of his horse Khartoum's head in his bed. *The Godfather* location scouts had obtained use of one of the most glamorous residences in the country, the Guggenheim family estate on Long Island Sound, which had been donated to the state of New York.

Coppola and Ruddy had hoped to shoot the scene in a real Hollywood mansion during location shooting in Los Angeles, but the work scheduled for both Las Vegas and Los Angeles was canceled for lack of funds. The Las Vegas scenes were shot in New York with a montage of stock footage of Las Vegas in the mid-1950s as establishing shots. Because the front exteriors of the Guggenheim mansion, built in the style of a baronial hunting lodge, looked nothing like a studio mogul's residence, Coppola filmed the exterior of a real Hollywood mansion after principal photography concluded.

Scenes filmed at the Guggenheim estate included a walking tour of the estate with Hagen and Woltz, a visit to the stable to meet the still living horse Khartoum, conversations over dinner, and the discovery of the head. Because of overcast, "non-California" weather, some dialogue was edited and added to the discussion over dinner (scenes of Marley and Duvall talking as they overlooked the Long Island Sound were never used). Coppola shot these scenes and other interior shots of the house, including a scene later deleted from the film in which Duvall spots Janie, the studio chief's starlet, waiting for Woltz outside her bedroom (a scene restored in *The Godfather Trilogy*).

With all of the discussion of depiction of Italian Americans in the film, there was still room for issues regarding other ethnic American groups. Several Jewish members of the crew were bothered by the inclusion of a plate of matzo in the dinner scene; why push the fact that Woltz was Jewish? Remembering his lunches with Jack Warner while he worked at the Warner Bros. lot on several projects, Coppola believed that the matzo added a touch of authenticity to the scene. In the end, the plate of matzo was included in the shot, but next to Woltz's dinner plate, it is difficult to see. Of course, Coppola's insistence on including the matzo for the scene further irritated some in the crew, driving another wedge between director and staff.

On May 22, the crew was ready for the horse's head scene. Paramount had encouraged Coppola to use a fake horse's head, but the prop the studio provided was hardly appropriate. "The studio sent us this big shaggy thing with bulging eyes," remembered Ruddy. "It had a big crack in the middle of it."

Smith had worked diligently without success to make up the fake head; on-screen, no audience would be convinced it was from a real horse. Meanwhile, the production's location scouts had found a real horse ready for the slaughter at a rendering plant in New Jersey that looked like the horse playing Khartoum, except without the blaze of white on its forehead. The head arrived in a metal container loaded with dry ice and was gingerly placed on the bed, where Smith painted on the white patch. (Note: Some viewers noticed what they thought was a continuity

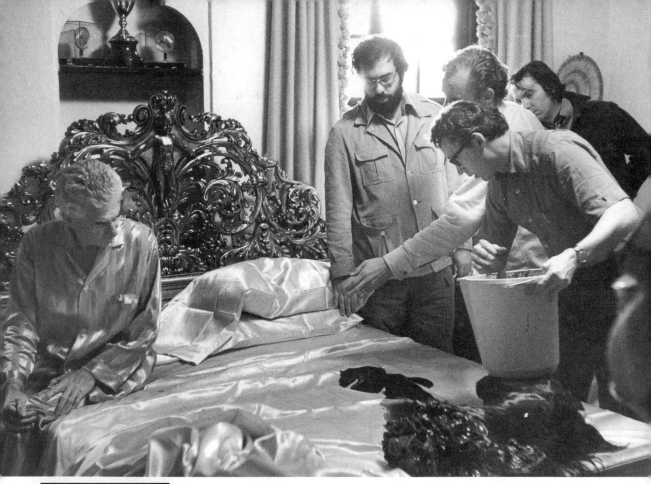

error in *The Godfather*, because the head appears to be shy a white blaze. The marking is indeed there, smeared with Karo blood and partially obscured by the sheet.)

"We added Karo blood to the bed, according to Coppola's direction," said Smith. "Before every new take we would add more blood. The level of Karo blood began to move up the bed toward John Marley like the tide; first to his knees, then to his crotch. Soon the sheets were soaked and Marley was covered."

Coppola treated Marley, who had appeared in films for some thirty years before *The Godfather*, with patient respect; appearing with such a hideous prop and soaked to the skin in blood—even Karo blood—was an unpleasant situation for even a veteran performer. The director coached the actor carefully for this brief scene; all involved knew the sequence would be one most anxiously anticipated by every reader of the book. At one point during rehearsal, Coppola climbed into the bed himself while Marley, wearing silk pajamas and draped with an overcoat, looked down at the director from the camera's perspective.

Coppola filmed Marley in bed from a number of angles before setting up the "payoff shot,"

in which the actor throws back the sheets and discovers the head, screaming in terror. Finally, when Coppola had enough takes to satisfy him and the gruesome scene was concluded, the head was repacked in dry ice and was given to the SPCA for disposal.

Several film historians have described the difference between the book and movie versions of the horse's head scene as a brilliant adaptation of literature to film; in the book, Woltz awakens to the sight of the head at the foot of the bed ("*Far down at the foot of the bed was a familiar shape. . . .*"). Coppola's handling of the scene is indeed an unforgettable screen moment, but the drama of Woltz pulling back the sheets was, in fact, the result of the director's misreading of the book.

"When I read the book, I read it wrong," Coppola said. "I thought the horse was *in the bed* with him. As I read it, that's the way it is in the movie. But in the book, the horse was there right in front of him."

The scenes featuring the horse's head were originally scheduled for the afternoon, but the schedule was switched due to the weather. As it turned out, the scene of the walking tour with

Marley and Duvall was shot after the gruesome head scene. Incredibly, Marley maintained enough composure to appear casual in the stable—only hours after being covered in blood while in bed with a thawing horse's head. (An imaginative viewer of the stable scene can *almost* hear a coarse roughness in Marley's voice from all the screaming he had done that morning.) The memory of the head stuck with him. "I still see it," he told a friend two weeks later.

By May 24, the production was ready to move back to Staten Island for Connie's wedding at the Corleone Mall. However, rain and other delays postponed shooting of the wedding sequences, which began a domino-effect of postponements of Brando's scenes, including the wedding, the Don's meetings with Michael, his visit to the hospital to see his dying consigliere Genco Abbandando, and his own death scene in the garden.

Several weeks earlier, it had become obvious that Brando would soon be in overtime on the project, to the tune of $40,000 per week—the penalty salary for problems on the production that he didn't cause. The Don's death scene, scheduled as one of his last, required a hot sunny day, presumably in the summer (the exact death date, though not mentioned in the film, is July 29,

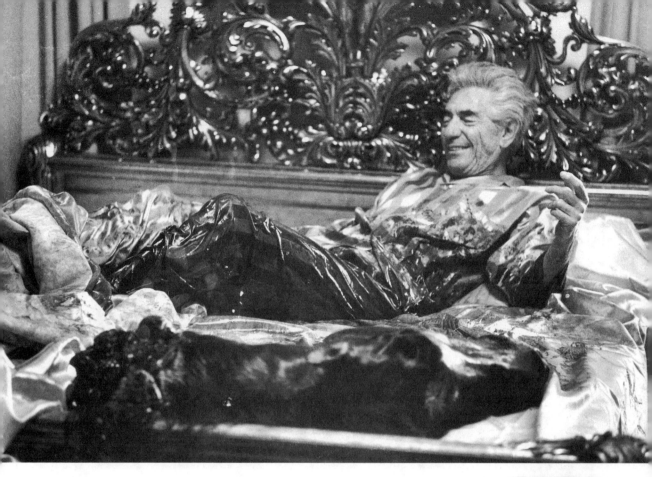

1955). The postponements were exacerbated when a rain squall nearly destroyed the Don's garden, which had to be replanted.

There were only two solutions for Ruddy—to eat the cost of Brando's overtime or offer the actor an alternative. Brando could have forced the production into weeks of overtime penalties amounting to tens of thousands of dollars, but instead he graciously chose to help.

"Francis was suicidal about the problems with Brando's scenes, so I told him, 'Let me go see Marlon and see what I can do,'" Ruddy said.

"So I met with Brando at his hotel. I told him, 'Marlon, look, the fucking wind has blown all the tomatoes down. To be honest, we don't have any money to keep paying you. So I'm prepared to glue the tomatoes on the fucking vines if that's what it takes to keep you working. However, if you're so inclined, I will buy you a ticket back to Los Angeles and a round trip ticket to get you back here. And we'll bring other tomatoes when everything has dried out.' He agreed and didn't charge us for the extra time.

"I got a call from Brando's agent, and he was fucking irate," Ruddy recalled. "'How dare you guys do that to my client! You know what the fucking deal was.' I said, 'I'm sorry, but I'm

THE CORLEONE RESIDENCE (LEFT). A WALL TURNS A STATEN ISLAND NEIGHBORHOOD INTO A MOB FAMILY FORTRESS.

doing this for this movie. We don't have any more money, I offered this to Marlon, and I'm doing it to support Francis.'"

By May 25, the weather appeared to be clearing, and Coppola decided to move forward with the shooting of the wedding—a sequence that, even before the elaborate production was filmed, required a complex choreography of arrivals at the site: caterers to supply party food, musicians, 350 extras brought in by bus, and temporary production assistants to control the crowd. Seduced by the colorful setting, Coppola again violated the original cinematography scheme and brought in four extra shoulder-mounted cameras to shoot in the crowd, as well as a helicopter to shoot aerial views of the wedding in progress.

The wedding scene was planned as period photography at its most vivid. Tavoularis designed a flawless re-creation of an Italian family wedding in the closing days of World War II, complete with thirty period cars, Johnstone's costume designs, food, glassware, and Italian festival lights.

Specially designed floral arrangements added a colorful complement to every scene of the wedding. Florists Herbert and Abram Gottlieb of Richmond Floral Co. in Staten Island fashioned

bouquets, boutonnieres, and various other bridal blooms for the six-day wedding scene shoot, all designed to resemble those favored by first-generation Italian Americans at that time.

Connie's bridal bouquet consisted of white orchids and stephanotis while the maid of honor held an arrangement of red American Beauty roses, pink bridal roses, and baby's breath. Brides-maid bouquets—complete with the long ribbon streamers popular in the mid-forties—were arranged in pink carnations and baby's breath. The Gottliebs also prepared boutonnieres for the men and, of course, "a special boutonniere for Marlon Brando," said Gottlieb. To maintain the continuity of the shots over the course of nearly a week of wedding shooting, the flowers had to be refreshed daily and matched to photographs of the original displays.

"Not only did we take pictures of the floral pieces so we could duplicate them day after

"STRICTLY PERSONAL— NOT BUSINESS." ON-SCREEN ENEMIES RICHARD CONTE (BARZINI) AND RICHARD CASTELLANO (CLEMENZA) ENJOY A PAUSE IN FILMING DURING THE WEDDING RECEPTION SEQUENCE.

day," said Gottlieb, "but we also had the same designers work on the same bouquets to avoid slight differences in designing."

The Gottliebs used more than three hundred white orchids to create the bridal bouquets and about one hundred canhaminia orchids for corsages. "Canhaminia orchids were used because they were very popular during the forties," added Gottlieb.

Many of the wedding shots captured festive behavior that was no playacting; because much of the sound was added later, extras and stars could say what they pleased as they danced, drank, and ate. Off camera, Brando signed autographs for several of the children acting as extras.

Given the near-constant stress early in the shooting, the filming of the outdoor wedding sequences provided a welcome setting for a display of the production's most popular form of practical joke. On the first day of the wedding shoot, Duvall and Brando planned a "sneak attack" on the entire production. While a shot was being set up for the family wedding photograph, Brando and Duvall calmly pulled down their pants, bent over, and pointed their bare bottoms at more than four hundred actors and crew. Needless to say, the stars' mooning caused an uproar on the grounds.

JAMES CAAN
DOES HIS CAGNEY
IMPRESSION.

Humor played an integral role in cutting tension on the production. Duvall and Caan, while superb professionals on camera, were often the instigators of high jinks on the set off camera. Even film of early rehearsals shows the pair clowning, hitting each other, and torturing Pacino by intentionally making him break into laughter during his scenes. To break the tension, Caan would commandeer props and perform a behind-the-scenes show; Pacino's cane became a sword with which he dueled the camera, and a pistol became the catalyst for a Jimmy Cagney impression.

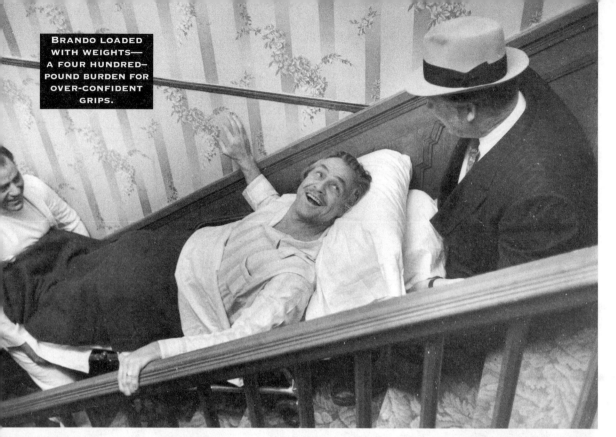

BRANDO LOADED WITH WEIGHTS—A FOUR HUNDRED-POUND BURDEN FOR OVER-CONFIDENT GRIPS.

DUVALL AND BRANDO: ALWAYS LOOKING FOR WAYS TO EASE THE TENSION.

But the wildest joke was mooning—the more public the better—with Caan and Duvall the usual conspirators (although Brando couldn't resist the audience at the wedding set for a moon of his own).

"My best moon was on Second Avenue," remembers James Caan. "Bob Duvall and I were in one car and Brando was in another, so we drove up beside him, and I pulled down my pants and stuck my ass out of the window. Brando fell down in the car with laughter."

Pacino was no mooner, but had his own variation on the pants-down high jinks on the set.

"We all pulled gags to relieve the tension," Pacino said. "In a scene where I sit behind the desk, wardrobe made this big fuss about getting me a shirt with a smaller collar. So while everyone was looking at the shirt, I took off my pants. When I came out from behind the desk, I got a laugh, even though we had to do the scene over."

Brando also pulled a practical joke that involved almost the entire

PACINO TAKES A BREAK.

production company—except the two victims. On May 7, the production filmed the Don returning home from the hospital. The scene calls for Brando to be carried up the stairs on his stretcher, and two burly grips, overly confident in their ability to lug Brando up the stairs, were given their chance to appear in the film as orderlies. While the grips got into costume, Brando loaded up the stretcher with weights to create, including his own weight, a near-four-hundred-pound load. Keeping a straight face, Coppola actually filmed the scene of the orderlies struggling up the stairs with their burden, before the entire production exploded with laughter.

Even Lenny Montana, who would have so much trouble with Brando in the Don's study, contributed to the on-set games. After struggling unsuccessfully through several of his takes

with Brando, the cast took a break. When Montana restarted the scene, instead of speaking, he stuck out his tongue at Brando; across his tongue was a piece of white tape, and on it was written FUCK YOU.

"It was a hilarious scene on the set when Lenny did that," Ruddy said. "At times like that, the humor really was a relief."

There were other pleasant moments. Dick Smith, a talented artist in other media besides makeup, would keep busy during lulls on the set by carving miniature sculptures of cast and crew out of modeling wax (his bust of Brando as the Don, only a few inches high, would later be photographed for the cover of *The Godfather* souvenir program).

Lunch at local Italian restaurants became a regular routine. On Al Lettieri's recommendation, Vincent's Restaurant became a favorite haunt for dining out or delivering food to the set. One of Brando's favorites was the spicy squid. He would also eat it on the set; on at least one occasion, when mourning over Sonny's body in the morgue, he held his lunch out of camera range as he was filmed.

The production staff also worked hard to keep spirits up by creating celebrations, birthday

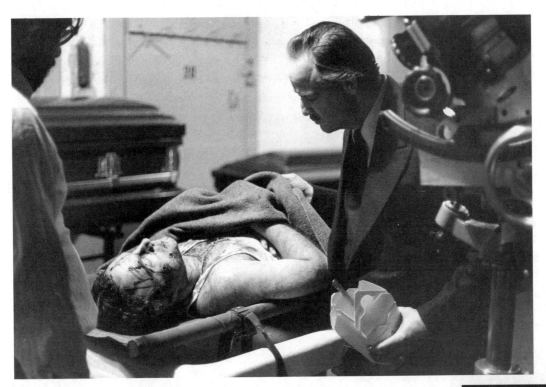

BRANDO RE-
HEARSES WITH
ONE HAND, AND
HOLDS HIS LUNCH
WITH THE OTHER—
ANOTHER ORDER
OF SPICY SQUID
FROM VINCENT'S
RESTAURANT.

parties, or get-togethers for the staff—in particular for the union staff. Good-natured celebrating created the goodwill that could allow the producers to smoothly work out differences without holding up production. Provisions supposedly destined for use in scenes, including large quantities of food, beer, and wine, would instead often wind up in postshoot parties, courtesy of production manager Fred Gallo.

On one occasion, one of these happy get-togethers on the set also provided a less-pleasant reminder that there was indeed a real world outside the realm of *The Godfather* production. The party was a send-off for a crew member whose National Guard unit had been called to active duty in Vietnam.

Once Coppola stopped worrying about being fired and was simply tense about the production and constant bickering with the studio, he had plenty of tangible and costly problems to handle. Shooting a period film—particularly in New York—presented logistical problems that continually plagued the production. Breakdowns of antique cars and other equipment were constant, delaying, among other shots, the scene in which the Don is wounded and the scene in which Sonny's body is brought to Bonasera's Funeral Parlor (shot in a morgue room at Bellevue).

Still other delays were costly. On March 23, during filming of the scene in which Sollozzo kidnaps Hagen, a window was broken, costing the production an hour's delay—$5,000 worth. In June, while shooting the Don's funeral, when lunch for the company did not arrive on time, union rules forced a meal penalty totaling $6,000. Several times, an entire day of film was ruined by the lab, which forced reshoots. While insurance covered those costs, lost days could not be recovered.

Beyond logistical obstacles, personal issues also complicated the shooting. Pacino had already been injured; Frank Puglia, a veteran character actor who had appeared in films for nearly fifty years, fell ill only a few weeks before his scenes were to be filmed; and Gianni Russo suffered a chipped elbow and two cracked ribs during the scene in which Sonny beats Carlo on the street (while a stunt double handled many of the most violent scenes, apparently James Caan's ardor overwhelmed him in the close-ups).

Of course, many problems were just part of the normal routine of making a film in the world's busiest city. Filming *The Godfather* was, reported the *New York Times*, "the biggest show in town." Thousands of onlookers continued to follow the production to its location shooting, and the cinemobile bus, with its *Godfather* logo painted on the side, was a dead giveaway to the location scenes. "We finally had to paint out the logo," Al Ruddy said. Meanwhile, during filming of the wed-

COPPOLA PREPARES TO FILM VICTOR RENDINA AS PHILLIP TATTAGLIA (OFF CAMERA) DURING THE MEETING WITH THE DONS.

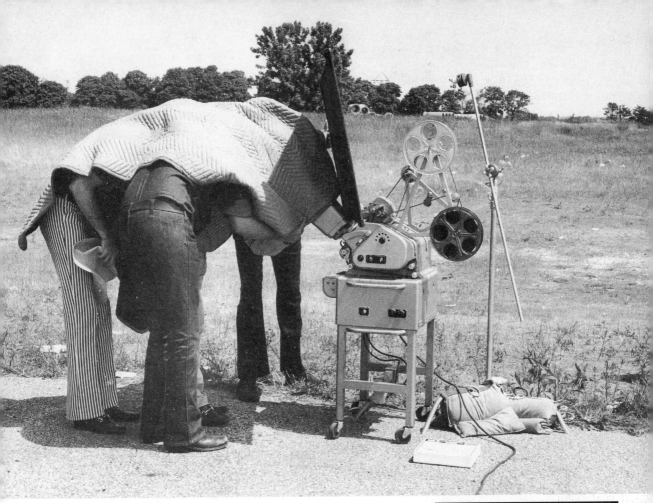

ding sequence, an otherwise perfect shot was ruined when a jet roared across Staten Island.

The need for matchless locations often compounded the crowd problem. The murder scene of Don Barzini was filmed July 1 on the steps of the Justice Building at 60 Centre Street, near City Hall—one of the busiest neighborhoods in Manhattan. Scheduled for the second-to-last day of shooting, the crew, by that time exhausted, had a 5 A.M. call to the site to get as much work as possible accomplished before traffic and bystanders jammed the streets. Even the early hour and the timing of the shot the day before the long Fourth of July weekend failed to stop a crowd of fifteen thousand onlookers.

On the other hand, some problems produced fortuitous results. On April 28, to save time shooting the meeting of the dons in the boardroom of the Penn Central Railroad above Grand Central Station, Coppola canceled plans to film close-ups of Richard Conte as Don Barzini. The distant shots unintentionally produced an effective hands-off aura around the character of Barzini. For the wedding sequence, the supplementary footage shot by handheld camera or helicopter turned out to be unusable, so the wedding shots remained as Willis had envisioned them—as stationary portraits of a colorful 1940s celebration, without intrusion of contemporary techniques. (To judge how the shots might have looked, compare them to a brief shot of Michael and Apollonia walking with their wedding party. For that sequence, Coppola had insisted on one handheld shot of the group as they walk from the church; after Willis's careful framing and camera placement for every other shot, this single exception does indeed seem jarring.)

A seventy-day shooting schedule in New York spread out over three months was scarcely enough time to shoot the bulk of a three-hour film, even when supplemented by twelve days in Sicily. While shooting slipped behind schedule early in the production, Coppola managed to catch up, only to be flummoxed again by other time-consuming work. Rehearsals moved to evenings, which eliminated the time to view dailies (the footage just completed). As a result, dailies were viewed only once a week. When it became critical to view particularly important scenes, the footage was brought to the set or, in at least one case, to a location site. While filming the "leave the gun, take the cannoli" scene in New Jersey, for example, a portable viewer was brought to the site. Ruddy, Coppola, Willis, and others were seen hunched over the tiny screen while all were covered with a blanket to block out the light—looking like some odd, creatively perfectionist animal.

Even during the happy and productive moments on the set, conflicts with the studio were never far away. Paramount staff in both New York and Los Angeles kept in constant communication with Coppola—not to interject the studio into creative decisions, but rather to ensure that the director was maintaining the pace and staying on budget. While Coppola often dealt directly with Evans, the director's chief adversary was Jack Ballard, Paramount head of production from California, who during much of the production was Evans's ears and eyes in New York. On several occasions, Ballard ordered Coppola to continue work late into evenings or in weather inappropriate for shooting, simply to maintain the schedule. In one particular instance—the filming of Kay and Michael in conversation at the wedding—Coppola had to shoot in dwindling light long past the point when footage would be usable, even though he knew the scene would have to be reshot.

"They let us make the picture, even with the concerns they had before shooting began, because we told them we'd stick to the budget," Ruddy said. "But they kept after us constantly."

The budget was so tight that after principal photography was concluded, the production team had to complete a complex shot without the coordinated—and expensive—support of the city or the police. To get the needed shot of Sollozzo's sedan after it picks up Michael in front of Jack Dempsey's, several in the production crew drove the vintage sedan and other period vehicles onto the 59th Street Bridge. Ruddy, Willis, and the camera operator stalled modern station wagons at the end of the bridge as Willis filmed the scene with just the old cars.

"By the time I said, 'Let's hit it' and got the hell out of there, there was a solid jam of cars all the way down the bridge and down Third Avenue, and the cops running up the street to get us," Ruddy said. "We did all these insane things because we didn't have money."

Through all the budget battles, Ruddy would be the peacemaker, calming Coppola with reassurance, gentle joking, and a sympathetic ear. Although Ruddy had his fair share of talks with the studio about the production's progress, Coppola often faced these confrontations directly, in countless angry phone calls and face-to-face meetings with Ballard and others from Paramount. Such frustrations would remain fresh in Coppola's mind when Paramount offered him the opportunity to direct *The Godfather Part II.* In that case, he demanded near-total control of the project—and got it.

Complications aside, Coppola was often his own worst enemy during *The Godfather* production. With the budget and logistical limitations, plus the constant battles with the studio, he was plagued by

COPPOLA: CREATIVE, DEMANDING, VASCILLATING.

pangs of tremendous self-doubt. With only a few weeks left in New York, Coppola told a young colleague, "Do you still want to direct films? Always remember three things: Have the definitive script ready before you begin to shoot. There'll always be some changes, but they should be small ones. Second, work with people you trust and feel secure with. Remember good crew people you've worked with before and get them for your film. Third, make your actors feel very secure, so they can do their job well."

Then he concluded, "I've managed to do none of these things on this film."

As alluded to previously, Coppola even butted heads with Gordon Willis, the man he relied upon the most. Later, Coppola and Willis would develop a strong respect for each other's work and collaborate on *The Godfather* sequels. But on the set of their first project together, their problems were loud and public. Willis—experienced, methodical, displaying little patience for actors but with a firm grasp of his domain—viewed Coppola as a neophyte. Coppola, however, was equally demanding and impatient, not to mention vacillating—traits that would not fail to set the cinematographer's teeth on edge.

"Francis would drive Gordon nuts," Dick Smith said. "Francis would say, 'We're going to do the master shot here, and shoot that way.' Gordon would get all set up, and then Francis would come in and say, 'No, we'd better do it from the other side.' Gordon would tear his hair out."

Another catalyst for conflict was the carefully laid-out photographic plan for the production, which Willis always remembered but Coppola frequently didn't.

"I would say that Francis forgot our discussions twenty minutes after we started the movie," Willis said. "So I spent five or six months executing it as discussed and reminding him that that's the way we had talked about it. He would veer between one thing and another; he'd want to do something cinema verité one day and want to use a thousand-millimeter lens the next day."

Clashes became inevitable—and frequent.

Although Coppola freely recognized the unsurpassed quality of Willis's work, the director chafed at his cinematographer's methodical control of the number of setups required for each day's shoot.

"With Gordy you're going to get five or six spectacular shots a day, but you are not going to get twelve," Coppola said. "And that means you very often have to forgo a shot that might have been very useful for many reasons. Sometimes I envy directors who have more shots to work with."

In spite of his concerns about the pace of setups, fortunately Coppola didn't tamper with Willis's set preparation, lighting, or photographic mood. Willis shot with flat, rich lighting, using a system of his own design of inverted overhead lights that bounced into diffusing frames.

To make up for the low number of shot setups, Coppola filmed an abundance of takes. "One last one" became such a familiar phrase that Smith finally asked Coppola not to say it anymore.

"When you say 'one last one,' Francis, you do five or six more," Smith said.

The conflicts erupted on a number of occasions, during which "Francis would lock himself

in his office, and Gordon wouldn't come out of his trailer," Ruddy recalled. "They actually got the best out of each other, but there was a lot of conflict."

The confrontation came to a head during the setup of the dinner scene with Sonny at the head of the table while the Don recovers from his wounds. Rehearsal went poorly, and Willis and Coppola descended into a shouting match that resulted in Willis walking off the set, shouting, "You don't know how to do anything right!"

Coppola continued to work on the scene, ordering the camera crew to proceed without Willis. They froze, and Coppola exploded, screaming, "Fuck this picture! I want to make the fucking shot now, and we will, even if the fucking director of photography has to be thrown off the picture!"

Then Coppola, too, walked off the set, returned to his office, and destroyed the door.

Brando, who had his share of highly charged conflicts during other productions, was remarkably calm about the strife on *The Godfather* set. After one particularly nasty confrontation, Brando turned to a crew member and said, "What are they getting so excited for? It's only a gangster picture."

• • •

Coppola and Paramount would continue to squabble throughout the entire production, usually over insignificant details or minor budget issues, and the clashes between the director and his crew would burst forth and die away with the regularity of a geyser. Despite the conflicts, however, it was becoming obvious that the team was producing cinematic moments of magic. The studio, Coppola, and Ruddy were beginning to realize that they were putting together a project with tremendous possibilities. The studio's growing enthusiasm about *The Godfather* was no doubt buttressed by the fact that months before it was released, it had already turned a profit without one ticket sold. Theater owners had prebooked the film with orders of $13 million—nearly *twice* the production budget.

As the filming approached the end of its second month, Coppola was still struggling with one tangible problem that had nothing to do with the studio or the budget—namely, how to revise the scenes of Michael and the Don? To solve this problem, Coppola would have to enlist one of the most talented writers in Hollywood to produce a last-minute fix that came together with literally hours to spare.

The Script Doctor

AS PRODUCTION entered the final days of May, shooting was completed on a number of key scenes: exteriors of the wedding, interiors of the Don granting favors, the horse's head scene, shots of Hagen visiting Woltz's studio, and Michael holding his first meetings as head of the family.

Work with Brando proceeded smoothly, but his commitment to the picture was quickly drawing to a close. Even with the extra time bought with his storm-induced hiatus, his contracted time would conclude during the first week of June.

At that point, Brando was not a problem. Shoring up the script for the key scene that remained for him to shoot, however, was an obstacle. In spite of near-constant tinkering with key elements in the script throughout the production schedule, perhaps the most important section—the transition of leadership between Michael and the Don—was not satisfactory to anyone; it lacked the power and emotion needed to bring completion to the two characters' relationship.

The problem is apparent in the March 29 script, in the dialogue after Michael has returned from Sicily. In this draft, Michael returns to America in spring 1951. The Don is already much weaker. As Michael steps from the car, he sees the Don working on his beloved garden. They embrace, and the Don entreats, "Be my son."

Later, the Don and Michael walk through the olive oil factory. Here, Michael finally learns about his father's hopes for his future.

VITO CORLEONE

This old building has seen its day. No way to do business . . . too small, too old.

(As they enter the office)

Have you thought about a wife? A family?

MICHAEL

No.

VITO CORLEONE

I understand, Michael. But you must make a family, you know.

MICHAEL

I want children, I want a family. But I don't know when.

VITO CORLEONE

Accept what's happened, Michael.

MICHAEL

I could accept everything that's happened; I could accept it, but that I never had a choice. From the time I was born, you had laid this all out for me.

VITO CORLEONE

No, I wanted other things for you.

MICHAEL

You wanted me to be your son.

VITO CORLEONE

Yes, but sons who would be professors, scientists, musicians . . . and grandchildren who could be, who knows, a governor, a president even, nothing's impossible here in America.

MICHAEL

Then why have I become a man like you?

VITO CORLEONE

You are like me, we refuse to be fools, to be puppets dancing on a string pulled by other men. I hoped the time for guns and killing and massacres was over. That was my misfortune. That was your misfortune. I was hunted on the streets of Corleone when I was twelve years old because of who my father was. I had no choice.

MICHAEL

A man has to choose what he will be. I believe that.

VITO CORLEONE

What else do you believe in?

(Michael doesn't answer)

Believe in a family. Can you believe in your country? Those *pezzonovante* of the state who decide what we shall do with our lives? Who declare wars they wish us to fight in to protect what they own. Do you put your fate in the hands of men whose only talent is that they tricked a bloc of people to vote for them? Michael, in five years the Corleone family can be completely legitimate. Very difficult things have to happen to make that possible. I can't do them anymore, but you can, if you choose to.

(Michael listens)

Believe in a family; believe in a code of honor, older and higher, believe in roots
that go back thousands of years into your race. Make a family, Michael, and protect
it. These are our affairs, *sono cosa nostra,* governments only protect men who have
their own individual power. Be one of those men . . . you have the choice.

(The reference here to the *"Cosa Nostra"* was the single offending reference that remained
to be removed as part of Ruddy's deal with the Italian-American Civil Rights League; the two
"Mafia" references were long gone.)
Later, after Kay makes an abrupt appearance in the script as a wife and mother, Michael and
the Don are again talking in the garden. Al Neri, Michael's trusted new assistant, has just left the
pair, and they begin to talk about Michael's future as the head of the family.

VITO CORLEONE

I see you have your Luca Brasi.

MICHAEL

I'll need him.

VITO CORLEONE

There are men in this world who demand to be killed. They argue in gambling
games; they jump out of their cars in a rage if someone so much as scratches their
fender. These people wander through the streets crying out "Kill me, kill me." Luca
Brasi was like that.
And since he wasn't scared of death, and in fact, looked for it . . . I made him
my weapon. Because I was the only person in the world that he truly hoped would
not kill him. I think you have the same with this man.

(Michael and the Don walk through the garden)

VITO CORLEONE

Barzini will move against you first.

MICHAEL

How?

VITO CORLEONE

He will get in touch with you through someone you absolutely trust. That person will arrange a meeting, guarantee your safety . . .

(He rises, and looks at Michael)

. . . and at that meeting you will be assassinated.

(Pause)

Your wife and children . . . you're happy with them?

MICHAEL

Yes.

VITO CORLEONE

Good.

(Michael wants to express something . . . hesitates, then)

MICHAEL

I've always respected you. . . .

(A long silence. The Don smiles at Michael)

VITO CORLEONE

And I . . . you.

This dialogue, which draws heavily on lines from the book, fails to convey the love and respect that father and son feel for each other, nor the passing of power from one generation to the next. Earlier in production, Coppola could tinker with an occasional passage in on-set improvisations, but he was too absorbed in direction to wholly restructure one of the most important scenes of the picture. Clearly, outside help was needed, and Coppola called on a colleague from his days with Roger Corman, a writer who was known as the most talented script doctor in Hollywood.

Robert Towne had, like Coppola, used his time with Roger Corman as a training ground for a career in filmmaking, and for two years he roomed with another Corman protégé, Jack

Nicholson. While Coppola headed toward film direction, Towne had moved into full-time screen writing (he would venture into directing in the 1980s). Towne worked on several Corman films, including *The Last Woman on Earth* and *Tomb of Ligeia*, and occasionally on television projects, before an extensive rewrite of *Bonnie and Clyde* and other successes opened opportunities for original projects and rewrites for mainstream films. By the time Coppola called for help, Towne was considered *the* writer to get when a script was in trouble—a fast and effective dramatist who solved script problems large or small and polished the script to a fine sheen.

"I would rather have the next five commitments from Robert Towne," Evans would later say, "than the next five from Robert Redford."

Towne arrived on *The Godfather* set June 2. Later, Towne would tweak several scenes with minor editing and additions; he described most of his script doctor duties for *The Godfather* as "not a major operation—just spot surgery." He wrote minor adjustments for, among other scenes, Michael's declaration that he would shoot Sollozzo and McCluskey.

His principal assignment was the transition-of-power scene.

"Mainly, Francis was perplexed," Towne said. "In the book there wasn't any resolution between Vito Corleone and his son Michael. He needed a scene between the two of them. Francis kept saying, 'Well, I want the audience to know that they love each other.' But you couldn't do a scene about two people loving each other."

His work may have been only "spot surgery" for the other scenes in the movie, but for the transition-of-power sequence, he would need to create a complicated transformation. The production was scheduled to shoot the scene of Michael and the Don just one day after Towne arrived in New York. The following day was reserved for filming the Don's death. After that, Brando would leave the production—assuming all went according to plan.

"That was the scariest situation I've ever been in," Towne said. "It was a tense situation at that particular point, because no one figured that the film was going to be the big hit that it was."

Most of Towne's previous work as a script doctor had involved rewriting or restructuring entire scripts—and not just reworking a single key scene, which is an assignment fraught with risk.

"I wasn't rewriting the script from beginning to end, which I've done most often," Towne explained. "Instead, I was adding outside material and had to fit it in with what existed, make it consistent—and this meant knowing everything that had been shot and everything that the director had in mind. An interesting problem. Usually you're rewriting right along with the director and you know where you're going."

In the process of preparing for his assignment, Towne provided one of the first indications from an outsider of *The Godfather*'s potential.

"I saw about an hour of assembled footage, and I thought it was brilliant," he said. "I couldn't get over it. The footage was so extraordinary. I felt that I was going to make a contribution to a film that was virtually assured of being a major hit, although that was not the prevailing opinion on the set."

Towne then met with Coppola, Brando, and Pacino and listened to their appraisal of the material and their characters' relationship.

"I took a lot from Marlon and Al," Towne remembered. "Particularly Marlon. So I took the notion that he wanted to have this man try to express himself . . . of Vito Corleone trying to talk, then, rather than having him give sage nods. Through most of the film it is the power of silence that carries force . . . the power of the character is conveyed through pregnant silence. But in the situation I was asked to write, he actually talks."

Working from the original father-son conversations, Towne needed to create new material that combined an explanation of events to come in Michael's life—a subtle transfer of power, expressions of love, respect, life philosophy, and parental regret—all shrouded in the context of gangland scheming and murder plots.

Towne took his notes and the original script and wrote all night, finally finishing the scene at 4 A.M.

"I wrote a scene about the succession of power, and through that it was obvious that the two men had a great deal of affection for each other," Towne said. "Through Brando's anxiety about what would happen to his son, and his anxiety about giving up his power—his ambivalent feelings about, in effect, forcing his son to assume his role, and having to give up his role—that was the key to that scene.

"The Don is saying, 'We've got to see about this,' and Michael is saying, 'Dad, I told you I'd take care of it, and I'm taking care of it.' What seems to be a kind of absentmindedness on the part of Vito Corleone is really his unwillingness to accept the position he's placed his youngest son in.

"In the course of the scene, the two men really accept the dictates of fate. It's sort of a perverse noblesse oblige: Vito is obliged to pass the cup, and Michael is obliged to take it. He does, and through that you see that the two men love each other very much, rather than my writing a scene about love, which wouldn't have worked in that movie. It's illustrative in a way of writing in general. Most scenes are rarely about what the subject matter is."

The scene is set in the Don's garden, after Kay has passed along Connie's request that Michael be the godfather of her baby. Michael sits on the edge of a lounge chair, leaning toward his father. The Don leans back in a wicker chair, nibbling on bits of fruit and drinking a glass of red wine.

VITO CORLEONE

So, Barzini will move against you first. He'll set up a meeting with someone that you absolutely trust, guaranteeing your safety. And at that meeting, you'll be assassinated.

> *(The Don pauses for a sip of wine, giving Michael a chance to ponder the calm delivery of news about his own impending murder)*

I like to drink wine more than I used to. Anyway I'm drinking more.

MICHAEL

It's good for you, Pop.

> *(The Don looks at the glass)*

VITO CORLEONE

I don't know . . . your wife and children—you happy with them?

MICHAEL

> *(Nods)*

Very happy.

VITO CORLEONE

That's good. I hope you don't mind how I keep going over this Barzini business.

MICHAEL

No, not at all.

VITO CORLEONE

It's an old habit. I spend my life trying not to be careless. Women and children can be careless, but not men.

(The Don pauses)

How's your boy?

MICHAEL

(Smiles)

He's good.

VITO CORLEONE

You know, he looks more like you every day.

MICHAEL

He's smarter than I am. Three years old, and he can read the funny papers.

VITO CORLEONE

(Grins)

. . . read the funny papers.

(The Don drifts away for a moment, looks up, and remembers something)

Uh, I want to arrange to have a telephone man check all the calls that go in and out of here. . . .

MICHAEL

I did it already, Pop. . . .

VITO CORLEONE

You know, it could be anyone. . . .

MICHAEL

Pop, I took care of that. . . .

VITO CORLEONE

Oh, that's right, I forgot.

(The Don frowns, hesitates, and rubs his chin)

(Michael leans closer and pats his father's knee)

MICHAEL

What's the matter? What's bothering you? I'll handle it. I told you I can handle it—
I'll handle it.

*(The Don pauses, thinks for a moment, stands and walks slowly to the other side
of Michael's lounge, looking away from his son)*

VITO CORLEONE

I knew that Santino was going to have to go through all this. And Fredo . . . well.

(The Don sits at the end of Michael's lounge chair)

Fredo was . . . well . . . I never . . . I never wanted this for you. I work my whole
life—I don't apologize—to take care of my family. And I refused to be a fool, dancing on a string held by all those . . . big shots. I don't apologize—that's my life—
but I thought that . . . that when it was your time, that . . . that you would be the
one to hold the strings. Senator Corleone. Governor Corleone . . . something.

MICHAEL

(Looks up)

Another *pezzonovante*.

(*The Don turns to his son*)

VITO CORLEONE

Well . . . there wasn't enough time, Michael . . . wasn't enough time.

MICHAEL

We'll get there, Pop. We'll get there.

(*The Don holds Michael's head in his hand, kisses him, and pats his cheek*)

VITO CORLEONE

Hm. Now listen. Whoever comes to you with this Barzini meeting—he's the traitor. Don't forget that.

(*The Don stands and sighs, and Michael leans back in the chaise, deep in thought*)

The scene, as typed for the script, would fit on little more than three sheets of paper; single-spaced, it could be condensed to a single page. On screen, it would run only three minutes and forty-five seconds, including an exquisite master shot of Brando's speech about his dreams for Michael that ran nearly two minutes without a cut.

Yet in spite of its brevity, Towne had created a masterpiece of screen writing that remains one of the most memorable scenes in cinema history. The revised script, combined with Coppola's gentle direction and superb performances by Brando and Pacino, supplied precisely the emotional interlude so essential at this pivotal moment in the film.

Towne would be remembered for his uncredited contributions to *The Godfather*. The garden scene was used in the Academy Awards broadcast as the showcased clip from the film during the nominations for Best Picture, and Coppola acknowledged Towne when he received his Academy Award for best screenplay.

"I'd like to thank Bob Towne, who wrote the very beautiful scene between Marlon and Al Pacino in the garden," Coppola said at the Oscar ceremony. "That was Bob Towne's scene."

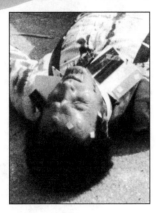

"These Guys Don't Go Around Shooting Each Other Anymore"

O N JUNE 4, Brando appeared in his last scene: the death of the Don. Smith created makeup that reflected the character's age and weariness. The actor's hair was askew in the carelessness of old age, his neck extra-wrinkled, his teeth an unappealing shade of yellow-brown.

The scene required a friendly bond between Brando and Anthony Gounaris, the three-year-old boy who appeared as Michael's son, who was also named Anthony (Coppola used the boy's real name to simplify work with

the toddler). Off camera, Brando tried to make friends with the boy by play-ing "monster"; Brando shoved a piece of orange peel in front of his teeth and growled. Instead of laughing, however, the child was terrified and started to cry. Brando did eventually soothe the boy, leaving Coppola captivated by the trick. "After having seen him like that," Coppola said, "I couldn't film the scene any other way."

Brando developed the scene as one of an old man playing with a child he loved. Coppola, on the other hand, considered it something more sinister; namely, the ironic death of the Don dying as a monster. Regardless of individual perspective, the truly extraordinary scene of the Don and Anthony running through the tomato plants and the Don keeling over in death as Anthony says "I love you" is a magical screen moment. "Sometimes," Coppola remembered, "you catch lightning in a bottle."

Brando was finished with the picture—an excuse for a shrimp and champagne party. When he emerged from removing makeup for the last time, he had also shaved the moustache he grew for the part, providing many in the crew with their first opportunity to see the actor's natural ap-pearance. With most of the cast in attendance, he was given a grand send-off. Thus Brando completed his work as Vito Corleone with little fuss, no major hassles, and none of the histrionics that Paramount thought he would bring to the production. Instead, he left the film with one of the most subtly powerful and memorable performances in cinema history.

With many of the film's more complex scenes completed, production would proceed quickly on a number of shots. On June 7, Coppola shot the exteriors of the baptism scene for Connie and Carlo's son—with Coppola's own daughter Sofia substituting for the child. (The interiors were shot on June 21 in Old St. Patrick's Church on Mulberry Street.) On June 8, the crew filmed Carlo's death at the hands of Clemenza—strangled in a moving car as he kicked out the windshield in his death agony. Gianni Russo was extensively rigged for the execution—his legs were padded to protect him from breaking prop glass and the car frame as he kicked. To simulate the garroting scene, in which Clemenza nearly pulls Carlo over the top of the front seat, Russo wore a chest harness that could be pulled from behind. When Richard Castellano wrapped the garrote around Russo's neck, he appears to be pulling hard on the wire and dragging Russo; instead, he was pulling on the harness strap.

BRANDO GETS POSITIONED FOR A SHOT OF THE DON'S DEATH.

By June 9, the production was ready to wrap up its work at the Corleone Mall. Coppola filmed a long shot of the Don's death using a double, then reshot Kay and Michael's conversation at Connie's wedding.

On June 22, the production focused its efforts on one of the most complex shots of the picture: the assassination of Sonny Corleone. By then Paramount had a clear understanding of *The Godfather*'s potential as a blockbuster. Even though the studio had already killed plans to shoot in Las Vegas and Los Angeles, Ruddy had been able to persuade the studio to let the production spend some money on this important scene.

Coppola had originally planned to shoot at real tollbooths, but the traffic logistics proved impossible. Instead, Tavoularis created a realistic substitute on a runway at Floyd Bennett Field, a deserted airstrip near Mineola, New York. It made a quiet, peaceful setting for an execution, much like the one used for the spectacular death scene for another Tavoularis scorcher, *Bonnie and Clyde*. The set designers constructed a reproduction of three tollbooths, complete with curbs and lane markers (a billboard in the background not only added depth to the setting, but also screened a distant apartment complex from view). The assassination sequence alone, which took three days and required extras, technicians, and explosives, consumed about $100,000 of the budget.

JOE LOMBARDI'S
SPECIAL-EFFECTS
RIGGING, SET TO
DESTROY SONNY'S
LINCOLN.

"It reflected the feeling of all of us that we could keep reaching for a little more quality—at moments—and that every dollar we spent would be money well spent both in terms of the creative return on the film and the financial return on the film," Ruddy recalled.

Sonny's execution was designed to be an especially thorough job, accomplished by a squad of machine gun–toting hit men. As a result, Caan was rigged for the simulated strafing by dozens of .45 caliber bullets across his entire body. In addition, he was also fitted with eight "face hits," or small plastic blisters filled with film blood, each attached to extremely thin fishing line. When the line was pulled, the blister would rip open and the blood would flow. Rigged for a take with

lines hanging from his face, Caan looked like a hapless fisherman who had caught fishing hooks in his face. With a sip of Karo blood to spurt from his mouth at the appropriate moment, Caan was ready to be killed.

The prepared Caan was, in Ruddy's words, a "walking bomb." He was rigged with more than one hundred explosive squibs—more than had ever been attached to one person before. The electric wires to activate the squibs led down his back, through his left pant leg, and into a firing console behind the car (which is why, in the master shots, Caan's left foot is not visible).

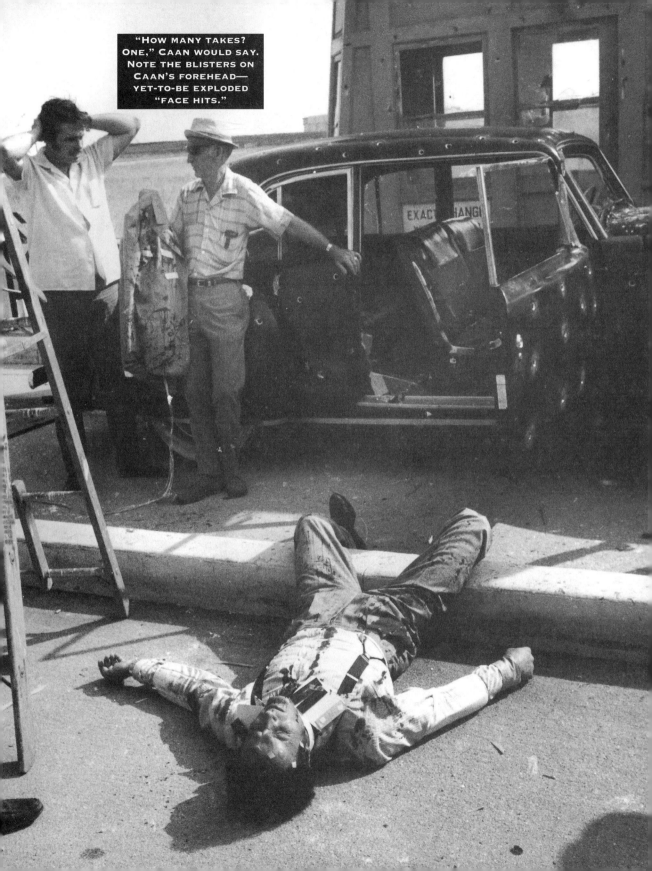

"HOW MANY TAKES? ONE," CAAN WOULD SAY. NOTE THE BLISTERS ON CAAN'S FOREHEAD—YET-TO-BE EXPLODED "FACE HITS."

As Caan was prepped for the scene, Ruddy decided to have some fun with the actor. "An hour before we started filming, I told Caan, 'I'm really nervous. We need you for another two weeks, and you could really get hurt in this scene. It would ruin our shooting schedule for the rest of the picture. So be careful.' Jimmy turned very, very pale." Similarly, as Caan was being prepared for the scene, one of the effects technicians leaned to him and whispered, "I've never put this many squibs on a guy in my life."

Caan quipped, "I don't think it was necessary for you to tell me that *now*."

The other victim in the scene was Sonny's 1941 Lincoln Continental. The car had been pristine when purchased, but for the scene, the crew drilled dozens of holes in the body, bent the metal to simulate the impact of a half-inch-wide bullet, then filled each hole with a small explosive charge. Of course, they had to putty and paint the whole car again afterward to bring it back to showroom condition. The rest of the set was then prepared in the same manner as the car. The rigging of Caan, the car's body, the upholstery, and the tollbooths required more than four hundred charges.

Over the years, when asked how many takes were needed to film the scene, Caan reveled in replying, "How many takes? *One.*" But that answer implied that the shot was filmed in one long take, after which everyone went home. That was hardly the case. Of course, after the teasing he took on the set during this shot, no one can begrudge Caan the luxury of remembering the scene any way he wants. In fact, Caan was telling the truth—in part—about the number of takes. The principal take of the shooting was indeed a single shot; all of the explosive choreography worked perfectly as hundreds of charges were exploded in rapid sequence, shattering glass, blasting wood and metal, and exploding through Caan's clothing as he simulated writhing in agony.

"In the middle of that scene, I thought they'd blow my whole suit apart," Caan said. "But I wasn't hurt. And you can see how realistic the results were. I didn't mind the scene too much, but I wouldn't be honest if I said it didn't make me a little nervous."

While the master shot was flawless, the preparations, shots from other angles, and close-ups would require two days to complete. In between takes, Caan would be seen sitting patiently on the set awaiting his cue, his clothes torn to rags and his body covered with Karo blood.

In the waning days of the production, another A. D. Flowers–orchestrated effect would require a much simpler but still delicate touch. When Moe Greene is shot, the bullet rips through the right lens of Greene's glasses and into his eye. All effects that involve eyes are potentially dangerous, but

CAAN TAKES A BREAK FROM THE MASSACRE.

Flowers and his crew rigged the effect so the glass appeared to be crushing inward, although it was actually blowing outward. For the scene, Alex Rocco, who played Greene, lay on his stomach getting a massage as the hit man came into the room. Rocco put on a real pair of glasses, and the camera stopped rolling. Then Flowers brought in a pair of glasses rigged with sugar glass and plastic tubes running down the stems. One tube contained thinned Karo blood; the other tube—connected to a cannister of compressed air—contained a tiny pellet. To create the effect, the pellet was fired through the lens *away* from Rocco, then the blood in the other tube was released to create the gory simulation of Greene being shot in the eye.

In the film, viewers see Rocco pick up his glasses and put them on as the hit man enters the massage room. The scene then cuts to a close-up of Rocco (already now wearing the prop glasses) as the shot is fired, the glass explodes, and the blood flows. Only knowing how the effect is done and a frame-by-frame viewing reveals the delicate technique: As the shot is fired, a small puff of air lifts Rocco's hair momentarily, and in one frame the pellet can be seen moving away from Rocco's face.

On June 28, after days of machine gun assassinations, beatings, and garrotings, the scene being shot was as far removed from images of violence as the production could get. In a suite at the St. Regis Hotel, Coppola filmed intimate scenes of Kay and Michael for use early in the film. (One of the shots, a scene of the couple in bed together, was deleted from the film but was restored in both *The Godfather Epic* and *Trilogy*.)

Late in the afternoon, startling news arrived from the annual Italian United Day celebration in Columbus Circle: Joe Colombo had been shot. Literally a few feet from the Gulf+Western headquarters, in front of thousands of shocked onlookers and despite a cordon of heavy police security, the founder of the Italian-American Civil Rights League was shot twice in the head at close range. The assassin—who had gotten close to Colombo because he carried a press identification card—was shot and killed immediately (the killer of the assassin was never identified).

Colombo wasn't killed instantly, but the wounds would later prove fatal. He suffered substantial brain damage and was left almost totally paralyzed, and in May 1978 he died of cardiac arrest, a condition his doctor said stemmed from his gunshot wounds.

Suddenly, the Mafia wasn't so glamorous anymore.

"I was shocked," Ruddy said. "This was a nightmare."

After filming was over for the day, several in the crew, including Coppola, watched the news report. "Before we started working on the film we kept saying, 'These guys don't go around shooting each other anymore,'" Coppola said. We thought one of our problems was to make the film relevant."

Police informants speculated that Colombo's shooting was part of an escalation of Mob violence that may have been spurred by dissension within the Colombo crime family. That conflict would spawn other violence that would continue for months, including in the days immediately following the release of *The Godfather*.

Meanwhile, on June 29, filming continued at the St. Regis with an eerie reminder of the previous day's events. In an upstairs hallway, Castellano was filmed firing shotgun blasts into an elevator for a scene of Don Strachi's murder. Coppola requested take after take, and with each new scene, the sounds of the shotgun blasts rumbled like explosions through the building.

By this time, the production in New York was winding down. Most of July 1 was taken up with filming the murder of Barzini outside the Justice Building. The next day, the last of principal photography, started more slowly than usual, because everyone was still recovering from the wrap party the night before. Since the actual last day of production included a night shot, the wrap party was held a day early at the Cornish Arms Hotel.

In the March 29 *Godfather* script, Michael finds Fabrizio, the traitorous bodyguard responsible for killing his Sicilian wife Apollonia, in New York. After Barzini and the other dons are eliminated, Michael and Neri travel to the pizza parlor where Fabrizio works, and Michael cuts him down with blasts from a *lupara* (the short-barreled shotgun the Sicilian bodyguards carry in the film). Before Michael exits the pizza parlor, he leaves the *lupara* on top of Fabrizio's body; presumably the weapon was Fabrizio's own gun, which Michael brought home from Italy for just this occasion.

COPPOLA FILMS RICHARD BRIGHT AS NERI IN THE REVERSE SHOT OF THE MURDER OF BARZINI.

MICHAEL PRE-
PARES TO KILL
THE TRAITOR
FABRIZIO IN A
SEQUENCE
DELETED FROM
THE FILM.

ON THE SECOND-
TO-LAST DAY
OF SHOOTING,
MICHAEL ENTERS
A PIZZA PARLOR
TO MURDER
FABRIZIO. THE
LUPARA (SHOT-
GUN) IS UNDER
HIS COAT.

On July 2, Coppola and his team attempted to film the scene at the Imperial Pizza Parlor on 35th Street. Coppola shot footage of Michael's entrance into the restaurant with the *lupara* under his overcoat, then his exit without the gun. Unfortunately, the location was on a heavily traveled street and shooting inside was impossible because of Fourth of July weekend traffic. As an alternative, the murder was filmed in a restaurant in Sicily decorated to look like an American pizza parlor. Strangely enough, although eventually Fabrizio's death was deleted entirely from the film, a photograph of Pacino in this scene—wearing a dark suit and a white hat—would become one of the most popular publicity stills of the young actor when *The Godfather* was released; *Saga*, a men's magazine of the 1970s, even featured Pacino on its cover, blasting away with Fabrizio's shotgun—a photo which must have mystified anyone who had seen the film. Paramount released several versions of the photograph; in one, the shotgun and coat are plainly visible.

The night of July 2, *The Godfather* production crew would film the last shot of principal photography in New York: Michael's pickup by Sollozzo and McCluskey in front of Jack Dempsey's restaurant. It was a grand public finale for the production; the warm July evening drew a crowd of thou-

PACINO, IN THE HEAVY MAKEUP THAT SIMULATED A BROKEN JAW, PREPARES TO FILM THE LAST SCENE OF PRINCIPAL PHOTOGRAPHY IN NEW YORK: MICHAEL'S PICKUP BY SOLLOZZO AND MCCLUSKEY.

sands for the simple scene of Pacino, in winter clothes, climbing into the big sedan and driving away. With sighs of relief all around, principal photography in New York was completed.

Coppola requested and received a two-week break before taking his crew to Italy for the Sicilian shoot. The break gave the director and his editors a chance to work on a rough cut of about three hours. The editing continued while Coppola was overseas and then over the next five months.

In preproduction, Coppola had convinced Evans—in one of their countless phone arguments about the script—that the Sicilian sequence was critical to the production, providing a brief respite from the treachery of the New York underworld. Of course, before shooting began, Evans had little to lose by agreeing: If the New York production went well, the Sicilian footage would be a welcome addition; if Coppola flopped, the studio could cancel the trip. By July, everyone at Paramount knew the production had gone very well indeed.

Coppola went to Italy, but with only a skeleton crew. Associate producer Gray Frederickson assumed the responsibilities of first assistant director. Although Willis shot the film and Tavoularis handled the design, the

A SKELETON CREW IN SICILY FILMS FABRIZIO (ANGELO INFANTI), MICHAEL, AND CALO (FRANCO CITTI).

PACINO RECEIVES
A SCALED-DOWN
MAKEUP JOB IN
SICILY. "IT WAS
PRETTY AWFUL
MAKEUP," DICK
SMITH SAID.

studio wouldn't cover the costs of sending Dick Smith along to handle makeup. As a result, the work was turned over to a local Italian makeup technician. Although there was no impact on basic makeup, Pacino's makeup suffered. At that point in the film, Michael's broken jaw was still healing, so Smith created a foam latex appliance that suggested the slight caving-in of the cheekbone. Smith sent the appliance, along with instructions, to his Italian counterpart but Smith said it didn't look like the application was used. It seemed as if the cheekbone had simply been smudged to give the impression of bruising. "It was pretty awful makeup," Smith said. When the later-to-be-deleted scenes of Michael killing Fabrizio were being prepared, the Italian makeup technicians soaked actor Angelo Infanti in so much blood, it looked as if it was applied with a paint roller.

Meanwhile, filming in Sicily gave Pacino a chance to think about his roots.

"My parents came from here," he said, "although I never thought much about it. How strange I should wind up playing a Sicilian."

"THESE GUYS DON'T GO AROUND SHOOTING EACH OTHER ANYMORE"

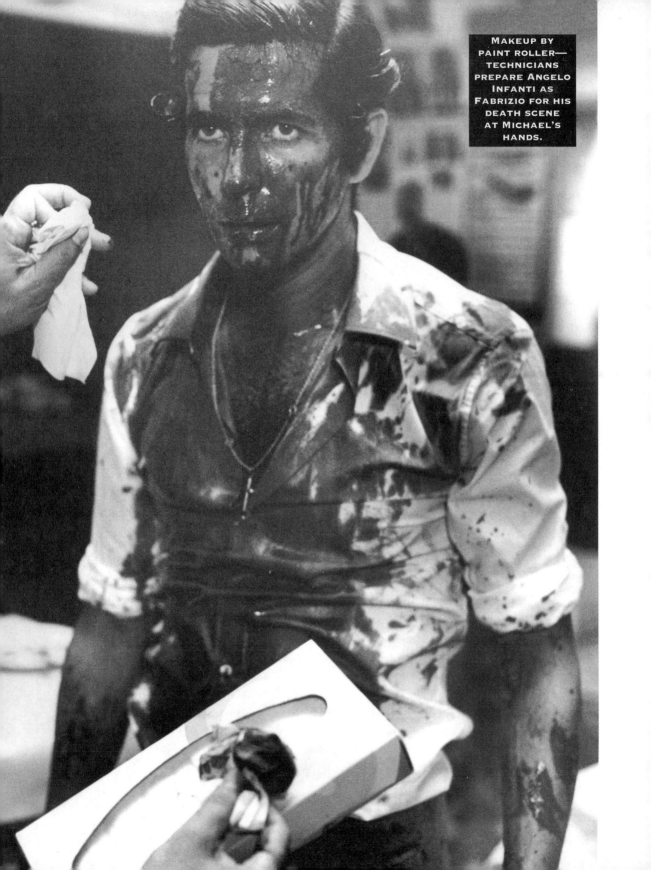

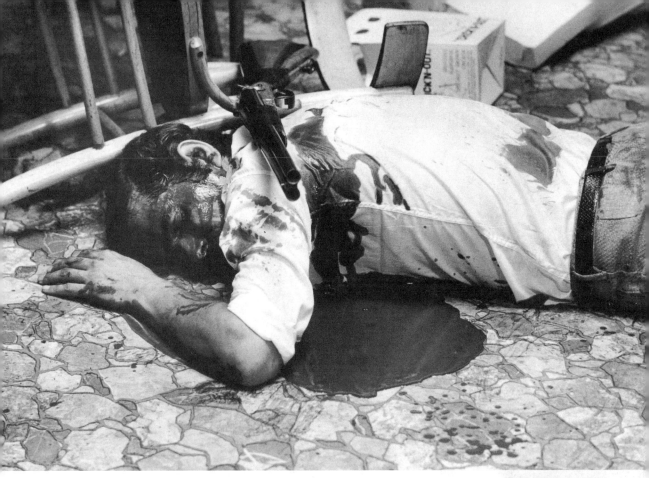

For Coppola, working in the Sicilian countryside—and six thousand miles farther from the studio—was a blissful contrast to the pressure-cooker setting of New York. Most of the scenes were shot in the region outside of Taormina, a resort town in eastern Sicily near Mt. Etna.

"For Francis, it was paradise," Ruddy said. "We came in, we didn't make any noise, and there was no fanfare—no one really knew we were there. The shooting itself was fairly uneventful. Everything went like clockwork. We did our stuff and got out."

By the time Coppola left for Sicily, Paramount was not only eager to release the film, but to give it exceptionally broad play as its major release of the year.

As production lingered, the studio had to accept the inevitable: It would be impossible to release *The Godfather* for Christmas. A December release would require finishing work in Sicily, editing the film, and completing all postproduction in only three and a half months—a feat impossible for a motion picture of such scope. On July 20, the studio finally broke the news publicly that many had long suspected: *The Godfather* would be held for the spring.

"It doesn't make sense to not keep faith with the book, with the production, and with the public," said Paramount president Frank Yablans, who had taken the top job when Stanley Jaffe resigned in March. "*The Godfather* is the most presold commodity on the market today; everyone wants it."

"The rushes have such a fantastic look," said Yablans, "we will not sacrifice one-tenth of one percent of the quality just to hit a release date."

Yablans could afford to wait. Even though *The Godfather* would deny the studio a major hit in the crucial Christmas season (instead, it released *Star Spangled Girl,* a modest Neil Simon effort), the extra time would ensure that the final version of *The Godfather* would be a film to remember. Thanks to the success of *Love Story* through most of 1971, the year would be a happy one for the studio. Of course, it could have been a happier one if *The Godfather* had been ready on time, but any gloominess about the delays would soon be dispelled. Yablans's casual approach to the delay sent an important message to theater operators: *The Godfather is going to be something very special.*

"I Believe in the Mafia"

THE **TWO-WEEK** break in filming, plus the relatively peaceful shoot in Sicily, had a calming influence on the production. By August 1971, when postproduction began, the enthusiasm was palpable.

While principal photography was completed in Sicily, a few inserts and one short scene remained. The exterior of a Hollywood mansion was filmed to double as the exterior of the Woltz estate. Later, the reconciliation scene between Kay and Michael was shot in Ross, a small town in Northern California. Because the scene was shot in early autumn, Ross substituted nicely for New Hampshire on a clear fall day, with leaves blowing and trees bright with autumn colors.

While the troubles on the set were just a distant memory, plenty of fireworks remained before the film was completed. During postproduction, controversy would boil over about the most important aspect of the film—its length.

Since May, a team of editors had been pulling together rough assemblies from the endless stream of dailies that poured from the set. By the time principal photography was completed, Coppola had shot 500,000 feet of potentially usable footage, or more than ninety hours of material. Among the six editors working on the project were William Reynolds and Peter Zinner, who earned the screen credit for editing. To speed the editing process, Ruddy and Paramount agreed to let Coppola work on the rough cut in San Francisco. Final edits and other elements of postproduction were completed at Paramount in Los Angeles.

"I felt that we would probably get through that maze much more rapidly by letting Francis live at home and work at his own facility," Ruddy said.

Tinkering with editing was—and is—a Coppola forte; the director indulges in massaging every scene, collaborating closely with his editors, and experimenting with varying takes of scenes. Years later, Coppola's wife, Eleanor, remembered a conversation the couple once had about filmmaking as a metaphor for life. When talking about editing, Francis said, "I am willing to sacrifice my best scene to make the film better . . . anything . . . I can always put it back. That's the difference with life—you can't put it back."

Over the last five months of 1971, Coppola would indeed take out scenes and put them back again and again, in an effort to both satisfy himself and appease the studio—a task that would not prove easy to achieve.

While editing proceeded, so did other integral elements of postproduction. As the film was pulled together, *The Godfather* crew would again be staffed by the best in the business, a postproduction team that matched the skill and expertise of the group that brought the images to film.

Among the most important elements of the film to mold into shape after shooting concluded was the sound, which was recorded on the set by Christopher Newman and rerecorded by Bud Grenzbach and Richard Portman. Ruddy and Coppola considered sound mix critical to the success of the film and were wary of studio interference. More than once Coppola had to, in his words, "ride to the rescue of my sound mix" as the studio staff attempted to tweak the sound to suit conventions at Paramount. *The Godfather* is awash in sound elements that support the story, from the loudest explosions to the most subtle background voices, hums, jangles, and buzzes. As Sonny arrives at the tollbooths moments before his death, for example, a baseball game plays softly in the background; when Bonasera exits the Don's study, the sound of musical instruments tuning up for the wedding reception is heard through the open door—an audio cue of the blast of music to come a few moments later with the first exterior shot of the film.

Much of the wedding was filmed without sound; later, the careful blending of sounds provided a seamless transition to the scenes shot during the full wedding sequence, isolated shots of individuals at the wedding (such as Kay and Michael talking), and the interior scenes in the Don's office and the hallway. In Little Italy, before the Don is gunned down, the cacophony of sounds in the crowded community provide the unseen backdrop of a busy tenement district—people talking, the soft rush of nearby traffic, and a single trumpet playing scales in practice drills. When Michael and Enzo the baker rush outside to scare off the Don's potential assassins, the distant rumblings of a storm can be heard, the perfect setup for the arrival of Captain McCluskey simultaneous with a loud clap of thunder. Later, when Sollozzo, McCluskey, and Michael are driving to their fateful meeting, the singing of the tires on the bridge's metal grate makes an eerie sound akin to a human chorus.

Of the individual sounds in *The Godfather*, perhaps the most potent are heard in Louis Restaurant in the Bronx, in concert with Michael's churning emotions as he prepares to kill Sollozzo and McCluskey. When Michael leaves the bathroom with the gun, the sound of the elevated train can be heard screeching outside; as an audio complement to Michael's apprehension, the roar of the train and screech of brakes perfectly match his anxious expression as the moment of execution approached.

Beyond individual sounds, creating a potent mix of existing sound was vital to the production. If, for example, one listens with eyes closed to the scene of Connie and Carlo fighting, the jarring blend of shouts, screams, pottery breaking, glass shattering, and Carlo's leather belt whipping Connie's body is chilling, as vivid as a domestic dispute recorded in a 911 call.

Some rerecording of individual voices was necessary, but concerns about Brando's legendary mumbling were unfounded. Brando was easily understood in most takes, although he did rerecord a few takes, and some added dialogue—later deleted—for a scene between Michael and the Don walking in the garden. The principal problem with Brando's dialogue came from another source—a small, furry source. The kitten Brando held during the scenes in which the Don meets with Bonasera the undertaker wreaked havoc with the sound recording; the equipment picked up more purring than dialogue.

"The cat nearly cost us Brando," Ruddy joked. "After Evans saw the scene, he called me. He said, 'What the fuck is going on? We're going to have to put subtitles on this whole movie. We can't understand Brando.' The problem wasn't Brando—it was the cat purring off camera!"

For the musical soundtrack, Coppola turned to one of the film industry's most distinguished composers. Nino Rota composed his first film score in 1933, when he was twenty-two years old, but after that project he would focus his attention for the next ten years on creating operatic works, symphonies, and classical compositions. Beginning in the mid-1940s, however, Rota again devoted much of his creativity to film music. He would become one of the motion picture industry's most popular and prolific composers, often producing as many as three film scores per year. Rota was perhaps best known for his association with Federico Fellini, composing every musical score for the director's work from *The White Sheik* in 1951 to *Orchestra Rehearsal* in 1978.

Using original material, as well as excerpts from the score he wrote from Fellini's 1958 production *Fortunella*, Rota created for *The Godfather* a powerful musical score that would include themes that have become some of the most memorable and popular in cinema history. From the film's opening "Godfather Waltz," performed on solo trumpet, to the heavily orchestrated arrangement that accompanied the credits, the score was laced with intricate melody, Italian-tinged passages, and hauntingly tragic themes. To complement the tension of several scenes, Rota also wrote passages of dramatic piano music; particularly noteworthy is the passage that accompanies Michael's visit to see his father in the hospital.

Rota also composed a suspenseful segment heavy with saxophone and jazzy piano called "The Pickup" reminiscent of 1950s film noir, little of which was used in the film. A short and subtle eleven-note theme for flute, piano, and clarinet titled "The New Godfather" serves as a theme for Michael's rise to power in the family. The passage can be heard, among other places, during the first few seconds of the reconciliation scene between Kay and Michael, and often bridges to the main *Godfather* theme, offering a delicate musical suggestion of Michael's rise to power in the Corleone family.

While Rota wrote most of the music, the soundtrack also includes incidental music from eight Italian and American popular songs, including "Manhattan Serenade" by Louis Alter, "I Have But One Heart" by Johnny Farrow and Marty Symes, "All of My Life" by Irving Berlin, and organ music for the baptism scene composed by Johann Sebastian Bach. On several occasions, the background music shifts seamlessly from background score to on set source music. For example, "Have Yourself a Merry Little Christmas" is used to establish the setting in front of Best & Co. when Michael and Kay are shopping, when the scene shifts to Luca Brasi putting on his bulletproof vest, the song is playing scratchily on the radio in his apartment. In the montage of the war among the five families, the tinny piano music in the background comes from the piano in the Corleone hideout as performed on set by Carmine Corleone.

The director's father was also among the composers whose work was included in *The Godfather*. Carmine composed much of the music used in the wedding sequence; his music, a jaunty piece ideal for wedding dances, is heard in the first outdoor scene of the film. In addition, he wrote an Italian-tinged waltz that was used in the wedding sequence when the Don and his wife dance. With his work on *The Godfather*, Carmine Coppola finally got his break in motion pictures. He would soon be regarded as an influential film composer and earn justified acclaim for his work on *The Godfather* sequels and other projects. "At long last," Carmine sighed, "I was on my way."

While individual elements of postproduction were coming together, the film was evolving, slowly but surely, as Coppola envisioned it. By September, however, the director and his editors had still not reached the point where they were able to fine-tune with a snip here or there. Instead, they required a machete to cut through the miles of extra footage. To bring the film even close to a manageable length, whole scenes and sections had to go. (Note: Many of the deleted scenes below were restored by Coppola in *The Godfather Epic* and/or *The Godfather Trilogy.*)

By September, a rough final cut was being viewed. Gone was the original flashback structure of the book and the final script; the film was cut in a more linear arrangement. Also gone were several complete scenes, including the death scene of Genco Abbandando, the Don's original *consigliere*. The scene of Genco in the hospital, which occurred after the wedding, was not deemed necessary to advance the film, but since its deletion removed almost all mention of the Don's most trusted adviser, viewers who had not read the book may be confused by an argument later in the film between Sonny and Tom, in which Sonny blurts out, "If I had a wartime *consigliere*—a Sicilian—I wouldn't be in this shape! Pop had Genco—look what I got." The scene also would have more fully explained Tom's role in the family at the start of the film; with the inclusion of the scene, viewers would have known that Tom was *consigliere*-in-training as Genco was dying.

> **THE VISIT TO SEE GENCO IN THE HOSPITAL—A SCENE DELETED FROM THE FILM. "WHEN YOU FINISH SCHOOL, I WANT YOU TO COME AND TALK TO ME, BECAUSE I HAVE PLANS FOR YOU, YOU UNDERSTAND?"**

By deleting Genco's death, the rough cut lost an important conversation between the Don and Michael, which occurs in the hospital corridor.

VITO CORLEONE

(The Don gestures at Michael's battle decorations)

What are all these Christmas ribbons for?

MICHAEL

(Pauses)

For bravery.

VITO CORLEONE

What miracles you do for strangers.

> *(Michael starts to walk away, then the Don stops him and holds him*
> *gently by the arms)*

Just a minute, Michael. I wanna talk to you. Now what are your plans when you get out?

(The Don puts his hand on Michael's shoulder)

MICHAEL

Finish school.

VITO CORLEONE

That's fine. I approve of that. Michael, you never come to me as a son should, you know that, don't you? When you finish school, I want you to come and talk to me, because I have plans for you, you understand?

(The Don pats Michael on the cheek)

MICHAEL

(Not convinced, mumbles as he turns away)

We'll see.

The inclusion of this scene would have established that the Don had unspoken plans for his son—plans that Michael no doubt assumed had to do with his role in the family business. The deletion of the sequence removed the sad irony that would have accompanied the garden scene, when viewers discover that the Don "never wanted this" for his son and instead had loftier—and legitimate—aspirations for him.

Another surprising deletion comes after Michael has returned from Sicily. He and the Don are walking in the Don's garden and talking about revenge.

VITO CORLEONE

Look at this—tomatoes, peppers—all of this—perfecto. . . .

MICHAEL

Pop, what about Sonny?

(Then)

What about Sicily?

VITO CORLEONE

I swore that I would never break the peace.

MICHAEL

But won't they take that as a sign of weakness?

VITO CORLEONE

It is a sign of weakness. . . .

MICHAEL

Oh. You gave your word that you wouldn't break the peace, I didn't give mine. You don't have to have any part—I take all responsibility.

VITO CORLEONE

Well, we have a lot of time to talk about it now.

Had it remained in the film, this brief scene would have helped establish the beginning of the transition of power between the Don and Michael. (Oddly enough, this important scene was added to *The Godfather Epic,* but not to *The Godfather Trilogy.*)

In other cases, scenes were retained, but chunks were excised. In Michael's first meeting with Tessio and Clemenza after assuming command of the family, for example, he tells the group that Hagen is no longer *consigliere*—he will instead be the family lawyer in Las Vegas.

In the final cut, Hagen's first line in this scene is "Mike, why am I out?" But as originally shot, other dialogue precedes that line.

TOM

Michael, why are you cutting me out of the action?

MICHAEL

We're going to be legitimate all the way—you're the legal man. What's more important than that?

TOM

I'm not talking about that—I'm talking about Rocco Lampone building a secret regime. Now why does Neri report directly to you instead of through me or the *caporegimes?*

MICHAEL

How'd you find that out?

TOM

Well, Rocco's men are a little too good for their jobs. I mean, they're getting more money than the jobs are worth.

VITO CORLEONE

I told you this wouldn't escape his eye.

The scene, while containing extraneous material, would have reinforced Michael's intention to get his family out of illegal businesses. With the untimely death of his father, it is clear the process will take longer than he hoped, and as viewers would see at the end of the sequel, Michael eventually gives up all hope of becoming legitimate.

Many other sections were cut from the existing scenes that remained, in trims that ranged from a few seconds to more than a minute: most of the birthday party at the Woltz studio; scenes of Hagen at Woltz's mansion (and seeing the starlet and her mother upstairs outside a bedroom); Clemenza working on his car, then giving Rocco Lampone the gun he will use to kill Paulie Gatto; Clemenza leaving Rocco and Paulie in a car while he has lunch and picks up cannoli.

In a scene to appear before the Don is shot, Michael and Kay are sleeping together in a New York hotel room. When they decide to wait an extra day before going to the Corleone house, they call Tom Hagen to tell him they are in New Hampshire. The scene was an easy cut; however, its inclusion would have explained a line that remained. When Michael calls Sonny after he hears about the shooting, Sonny has no idea where his brother has been. Michael asks, "Didn't Tom tell you I called?"

From the Sicily footage, several brief scenes were cut, including Michael, Fabrizio, and Calo talking about America; the trio watching a communist party march; Michael's return to his father's ancestral home, only to discover that none of his family remains in the town of Corleone; and a scene of Michael in bed, barely conscious after the explosion that killed his new wife and begging Don Tommasino to find Fabrizio.

The fight between Connie and Carlo was trimmed from a slightly longer length, including scenes of Carlo in the shower asking Connie to make him dinner. This is why in the final film, Connie complains, "Look, you just told me to make you dinner!"

Later, when Paramount became more involved in the editing, they asked Coppola's final scene to be cut. Originally, the film was to end with a shot of Kay, the credits rolling, as she lights candles in church and prays for Michael Corleone's soul. But Evans persevered and Ruddy and Coppola didn't feel the shot was worth fighting for; instead the film ends with a chilling shot of Kay as the door to the new Don's office closes in her face.

In the tally of film deleted from the final cut, the biggest victim of the trims was clearly James Caan. Several of his lengthy scenes were removed, sequences that explored the sensitive side of the mostly explosive personality that remains on-screen.

Nearly all of the excised footage of Sonny comes from the sequences after the Don is shot: Sonny tells his mother about the shooting. He then goes to his father's office—deliberately avoiding sitting in his chair—and prepares to launch a defense of the family.

Had these scenes been included, not only would the role of Sonny have been more developed, but viewers would also have learned that Clemenza is a suspect in the Don's shooting. It was assumed that either Paulie or Clemenza was responsible for setting up the Don, which is why when Clemenza offers to send some of his people to guard Sonny's family, Sonny declines. (In the deleted footage, Sonny calls Tessio to ask him to send reinforcements. The scene also explains Clemenza's level of distress when Michael returns to the Corleone house. Clemenza is not only concerned about the Don, but he also knows he is a suspect and is terrified that he may be assassinated.) In another deleted scene, Sonny receives a call from his contact at the telephone company about the destination of calls made from a booth near his father's office confirming that Paulie—not Clemenza—is the guilty one.

"I was plenty steamed, because I'd done a lot of work in four or five major scenes that were cut," Caan said. "There were all kinds of nice moments. I worked hard on those scenes. They meant something to me as an actor. Little things—showing Sonny's inability to cry because he thinks it's unmasculine. But his voice cracks when he talks to his mother.

"It was like painting a fourteen-foot canvas and ending up with a three-foot canvas. I felt like telling everybody they ought to see the other eleven feet!"

In the end, Caan's footage was unnecessary to advance the story. However, these scenes, as well as many others, would be ideal to flesh out the Corleone family story in a longer project. Indeed, almost all of the deleted scenes would later be brought to light when Coppola would twice have the opportunity to recut his project without studio interference.

Finally, in November 1971, after months of broad cuts and subtle trims, Coppola and Ruddy completed a semifinal version of *The Godfather* that satisfied the production team. At two hours and fifty-five minutes, it was precisely what all involved had hoped for—or at least, as close to perfection as a collaborative art could create.

Right down to the final cut, Ruddy would stick to his deal with the Italian-American Civil Rights League: The word "Mafia" would not be spoken in the film. Or so Ruddy thought. During a screening of the semifinal cut, the producer had barely settled into his seat in the mixing room when the crew finally got even with the producer for all of the preproduction shenanigans with the League. The screen went dark, and the voice of the undertaker came up:

"I believe in the Mafia. The Mafia has made my fortune. . . ."

Ruddy's jaw dropped. "I said, 'What the fuck is *this?*' And then I heard all of them behind me laughing."

With the correct line ("I believe in America. . . .") tactfully reinserted into the soundtrack, Coppola's cut of *The Godfather* was ready for viewing by Robert Evans at the studio in Los Angeles, and Frank Yablans in New York.

Evans said it was lousy.

Twenty-five years after the editing of *The Godfather*, disagreements still remain about the events that led up to creating the final version of the film—in particular how much Robert Evans himself was involved in the editing and who was responsible for producing the cut that eventually became the final film.

"Francis worked on the first cut without anyone from Paramount looking in," Ruddy said. "I went up once a week but, basically, the first assembly of the film was done in San Francisco by Francis."

From here the stories vary widely, depending on the teller. Coppola and Ruddy remembered delivering a near three-hour rough cut to the studio. The first cut, according to Ruddy and Coppola, ran two hours and fifty-five minutes—close to the length of the final version.

As Ruddy tells it, "Bob loved the film at 2:55. He called Frank Yablans and told him. Frank went nuts. He was yelling, 'I won't risk any movie that's almost three hours! Get it down to 2:20.'

"Francis went back to editing to get a new cut into shape," Ruddy said. "He got it down to 2:20. We showed it to Evans again, and he said, 'This movie plays longer to me at 2:20 than at 2:55,' and he made that point to Frank. So it stayed exactly the way Francis wanted."

The "lousy" reference comes from Evans's recollection of the story; he recalled first seeing a short version of the film, then encouraging the director to restore material.

"The first cut Francis showed me was two hours and twenty minutes—and I told him it was lousy," Evans recalled. "He said he was just afraid to bring in a three-hour movie; every studio head he ever knew always said 'cut, cut.' So I told him to make it as long as he wanted and restore the texture, the family warmth."

What really may have occurred is that Evans recalled seeing the shorter version first because Coppola's contract called for a final cut shorter than 2:30. Longer than that and Paramount chiefs could wrest control of the edit from him and do the work themselves—a frightening prospect to a creative talent such as Coppola.

The true story is further obscured by Evans's remarks about his extensive involvement in the edit. The studio head would recall near-constant collaboration in editing *The Godfather*—work that he said would contribute to the failure of his marriage to Ali MacGraw.

"Toward the end it was seven days a week, eighteen hours a day," Evans said. "One columnist said the picture came between Ali MacGraw and me, and in a way that's true—I just wasn't home much for about six months."

At one point years later, such comments so incensed Coppola that he fired off an angry telegram to Evans about it.

"I've been a real gentleman regarding your claims of involvement on *The Godfather*," Coppola wrote to Evans in 1983. "Your stupid blabbing about cutting *The Godfather* comes back to me and angers me for its ridiculous pomposity."

The final word on the subject belongs to Ruddy—still the peacemaker even twenty-five years after the film's production.

"I tell my wife, I don't believe anyone cares about this anymore—what happened happened," Ruddy said. "Bob was going through some problems, and he was hanging around with us a lot at night. Bob's fine—nobody had any problem with him being there, and he was always very gracious.

"I don't want to take anything away from Bob, who backed us, always tried to be helpful, and was never an obstacle. But the final cut was Francis's cut—frame for fucking frame."

While Evans's involvement in editing may not be fully resolved by those who care to debate such issues, his role as the defender of the long version of *The Godfather* has never been challenged. All associated with the production agree that whenever it was that Evans saw the long cut, he approved it and steadfastly defended it to senior management at Paramount and Gulf+Western.

"I consider this Bob's big contribution to the film—standing behind us when we came in with a picture that was near three hours without an intermission," Ruddy said. "When Frank Yablans heard that, he nearly flipped out, but Evans backed us."

Confirmed Coppola, "As soon as he saw the film, Evans decided it would be a major hit. He was the guy who fought for the length."

By December 1971, *The Godfather* was a near-finished product, and late in the year and early in 1972, the film was screened for Paramount staff and exhibitors. Although theater owners and reporters enjoyed special screenings, the studio was still working hard to keep a tight lid on public pronouncements about the film until closer to its March release.

The lid came off on February 25, when Ivor Davis, a reporter for the *London Express*, was, as news reports described it, "smuggled into a private screening" and wrote a minireview that was distributed worldwide. In America, it was first published in the *New York Post*. Davis sneaked into a preview for exhibitors at a sales convention in Los Angeles on February 23. While other journalists had already seen the film on condition of holding back reviews until the release date, Davis was the first reporter who was able to write about it.

"Even the select audience gasped," wrote Davis. "Three minutes into *The Godfather*, the camera finally settled on the almost unrecognizable face of one of the world's most famous actors."

Davis described Brando's face as "squashed as if it had collided with a bulldozer and never fully recovered," his nose "slayed like an old wrestler," and his voice "old and weary, sometimes wheezing rasps out of the side of his mouth."

Davis called *The Godfather* a "tour de force" for Brando. "He gets a lot of competition, especially from handsome newcomer Al Pacino, with the looks of Alain Delon and the intensity of a young Rod Steiger, who plays son Michael. The picture is beautifully directed by Francis Ford Coppola, who manages to capture the late forties, and the whole Italian-American milieu of that time to perfection."

Davis would call his peek at *The Godfather* the "first-ever" screening of the picture, which was more than an exaggeration; among others, the movie critic for *Variety* saw the film on February 6. However, Davis's enthusiasm for *The Godfather* was sincere—and the first hint of the public enthusiasm to come.

By this time, Paramount had made a huge fuss over scheduling the film in a special world premiere booking in five of New York's most formidable theaters: The Loews State 1 and 2, Loews Orpheum, Loews Cine, and Loews Tower East. The premiere was set for March 15 in New York, with national release slated for March 29. The release was backed by extensive publicity, a simultaneous release of a sound-track album, and a special paperback book printing by Fawcett of 1.3 million copies, each with a special thirty-two-page insert of photographs from the film. Another one million copies of the hardcover edition were in print, poised for sale as soon as the picture opened.

As the premiere date grew closer, Coppola was at the same time both wildly enthusiastic and deeply uncertain about the success of his film. In one interview, he confided, "I was sure that people would feel I had taken this exciting best-selling novel and transformed it into a drab, ponderous, boring movie with a lot of actors who were known to be my personal friends." In contrast, Coppola was also quoted as proclaiming, "If it makes twenty to thirty million dollars, Paramount will think it's a failure. It should make at least twice that."

He would soon learn just how high his expectations should be.

"It Was Just a Fantastic Thing"

"**T**HE **GODFATHER**," the ad in *Time* magazine boasted proudly, "is now a movie." On March 15—three years after the book was published and eight days short of a year after the first scene was shot—*The Godfather* reached the screen.

As promised, the studio opened the film in a grand five-theater premiere in New York (first-night proceeds went to the Boys Club of New York). By movie marketing standards of the 1970s, it was a bold move unlike anything ever before attempted in New York.

"When I heard Paramount was opening *The Godfather* in five theaters in New York simultaneously, I was terrified," Ruddy said.

At the time, the plan for the premiere was a genuine gamble. In 1972, the marketing of a major motion picture was handled quite differently from the way it is done today. Back then, there were no 1,200-screen premieres in theaters across the country, $100 million first-week grosses, nor multimillion-dollar advertising budgets. The industry believed that a broad release would burn out interest in a hurry, and movie marketers snubbed the idea of big releases in hundreds or thousands of theaters, calling it "get-it-quick saturation."

When a film appeared—as the ads once said, "at a theater or drive-in near you," that could mean as few as one hundred to two hundred theaters nationally in its first-runs (in 1972, there were a *total* of ten thousand theaters in the entire country). Three hundred–plus screens would be reserved for only the most important or lucrative motion pictures.

Even for a motion picture as important as *The Godfather*, at that time a broad national release would not be the first and most logical step in the marketing plan. Amazingly enough, the industry believed that a limited run—in as few as one or two theaters—would build intense interest in the film for several days. Only then would the studio follow up with a national release. Among exhibitors and marketing executives, the technique was called "snowballing."

For *The Godfather*, the "snowball" quickly became an avalanche.

Even before the film opened, Paramount knew the film would be successful, but after its release, Evans and Ruddy quickly discovered they had a runaway hit on their hands. The first evidence of what was in store for *The Godfather* came to light on the early morning of March 15 as Ruddy rode to the Gulf+Western building in a heavy downpour.

"I remember driving in the rain down to the office that Wednesday," Ruddy said. "In front of the Orpheum there was a line for *The Godfather* around the block—at 8:15 in the morning. It was beyond anyone's dream."

No one could have anticipated the near-stampede of fans who descended on theaters at levels unprecedented in the history of the film business. From the office of *Variety*, the staff looked down to see the lines forming for the Loews State 1—a theater that was around the corner on Broadway. Patrons waited for hours—sometimes holding tickets for shows two or three screenings later. Scalpers sold tickets for up to twenty dollars each, and vagrants held places in line and peddled them as they approached the box office.

"It hasn't been this way ever before in terms of dollars and queues for one picture at five Manhattan theaters," wrote a stunned *Variety* reporter. "There were lines at the State 1, State 2, Tower East, Orpheum and the Cine extending nearly half a city block at each house to see *The Godfather*. On the basis of some brief chats, the people didn't seem to care (and actually didn't know) how long they would have to wait."

Even a boost in the ticket prices—$3.50 on weekdays, and $4.00 on Friday, Saturday, and Sunday (no passes honored)—could not slow interest in *The Godfather*. At the five New York City theaters, *The Godfather* screened at 9 A.M., 10 ,11 , noon, 1 P.M., 1:30, 2, 3, 4, 4:30, 5, 6, 7, 7:30, 8,

9 ,10, 10:30, 11, and midnight, plus some added extra-late-night shows. The five theaters had a combined seating capacity of 4,880, and attendance was near 98 percent for weeks—unheard of attendance by exhibitor standards in 1972.

Given the near-three-hour running time, the New York theaters scheduled only five minutes in between each show, so patrons were barely able to leave their seats before the next army of eager viewers started to enter. As schedules began to slip several minutes for each screening, the late show often started more than an hour late, which meant patrons of the last *Godfather* screening for the night often left the theater after 4 A.M.—only two hours before lines for the morning shows began to form. About the late finish of the movie, *Variety* reported, "There has been no bellyaching."

When reviews started to appear in the media, the critics were as excited as the patrons in line:

The Godfather, reported the *New York Times*, "is the year's first really satisfying, big commercial American film . . . a movie that describes a sorrowful American Dream as a slam-bang, sentimental gangster drama."

"*The Godfather* is a movie that seems to have everything—warmth, violence, nostalgia, the charisma of Marlon Brando in one of his finest performances, and the dynastic sweep of an Italian-American *Gone With the Wind*," wrote *Time.*

Not all reviews raved. In the most unyieldingly negative review, the *New Republic* blasted *The Godfather*, countering word for word the praise in other reviews. "Al Pacino rattles around in a part too demanding for him," the *New Republic* sniffed. "Brando's makeup is poor, the score by Nino Rota is surprisingly rotten, and the print had very washed-out colors." The critic also said "a lot of money" was spent on the picture—which must have amused Ruddy.

But negative or positive, Ruddy didn't care. "Frankly, the only statement I'm interested in ultimately is the bank statement."

In many reviews, Marlon Brando was singled out for his bravura performance, and the work that linked all other elements of the production.

Wrote Vincent Canby in the *New York Times*, "Marlon Brando has finally connected with a character and a film that need not embarrass America's most complex, most idiosyncratic film actor, nor those critics who have wondered whatever happened to him."

At the studio, Brando was forgiven for all past sins—and his superb performance probably earned him a few dispensations for the future as well. Even Paramount's Peter Bart, Brando's sharpest detractor, was as quick to praise as he was earlier to criticize.

"*The Godfather*," Bart said, "reminded the film community that Brando really is a legend, that he is a man of just luminous talent—impossible to deal with, risky, but one of the great actors in the history of the cinema."

Evans was thrilled with his star's performance—both on-camera and off.

"I had less trouble with Brando than with any actor I've ever worked with," he said. "He's a strange guy, of course, but he was always on time for shooting and was terrific with the other actors."

Critics raved about the entire cast, but singled out Al Pacino for his "overnight success" as Michael Corleone. Pacino was described by film columnist James Bacon as "Dustin Hoffman with sex appeal.

"The movies have a new superstar—a guy who was just another actor yesterday—in Al Pacino," said Bacon. "Pacino steals the movie even from Brando's best performance since *On the Waterfront.*"

Pacino, wrote the *New York Times*'s Vincent Canby, "is an actor worthy to have Brando as his father."

After half a lifetime of struggle, Pacino became a film superstar the moment *The Godfather* reached the screen. He was still struggling financially—most of the $35,000 he earned for *The Godfather* went to pay the legal bills that stemmed from the lawsuit by MGM over his appearance in *The Gang That Couldn't Shoot Straight.* After his work on *The Godfather* was over, he left immediately for Boston to appear in the play *The Basic Training of Pavlo Hummel*—for two hundred dollars a week. He would continue to appear in theater productions for low pay, but his days of five-figure film salaries were over.

Beyond the praise *The Godfather* received, critics and commentators also raised questions about the presentation of violence in the film. The violence—tame by today's film standards—was troubling in 1972, in part because it was so compelling, which led some film writers to suggest that Coppola was glorifying the Mafia.

"An east side audience last Friday night murmured with satisfaction every time an enemy of the family was dispatched," wrote Nicholas Gage in the *New York Times.* "The slaughter was choreographed with such precision that one member of the audience was heard to sigh 'Beautiful!' at a particularly sanguine execution."

What concerned critics most was realizing that characters so appealing and frequently so normal were, at the same time, sociopathic butchers.

"It is more than a little disturbing to realize that characters, who are so moving one minute, are likely, in the next scene, to be blowing out the brains of a competitor over a white tablecloth," wrote Vincent Canby in the *New York Times.* "It's nothing personal, just their way of doing business as usual."

If a popular film wasn't enough to spark a national debate about violence in America in the spring of 1972, one only needed to turn to the streets of New York for a vivid real-life example. In the early morning of April 7, Joseph Gallo, a longtime Mob leader, was gunned down in Umberto's Clam House in Little Italy as he celebrated his forty-third birthday with his family—one block from the headquarters of the New York Police Department and around the corner from the Mott Street site of *The Godfather*'s location for the Genco Olive Oil Company.

The assassination of Gallo—a popular underworld figure known as "Crazy Joe"—was the third gangland murder within twenty-four hours in Manhattan and Staten Island. It was a particularly public and ruthless killing. Sitting with his family and his bodyguard, Gallo was hunted down by an unidentified assassin who came in a side door of the restaurant firing a .38-caliber pistol. The bodyguard and another man in the restaurant fired back; eventually four guns were involved, and more than twenty shots were fired as the battle spilled out onto Mulberry Street. Hit four times, Gallo staggered out of the restaurant and collapsed as the assassin made his escape in a waiting car.

Police informants speculated that Gallo's murder was revenge for the shooting of Joe Colombo ten months before—even though Gallo had never been linked to the Colombo shooting. Regardless, the Gallo hit was only the latest act of violence in a decade-old war between Gallo and his brothers and the former boss of their family, Joseph Profaci, a war that mirrored the Mob violence portrayed in the film.

Examining the issues of violence in film and glorifying the Mafia would be high on Coppola's agenda when he began to prepare his sequel to *The Godfather;* in the second film of the saga, he would set out to destroy the Corleone family.

When *The Godfather* opened nationally in 316 theaters on March 29, the record-breaking pace continued on a broader scale. Only weeks after the film debuted, the movie was not only a success, but also a money-making machine unlike anything Hollywood had ever produced. What surprised the entire film industry was the speed with which *The Godfather* raked in money. By March 29, only two weeks after the premiere, the film had earned $7.3 million in 322 theaters in the United States and Canada. Of that total, $6.4 million had come from the film's appearance for only five days in national release, and by mid-April, *The Godfather* was appearing in 372 theaters and cracked the $25 million level in ticket sales. On April 14—a year to the day after Marlon Brando appeared in his first scene—*The Godfather* achieved an astonishing plateau: The film was grossing more than $1 million a day—a first in the history of motion pictures.

If these numbers seem low by current standards—*Jurassic Park* and *Independence Day* earned $1 million *every two hours* early in their releases—remember that *The Godfather* achieved its success at a time when the motion picture industry was flat on its back. We can only imagine how the film might have performed decades later, with the benefits of a thousand-screen opening, monstrous advertising budgets to back up the interest generated by the book, and eight-dollar tickets.

With the continued strong performance, the principals involved in the production saw their bank accounts swell. In a hard-nosed arrangement with theaters, Paramount took about three-quarters of the price of each ticket; a pretty return indeed. Paramount's share of the profits was 84 percent, with the rest of the split going to Ruddy (7.5 percent), Coppola (6 percent), and Puzo (2.5 percent), which transformed all three men into millionaires within months. The money would make Coppola a rich man (temporarily at least), clear his debt to Warner Bros., and help keep American Zoetrope solvent.

Having cleared its books of *Godfather* expenses only weeks into its run, Paramount would go on to earn more than $85 million on the film in its initial release—jacking up the price of Gulf+Western stock from thirty-eight to forty-four dollars. On the strength of *The Godfather's* earnings, the overall value of the G+W stock increased by $97 million.

With so much cash rolling in, all of the infighting between Coppola and the studio was quickly forgotten.

"We took a big chance with Francis," said Evans, "but it certainly paid off."

Peter Bart received the acknowledgment he so richly deserved for his behind-the-scenes role in the film's success: For nurturing Puzo while he wrote the book, for defending Coppola, and for standing behind the production team during the darkest moments of shooting.

"Bob Evans was always great to us, but Peter Bart had more to do with that movie than anyone else at the studio, including knowing when the script was right, and backing us up at critical times," said Ruddy.

Bart was equally complimentary, especially about Coppola.

"Francis's conceptualizing was brilliant, his casting was brilliant, his sense of production was brilliant, and his direction was brilliant," Bart said.

Even the cast forgot the hell of the production and offered only praise.

"All the credit for *The Godfather*," Duvall said, "belongs to Coppola. I think you could fault the picture a little bit for being romantic, but it was well done."

Regardless of blame or praise, one fact emerged—that everyone involved would get an enormous career boost.

"The thing that I like most about the film's success is that everyone that busted their hump on this movie came out with something very special—and good careers," Ruddy said. "Everyone on that movie needed it. Pacino had done only one movie. Brando was unemployable. Jimmy Caan was doing bullshit. Francis was doing bullshit. I had just done a motorcycle-racing movie— who the fuck were we? All of these people came together in one magic moment, and it was the turn in everybody's careers. It was just a fantastic thing."

Beyond the rave reviews and flow of cash, *The Godfather* transcended the status of a popular film. In the spring and summer of 1972, the film dominated American culture. News coverage highlighted the film's continuing success, and virtually every general-interest magazine in the country featured the movie and its stars. Many monthly magazines that normally developed articles with a leisurely lead time of three months or more scrambled to insert coverage of *The Godfather*. The film was "picture of the month" for the May issue of *Seventeen* magazine's—an interesting choice, given the strong adult theme and R rating, which meant that the magazine's primary audience could not see the film without a parent or adult guardian.

From March through September, standing in line to see *The Godfather* became a national pastime for an entire generation of moviegoers who had never waited more than a few minutes for even a top film—let alone hours.

"Remember when moviegoing used to be simple and fun?" joked the *Los Angeles Times*. "Well, it seems like all that has changed with the cataclysmic opening of *The Godfather*, the only film in memory that you have to audition to stand in line for. The lines are enormous. On a Saturday night, they're so long you could conceivably cross three zip codes."

The Godfather also became the inspiration for a flood of merchandise. The black-and-white poster of Marlon Brando as the Don was the most popular decoration of 1972, and for years it became a staple on bedroom walls and in dorm rooms across the country, joining the Beatles, Jimi Hendrix, and Jim Morrison as the most popular images of the early 1970s. The poster featured the line that Puzo had never expected to become famous: "I'm gonna make him an offer he can't refuse"; the phrase also wound up on millions of bumper stickers, lapel buttons, and coffee mugs. The movie inspired a board game, and the sound-track album was one of the most popular albums of the year.

The Godfather even inspired a return to old social customs among "the boys": FBI informants reported that within Mafia families, many of "the old ways" were returning to the underworld social rituals, such as kissing hands and referring to Mob chiefs as "Godfather."

"There is no doubt," said historian Arthur Schlesinger, "that *The Godfather* is the cultural phenomenon of the season."

Gangster films returned to a cycle of popularity. *The Godfather* spawned countless films that focused on crime and criminals—none of which approached it in quality and most of which fell far below it. The character of Vito Corleone even inspired a parody. In *Uptown Saturday Night* starring Bill Cosby and Sidney Poitier, Harry Belafonte appeared as an African-American Mob boss, his cheeks intentionally stuffed so full of cotton that he could barely speak.

Even the title of the film became a cultural milestone, reaffirming the status of the word "godfather" in the American lexicon. No longer only referring just to an appointed guardian or close friend of a family, its use was reinforced to be synonymous with "the paramount position" or "originator." When fans of performer James Brown called him "The Godfather of Soul," they were talking about the first and the best.

Of course, the domestic earnings from *The Godfather* were only the beginning of the film's earning power. In the summer of 1972, *The Godfather* began to be exhibited outside of North America. Evans personally supervised the creation of four foreign-language dubbings of the film, including a French version directed by Louis Malle.

In London, *The Godfather* opened the last week of August. Many English critics were disturbed by the violence, but even those critics who decried the violence had strong praise for

Brando. Brando's performance, wrote the *London Daily Mail*'s Cecil Wilson, "amounts in actual screen time to surprisingly little, but in dramatic power it dominates everything."

The Godfather also did record-breaking business in Japan, even then an important foreign market for American films. When it opened in Japan, more than one million people saw the film in its first seven weeks. When asked to explain the film's popularity in Japan, critic Tadao Sato explained that what appealed to Japanese audiences about the film is the strength of an organization under the boss-gang system, a fixture in Japan of generations before. "Behind the popularity of the movie, I can see Japanese nostalgia for the old family system . . . which modern Japanese society has lost," Sato said.

After months of foreign release, only one important overseas market remained, perhaps the most vital to the film's credibility—Italy. In September, *The Godfather* reached the ancestral homeland of the Corleones, and the picture was a sensation.

"Mafia country smiles Wednesday night," reported the wire services. "*The Godfather* finally came to town."

Screening across the country at prices increased 25 to 30 percent over the norm, theaters in Italy and Sicily were packed.

"Dubbed into Sicilian dialect, the dirty words were dirtier and the jokes coarser, much to the delight of the audience, which tittered at each bloodbath," said a bemused United Press International reporter.

"'That is only the first one,' clucked one mustachioed man when the first violent death smeared the screen," UPI reported.

"Marlon Brando is the envy of all the real Godfathers on the island," said Roberto Ciuni, the editor of Palermo's newspaper, who knew them all. "They wish they were that good-looking and suave."

Only a month after its release in Italy, *The Godfather* was headed toward becoming the country's all-time top-grossing film.

As *The Godfather* rolled on toward its sixth month of domestic release, the film industry began to recognize that its success did not have to be an isolated incident. *Love Story*, which eventually earned more than $105 million, had started the upward trend; together, *Love Story* and *The Godfather* proved that studios could actually plan projects designed to produce phenomenal profits. Film analysts began to speculate that an upturn for the business might be on the horizon—not just for profits, but for ongoing public interest in the movies. Throughout the film industry, *The Godfather* was considered a bellwether of new fortunes to come.

The Godfather, *Box Office* magazine suggested, "should prove that the movie audience is not 'lost'—but waiting to be thoroughly sold on the kind of pictures it wants to see."

Under the headline GODFATHER: BOON TO ALL PIX, *Variety* described how *The Godfather*'s success meant as much to the other studios as it did to Paramount.

"That Paramount's *The Godfather* is an historical smash of unprecedented proportions is not only generally conceded within the trade but it has also generated a newfound optimism of proportions rarely if ever experienced before . . . in what some regarded as a 'nervous' if not dying industry," *Variety* reported.

While *The Godfather*'s million-dollars-a-day pace had slowed somewhat during the summer, excitement about the speed of the film's earnings was replaced by interest in its total revenues. Tracking the money flow from *The Godfather* became a gleeful Hollywood ritual as the film rose closer to the all-time box office champion. Predictions that the film had the potential to earn $20 million were revised immediately after its release to at least $30 million and then doubled to $60 million. Over the Labor Day weekend, *The Godfather*'s earnings passed the $75 million mark. Finally, sometime in mid-September, *The Godfather* became the biggest domestic money-making film of all time, passing *Gone With the Wind;* what had taken David O. Selznick's masterpiece thirty-three years to accomplish had required only six months for *The Godfather* to surpass.

The Hollywood studios moved quickly to follow *The Godfather* example: investing more money in script development, bestselling books, and new technology; and using broad new marketing techniques, thus beginning a trend toward large-scale box office successes beyond anything ever seen before in the industry. In a formula as old as the film business, one Hollywood success had spawned others. In the case of *The Godfather*, however, it set the tone for the future of an entire industry.

By 1972, when *The Godfather* became box office champion, only two other films had earnings that approached it: *Gone With the Wind* (1939) and *The Sound of Music* (1965). *The Godfather* would remain box office champion just one year, until *The Exorcist* opened to terrify millions of movie fans in 1973. In the twenty years that followed *The Godfather*, fifty-eight movies would surpass it in earnings. Even rising ticket prices could not account for the stunning rebirth of good fortune in the movie business.

By the end of 1972, *The Godfather* was still making money, but its first release had run its course. After more than nine months in general release and with more than $110 million in revenue, on December 31 Paramount withdrew the film temporarily to strike new prints for a new round of exhibition timed to coincide with the presentation of the Academy Awards.

By the time the Academy Award nominations for 1972 were announced on February 13, 1973, Paramount already knew that *The Godfather* was a top contender for the industry's highest honors. Coppola had been awarded the Directors Guild of America Award for Best Direction—an especially coveted honor for the filmmaker—and the film was voted the best picture of the year by the readers of *Photoplay* magazine, the oldest and largest-selling movie fan publication. The film won five Golden Globe Awards from the Hollywood Foreign Press Association: Best Performance by an Actor, Best Score, Best Screenplay, Best Direction, and Best Picture. Marlon Brando was named the Golden Globe World Film Favorite for 1972 and would repeat his win in 1973. He would continue to make unusual films and often appear in less-than-bankable projects, but his position as a sought-after film superstar was secured.

Later in 1973, another award would provide a final footnote to the controversy over the image of Italian Americans projected in the film. While some Americans of Italian descent may have held grudges against *The Godfather*, Italians in Italy did not. In July 1973, Al Ruddy was named recipient of the 1973 David Donatello award as the best foreign producer of the year—Italy's highest prize for international films. Pacino also won the Donatello award for his performance.

The announcement of the Academy Award nominations would provide even more good news: *The Godfather* received nominations for ten Oscars: Best Actor (Brando), three Best Supporting Actors (Caan, Duvall, and Pacino), Best Screenplay (Coppola and Puzo), Best Editing (Reynolds and Zinner), Best Costume Design (Johnstone), Best Sound (Newman, Grenzbach, and Portman), Best Director (Coppola), and Best Picture (Ruddy). (The film also received an eleventh nomination—Nino Rota for best score—but the nomination was disqualified because the work included material from *Fortunella*.)

Paramount was ready for the Oscars. The day after the ceremony, *The Godfather* was scheduled to again open nationwide in a three-week run, for which exhibitors paid the studio a total of $2.5 million in advanced billings.

On March 27, 1973, the Academy Awards ceremony was broadcast worldwide from the Pavilion at the Los Angeles Music Center. At first, one by one, the Oscars went to other films.

Cabaret was the big Oscar winner for most of the evening, beating out *The Godfather* in every category the two films shared. The Bob Fosse–directed musical would receive eight Oscars that night, including Best Director. But Coppola himself would not go away empty-handed. He and Puzo won the Oscar for Best Screenplay. For the second time in three years, Coppola won the Oscar for the film work he loved best.

Wearing a blue velvet tuxedo jacket, Coppola accepted his Oscar, seemingly with some relief.

"When I came here, I was very nervous because I hadn't prepared anything to say should I come up here," Coppola said with a smile. "And then after about forty minutes, I thought of something to say but started to get very nervous that I would never get to come up here to say it. And I've forgotten it, whatever it was."

Coppola then thanked Robert Towne for his work on the film and acknowledged Peter Bart, "who was responsible for getting me this job in the first place, which sort of rescued me from my wonderful romantic escapade in San Francisco—which still lives," triumphantly raising his fist. He went on to congratulate Bob Fosse, then turned his attention to the three men from his extended "movie family" who had brought him professional satisfaction during an otherwise tortuous production.

"The best award a director could get would be to have three of his best friends and dear associates and actors—Jimmy Caan, Bobby Duvall, and Al Pacino—all get nominated in the same category," Coppola said, closing his remarks.

Late in the ceremony, the program finally came to the Best Actor award. Brando was up against particularly stiff competition: Michael Caine and Laurence Olivier for *Sleuth,* Paul Winfield for *Sounder,* and Peter O'Toole for *The Ruling Class.* Although he caused no trouble during production of *The Godfather,* Brando had the last word. Liv Ullmann and Roger Moore, the Best Actor presenters, gamely went through the nominees and requisite film clips. But when Ullmann announced Brando's name as the winner, his designated recipient was Sacheen Littlefeather, who identified herself as president of the Native-American Affirmative Image Committee. As Moore extended the Oscar toward her, she held up a hand. "No?" Moore asked. He shrugged slightly and stepped away to allow Littlefeather to deliver her remarks:

"Marlon Brando has asked me to tell you, very regretfully, that he cannot accept this very generous award because of the treatment of the American Indians today by the film industry, and on television and in movie reruns, and also with the recent happenings at Wounded Knee."

Littlefeather delivered her remarks to both a scattering of boos and an equal number of cheers, then left the stage to polite applause. Brando had made his point; his rejection of the Oscar and the reasons behind his decision became nearly as heavily covered in the media as was the outcome of the rest of the ceremony.

At the end of the evening, however, the focus was back on *The Godfather.* Presenter Clint Eastwood read off the nominees for Best Picture: *Cabaret, Deliverance, The Godfather, The Immigrants,* and *Sounder.*

Eastwood and Al Ruddy were old friends; the actor, who rarely attends award ceremonies, appeared on the program in part because he was convinced *The Godfather* would win and he could present Ruddy with the Oscar. Before the show, Ruddy had kidded Eastwood about the presentation. "I said, 'Clint, when you open the envelope and look at the card, you'll be the only one in the world who knows the winner, other than the guys at Price Waterhouse. If I don't win, just go ahead and say, "Al Ruddy for *The Godfather,"* tear up the card, and eat it.'"

Eastwood remembered Ruddy's remarks. When he opened the envelope, he grinned slyly, looked into the audience at Ruddy, and said, "Albert S. Ruddy, for *The Godfather.*"

As the audience roared its approval, Ruddy, who practically leaped to the stage, pulled Eastwood away from the microphone and quickly stage-whispered a question. Eastwood laughed and showed him the card.

"Just to show the state my mind was in, I actually believed for a split second that Clint said my name because he was a friend of mine," Ruddy said. "I whispered, 'Does it really say Albert S. Ruddy on the card?'"

Eastwood showed him.

Ruddy recovered quickly. "We were all getting nervous about this for a moment," he said with a laugh. Ruddy thanked Bob Evans, "for giving me more than any studio head should in time and creativity"; Frank Yablans, "for having the courage to sell this film and make my mother rich"; and Charlie Bluhdorn "for having the courage to finance films which, I guess, borders on insanity."

An Oscar heals all wounds.

In the spring of 1973, two years after production began for *The Godfather* and a year after it was released to critical and popular acclaim, some key questions about the film lingered: Could the film have been even better? Did Coppola achieve his vision for the project as he imagined it when he was hired two and one half years before? Would *The Godfather* have turned out to be a different film if Coppola had worked unfettered by studio interference?

More than two decades later, Ruddy offered answers.

"In my opinion, there is not another director in the world who could have made *The Godfather* besides Francis Ford Coppola," Ruddy said. "I can't imagine any other person in the world who was at the peak of his power and creativity, who could have done a better job than he did on that movie.

"The studio may have hassled Francis along the way about speeding up when they thought he was working too slowly on some big-budget scenes, and no one needs that kind of a hassle when you're trying to be creative," Ruddy said. "But the only creative constraints ever put on that movie were approving the cast and giving us a tight budget.

"Well, we got the cast we wanted, and the budget was tight, that's true, but sometimes you have to be more imaginative to get what you want for less money. Beyond those two constraints, there was nothing else the studio put on us—nothing. When the script was being written, that was entirely in our control. We had no constraints on what we shot. We got the cut we wanted. Evans even backed us on the length.

"After all the trouble in production," Ruddy said, "the irony of it is that the movie that we made is the movie we wanted to make."

The Godfather Legacy

THE **GODFATHER** was still months from release when Paramount began to plan a sequel. By the time Coppola returned from Sicily in August, the studio had given the green light to start a script for a second *Godfather* film. At one time or another, the proposed sequel was known by a host of names: *Michael Corleone*, *Don Michael*, *The Son of Don Corleone*, and eventually *The Godfather Part II*. In August 1971, Paramount signed Mario Puzo to write the script.

Puzo was the lone member of the production team

who was secured for the sequel. Coppola was still busy with *The Godfather*, mired in postproduction and the premiere still months away. A sequel was far from his mind.

One member of the production team who had decided not to return for the sequel was Al Ruddy. Although he had the option to continue with *The Godfather* saga, Ruddy turned down the opportunity to produce the sequel; he had the leverage he needed to develop any project he wanted. And for all his good-natured kidding and peacekeeping during the production, Ruddy felt profound relief that the work was over, the film was a success, and his brush with the criminal underworld was behind him.

"I was lucky to have gotten through the movie—skated through—keeping everybody happy," Ruddy said. "That was probably my greatest contribution. I didn't get hired because I was some kind of creative genius—that was Francis's job. I am probably the only person who was stupid enough and street-smart enough to enable us to keep going the way we did. Between handling the politics at the studio, the nonsense going on on the set, 'the boys,' and keeping it all going—it was a major contribution.

"But when I got through and Bob Evans asked me if I wanted to do a sequel, I said, 'Do it without me.' I didn't ever want to hear about *those people* again—and I wasn't talking about Francis or Peter or Bob or Al or Marlon."

Ruddy spent the year after *The Godfather* was released traveling around the world promoting the film, cashing his hefty royalty checks, and planning how to use the creative leverage he had gained from his work on *The Godfather*. Ruddy did what he had always wanted to do—produce youth-oriented popular films. His first project after *The Godfather* was *The Longest Yard*—one of Burt Reynolds's most successful films—and a string of other top box office hits.

While Puzo was the only principal from the production team who was definitely in, Ruddy was the only one who was definitely out. As late as April 1972—a month after *The Godfather* was released—Robert Evans bemoaned the fact that Francis Ford Coppola would not direct the sequel.

"I'd like to have him, believe me," Evans said of Coppola at the time. "He just has a number of other things he wants to do. In any case, I want Francis's stamp on it."

Coppola had plenty of reasons to bypass a sequel. At thirty-five, he was immersed in other projects during what had become the most creatively fruitful period of his life. After he finished *The Godfather*, he wrote a screenplay for Paramount's production of *The Great Gatsby*. He wrote, produced, and directed *The Conversation*, with Gene Hackman in the starring role, and executive produced George Lucas's *American Graffiti*, which became one of the biggest box office smashes of 1973. At the American Conservatory Theatre, he directed Noel Coward's *Private Lives*, as well as an operatic production, Gottfried von Einem's *The Visit of the Old Lady*, for the San Francisco Opera Company.

However, when the money started to roll in from *The Godfather*, Paramount recognized that such a valuable franchise needed its original guiding force. Simply put, Evans and Bluhdorn made the job irresistible. They offered near-complete creative control and an almost unlimited budget,

THE MICHAEL CORLEONE FAMILY

BOSS

MICHAEL CORLEONE
ALIAS
"DON CORLEONE"
FBI #861572

SUCCESSOR TO:

VITO CORLEONE
ALIAS
"DON CORLEONE"
FBI #397385
DECEASED

SANTINO CORLEO
ALIAS
"SONNY"
FBI #473001
DECEASED

KEY TO ACTIVITY CODE

- A CURRENTLY IN JAIL FOR NARCOTICS
- B AWAITING TRIAL FOR NARCOTICS
- C PREVIOUS CONVICTION FOR NARCOTICS
- D SUSPECTED OF BEING ACTIVE IN NARCOTICS
- E GAMBLING
- F SHYLOCKING
- G LABOR RACKETEERING
- H VENDING MACHINES AND/OR JUKE BOXES
- I EXTORTION, STRONG ARM AND MURDER
- J COUNTERFEITING
- K CRIMINALLY RECEIVING
- L ALCOHOL TAX VIOLATIONS

UNDERBOSS
FREDO CORLEONE
FBI #927431

CONSIGLIERI
THOMAS HAGEN
FBI #327461

CAPOREGIME

FORMER:

PETER CLEMENZA
ALIAS
"FAT CLEMENZA"
FBI #100375
DECEASED

SALVATORE TESSIO
ALIAS
"SAL"
FBI #320611
DECEASED

PRESENT:

AL NERI
FBI #563241
(G,I,K)

ROCCO LAMPONE
FBI #326412
(G,I)

FRANK PENTANGELI
ALIAS
"FRANKIE FIVE ANGELS"
FBI #641323
(E,G,H,K)

BUTTONS - SOLDIERS

LUCA BRASI
FBI #163432
DECEASED

PAULI GATO
FBI #742611
DECEASED

FRANCIS FORDUCCI
ALIAS
"THE KID"
FBI #324511

ANGELO GRANELLI
ALIAS
"THE TROJAN"
FBI #436661
(A,E)

GINO FREDONNA
ALIAS
"PRETTY BOY"
FBI #223314
DECEASED

FRANK DARRA
ALIAS
"FRANKIE DARE"
FBI #204325
(A,C,G)

CHRIS PENARRI
ALIAS
"THE MANAGER"
FBI #416311
(H, I.)

NINO ARNELDI
ALIAS
"THE PATCH"
FBI #312112
(G, H, I.)

RICARDO SIMINNI
ALIAS
"POWDER"
FBI #723412
(H, I.)

GINO CORSETTA
FBI #611294
(A, B,)

SABASTINO SABELA
FBI #333495
(A,B,C,D)

ALPHONSE EVOLLONI
ALIAS
"AL OVE"
FBI #177123
DECEASED

DONATO
TOLENTINICCI
FBI #134375
(G,H,I,)

VICTOR VINATONNI
ALIAS
"VICKY VEAL"
FBI #177321
(H)

FRANK CORTEALE
FBI #463011
(H,I,)

BARTOLO NENI
ALIAS
"O'NEAL"
FBI #547073
(A,B,C)

LAWRENCE TIPPIRRI
FBI #892538
(I,K)

PETER LEONE
ALIAS
"THE LION"
FBI #360644
(A,B,C,D)

GAETANO DE LUNA
ALIAS
"GARY DEE"
FBI #892668
(E,F)

CALOGERO RAOENI
FBI #144176
(H)

ETTORE RAOENI
ALIAS
"OILY HAND"
FBI #493493
(F)

JOESEPH BRONSKI
ALIAS
"JOEY JAIL"
FBI #467032
DECEASED

GAETANO SIRILLO
FBI #936000
(H,I)

CASSANDROS FRACCA
ALIAS
"DAVID GELLY"
FBI #428933
(H,I)

ROBERTO NELENZA
ALIAS
"THUNDER BOB"
FBI #339933
(E,F,G,I)

RAFILO GERNZO
FBI #416230
(I)

SALVATORE PLUMARI
ALIAS
"SALLY PEE"
FBI #210077
(L)

NATALE PARRI
ALIAS
"FAT NAT"
FBI #445512
(H,I)

TONY DINEGIO
ALIAS
"TONY DING"
FBI #133401
(E,H,I)

CHARLES LOCIRNO
FBI #136311
DECEASED

WILLIAM CICCI
FBI #473289
(E, F, G,I)

CARMINE CORONDA
ALIAS
"THE PLUNGE"
FBI #179205
(E,H,I,L)

SAMUEL COROCCO
FBI #329661
(E,H)

ALPHONSE BARINO
ALIAS
"AL BARRET"
FBI #279532
(G)

CARMEN DELLA
FBI #146372
(G)

CRISTOFORO D'BINNA
FBI #432411
(H,I)

as well as the studio's cooperation in scheduling the production so Coppola could work around his other projects. In addition, Coppola could bring back as many people as possible from the original cast and production team.

The money, too, was enticing. Coppola received $250,000 for writing, $200,000 for directing, and $50,000 for producing, plus 13 percent of the adjusted gross—enough to earn him millions if the sequel achieved even a portion of the success of its predecessor. "Charlie let me name my own price," Coppola summed up. "He said I could do anything I wanted with the sequel."

Coppola also had his "wonderful romantic escapade" in San Francisco in mind. "The way I set up the deal for *Godfather II*," he explained, "it promises to make me so much money that I'll be able to finance my own work. The fundamental use of wealth is to subsidize work."

For Coppola, his reasons to create a sequel meant far more than money; with his percentages of *The Godfather* and *American Graffiti* rolling in, money was, for once, the least of his worries. Rather, Coppola wanted to make a sequel that was necessary—or not make it at all.

"The only way *The Godfather Part II* can be an excellent film," Coppola explained, "is if when it is done and seen, the audience, including myself, looks at it and says that it was essential that it was made, and that it wasn't an appendix that came after the first."

Coppola signed to both direct and produce *The Godfather Part II*. Among his first decisions was hiring Gray Frederickson and Fred Roos as his coproducers. He succeeded in attracting virtually all of the other key members of his production team to the project, including Gordon Willis, Dean Tavoularis, Dick Smith, and A. D. Flowers.

Coppola also brought in some new faces: For costumes, he turned to Theadora Van Runkle, who in 1967 turned her first costume project, *Bonnie and Clyde*, into a fashion phenomenon of the mid-1960s. That work brought her some of the hottest productions of the late sixties and early seventies, including *I Love You, Alice B. Toklas; The Thomas Crown Affair; The Reivers; The Arrangement;* and *Myra Breckinridge*. Van Runkle had spent the year before starting *The Godfather Part II* at work on costumes for the lavish film version of *Mame*, starring Lucille Ball.

As his production team came together, Coppola explored new methods to present his film. In March 1973, he announced that *The Godfather Part II* would be released as a companion to the original film, with both features released simultaneously as a six-hour movie.

"I'm attempting something very exotic with it," Coppola said. "It's going to be a very unusual kind of film. It's being designed to fit with the first one so that the two of them may be played together."

That distribution plan fell through, but Coppola was still intrigued by the idea of weaving two separate, but related, stories into one motion picture. In the process, he also wanted to plunder the romance and the appeal of the Mafia family that had been so integral to the original film.

"I was fascinated by the idea of a movie that would work freely in time, that would go both forward and backward in time," Coppola said. "I thought it would be interesting to juxtapose the decline of the family with the ascension of the family; to show that as the young Vito Corleone is building this thing out of America, his son is presiding over its destruction.

"I felt that *The Godfather* had never been finished. This time, I really set out to destroy the family," Coppola said. "Yet I wanted to destroy it in the way that I think is most profound—from the inside. And I wanted to punish Michael, but not in the obvious ways. At the end he's prematurely old, almost syphilitic, like Dorian Gray. I don't think anyone in the theater can envy him.

"At the end of the first film, Michael, who started as a bright-eyed, idealistic, beautiful, tal-

ented man with all the potential in the world, was turned into this cold, intro-verted, loveless, horrible monster who closed out of his life the person he claimed to be closest to him, his wife. To quote from *The Magnificent Ambersons*, 'he got his comeuppance.' Perhaps that was not enough; to really show what he had become I had to go further, which all the more makes the second film not an appendix but an extension.

"But as I've said, this movie was never about a Mafia family. I think it was about a classic noble family. It could be about kings in ancient Greece or in the Middle Ages. It could just as well be about the Kennedys or the Rothschilds, about a dynasty that transcends even one's obligations to one's country. It is about power and the succession of power."

Or, as Talia Shire put it more simply: "Francis felt that he had to knock this family off."

Puzo and Coppola, working in unison but separately—as they had on the first film—used some of the structure and characters from the original *Godfather* book, plus a new plotline that carried forward with Michael's reign as head of the family, intrigues in Cuba, family betrayal, and Senate investigations of organized crime. Most of the film was set in 1958 and 1959, but a significant portion would be devoted to flashbacks to Italy and New York in the first quarter century.

The film would be produced in late 1973 and the first half of 1974, and release was scheduled for Christmas 1974.

"In basic content, *The Godfather Part II* is the inevitable continuation of the first movie," Coppola said. "And it's a challenge to take the same actors and try to make a movie that is better than the first one."

Most of the actors from *The Godfather* were enticed to return for the sequel—for considerably more money. Al Pacino and Robert Duvall were signed in July 1973; Pacino received $500,000 plus a percentage—the trade papers described it as "a near-2,000 percent raise." John Cazale, Diane Keaton, and Talia Shire were signed to return as Fredo, Kay, and Connie—each with much more substantive roles. Also rehired were Richard Bright and Tom Rosqui, who as Al Neri and Rocco Lampone would be elevated to *caporegimes* in the Corleone family, with additional screen time. Even characters killed in *The Godfather* would return—James Caan as Sonny, Gianni Russo as Carlo, and Abe Vigoda as Tessio were all signed for cameo roles in a brief flashback for the close of the film.

Two key performers, however, would not be back. Richard Castellano, who played Peter Clemenza in *The Godfather*, demanded too much money. So Clemenza inexplicably "dies" just before the 1959 sequences of the film begin. In his place, Coppola and Puzo created a new character, Frankie "Five Angels" Pentangeli,

PROPS IN THE LAKE TAHOE HOUSE: MEMENTOS OF THE CORLEONE FAMILY FROM HAPPIER TIMES.

MICHAEL GAZZO
AS FRANKIE PEN-
TANGELI AND
JOHN CAZALE AS
FREDO—LONGING
FOR THE GOOD
OLD DAYS.

a longtime associate of the Corleone family. Coppola cast Michael Gazzo, a veteran performer, producer, and director of films and who, in 1955, wrote the play *A Hatful of Rain*.

The original Don Corleone, Marlon Brando, would also not return. He, too, wanted too much—$500,000 plus 10 percent of the gross—just for the brief flashback scenes that Coppola and Puzo had written for him. (After the Academy Awards, rumors flew around Hollywood that Brando had no intention of appearing in the sequel because he resented Paramount president Frank Yablans's alleged negative remarks about Brando's fuss at the Oscar ceremony.)

Was Coppola upset about the absence of Castellano and Brando?

"Well, you know," Coppola recalled, "I think a writer or a director is like a good husband, in that he may desire to have a woman as his wife, but when he loses her and chooses another, then she becomes his only wife. And he forgets the former love. It may sound simplistic, but it's a good rule in life that whenever something doesn't happen that you want to happen, maybe it's all for the best."

Instead, Coppola added other formidable cast members. Gastone Moschin was signed as Fanucci, the Don of Little Italy in the flashbacks. Coppola cast Moschin "long distance" based on his performance in Bernardo Bertolucci's *The Conformist*. The Italian stage actor made his film debut in Pietro Germi's *Signore e Signori* and had been awarded the Nastro D'Argento, Italy's highest acting honor.

Bruno Kirby, who had appeared in *Cinderella Liberty* with James Caan, was cast as the young Clemenza who appeared in flashbacks. (At the time, Kirby used his given name, B. Kirby Jr. or Bruce Kirby.) Kirby was already familiar with Castellano's acting style and mannerisms, having played his son on the television series *The Super*. John Aprea—with his strong resemblance to a young Abe Vigoda—was cast as Tessio. Frank Sivero appeared in a brief role as the young Genco Abbandando, the Don's first consigliere, and Francesca De Sapio played Vito's wife as a young woman. ("Mama" Corleone's first name, which is never mentioned in *The Godfather*, was Carmella.)

For the brief but crucial role of Vito's mother, Coppola cast Maria Carta who, in addition

to performing as an actor was a noted interpreter of Italian folk songs. To play Vito as a boy, Coppola found Oreste Baldini, an eleven-year-old Italian boy new to acting. Mariana Hill, who had extensive experience on TV and in films, took on the role of Deanna Dunn, a character from the book linked to Johnny Fontane's Hollywood escapades. In a twist of the plot from the book, Dunn, an uncontrollable alcoholic, marries Fredo and becomes a family burden.

Other distinguished character actors were signed for brief roles. Troy Donahue, a film heartthrob of the 1950s, was cast as Connie's third husband, Merle Johnson (Merle Johnson Jr. was Donahue's real name). G. D. Spradlin, an attorney-turned-actor who was once a mayoral candidate in Oklahoma City, signed on as Senator Pat Geary.

To portray Kay and Michael's son Anthony as an eight-year-old, Coppola cast James Gounaris, the older brother of Anthony, who played the same character as a three-year-old in *The Godfather*. For Michael's bodyguard—who never utters a word—Coppola found Amerigo Tot, an Italian sculptor for whom acting was a hobby.

Some casting decisions were particularly notable because Coppola hired nonperformers to play characters similar in stature to that of the real-life individuals. The hundreds of extras at Anthony's First Communion party were primarily well-to-do retirees from the Lake Tahoe area or the families of executives and professionals—filling precisely the roles they were hired to play.

To portray U.S. senators in the congressional investigation of organized crime, Coppola hired several behind-the-cameras industry veterans, including some colleagues from his formative years in the business. Included in the Senate panel were Roger Corman, Phil Feldman (producer of Coppola's *You're a Big Boy Now*), and Buck Houghton (a TV legend best known for his work on *The Twilight Zone*). As extras in the background of the Senate scenes, Coppola cast primarily non-actors: news photographers played photographers, real reporters appeared as reporters. *Los Angeles Times* National Editor Ed Guthman, who won a Pulitzer Prize in 1965 for his coverage of Senate hearings, acted as adviser for these Senate scenes.

Coppola had no hesitation about using nonactors—an attitude that would cost him dearly during the production of *The Godfather Part III*, when he cast his daughter Sofia in a leading role. But in *The Godfather Part II*, the appearance of non-actors was an important—and appropriate—artistic decision.

LEE STRASBERG PREPARES FOR SCENES SET IN A CUBAN HOSPITAL.

"I like to cast relationships or actors—or people—who bring some natural tensions or prejudices to the scene, which are going to work in our favor," said Coppola. "The senators are all played by nonactors, but they are people of executive power and reputation in their own fields. These are roles that a beginning actor can do masterfully."

Perhaps the most notable casting of a film "newcomer" was that of an actor who had influenced generations of movie performers. At Pacino's suggestion, Coppola cast Lee Strasberg, the director of the famed Actors Studio and perhaps the world's most well-known acting teacher, in the role of Hyman Roth.

Despite his work with countless film performers, Strasberg had never appeared in a motion picture. Yet at seventy-four, he was an inspired choice to play Roth, a character that Coppola called the "wily, introverted wizard who could be an antagonist for Michael."

"My first reaction was that it sounded right—he was from New York, a Jew, and a man with a tremendous mastery he's known for in his classes," Coppola said. "I'd also heard it said that he was a very demanding and exacting teacher, a man with a tremendous background and very opinionated. I didn't know what to expect and I was a little leery of him, thinking, 'I'm going to have to deal with the country's expert on acting, and I'm going to tell him what I want and maybe he's going to come back at me with theories.' So I was a little frightened of it. I'm sure he was equally frightened, you know, of exposing himself, putting himself in my hands, trusting me."

Strasberg was intrigued by the role and agreed to appear in the film—especially because much of his work would be opposite Pacino.

"I find the things which ultimately made a film the most eccentric and the most beautiful are things that you can't quite put your finger on in any of the individual scenes, but which are there in the aggregate," Coppola said. "Lee was never really Al's teacher, but Al is a member of the Actors Studio and has done a lot of work there—of which Lee is the operating and spiritual head. So, there existed a warm relationship between them and one—although I wouldn't call it a total surrogate father and son—that possessed elements of it."

Of the new roles for *The Godfather Part II*, the most important was that of the young Vito Corleone, a character who figured prominently in virtually all of the flashbacks to old New York. The role would be one of the most difficult ever; not only did the part call for an actor with extraordinary screen presence, but the performance needed to presage the character interpretation that Marlon Brando had already created. Even more difficult, most of the character's lines were spoken in Sicilian or broken English.

For Coppola, the choice was never in doubt. Robert De Niro was signed for the role of young Vito without a screen test or competition.

Coppola, who had tested De Niro as Sonny and cast him as Paulie Gatto in *The Godfather* before releasing him to replace Pacino in *The Gang That Couldn't Shoot Straight*, already appreciated the actor's abilities. "I thought he was very magnetic and had a lot of style," Coppola said of De Niro. "However, my first impression was a lot different than my feeling about him now. He seemed like a crazy kind of kid with a lot of energy—maybe because he was trying out for Sonny."

Later, through director Martin Scorsese, Coppola got better acquainted with De Niro and began to envision him as something more than a crazy kid.

"As I was preparing to write *Part II*, it kept rolling around in my head that in a funny way, De Niro's face reminded me of Vito Corleone," Coppola said. "Not of Brando, but of the character he played with the accentuated jaw, the kind of funny smile. De Niro certainly is believable as being someone in the Corleone family and possibly Al's father, as a young man."

After Scorsese showed Coppola an early cut of De Niro's performance in *Mean Streets*, no doubt remained. "I just decided," Coppola said of De Niro, "that it would be him. Very early, I just made the decision, unilaterally, that he was right and that he could do it."

Filming *The Godfather Part II* would be a journey requiring nine months of filming in Lake Tahoe, Los Angeles, New York, Las Vegas, Santo Domingo (substituting for Cuba), Italy, and Sicily.

For the first stage of the journey, in October 1973 Coppola moved the Corleones into Fleur du Lac, the lakeside stone estate of Henry T. Kaiser built in 1934. Months before, Dean Tavoularis and a crew of greensmen and carpenters had descended on Fleur du Lac, transforming the estate from a spacious home into a cold facility more reminiscent of a glamorous fortress, complete with an imposing wall eight feet high and two-thousand feet long.

The first scenes shot were also the first that would appear in the 1958 sequences—the ritual of First Communion for Anthony Corleone. (The service was rendered by Father Joseph Medeglia, the same priest who performed the baptism of Michael Rizzi in *The Godfather*.) At a Lake Tahoe church, members of a recent Communion class repeated their religious initiation and joined the families—and some four hundred others—for two weeks of day-and-night shooting of the Communion party.

While filming of the 1959 sequences got under way, De Niro—armed with a tape recorder and a novice's knowledge of Sicilian—prepared for his role with an odyssey through the Sicilian countryside. De Niro's lines were scripted, so if he chose, he did not have to speak Italian well to deliver them. Other than a few words in heavily accented English, his entire part was delivered in Sicilian, which is considered by many linguists to be a language of its own. Yet the actor took

FILMING THE FIRST COMMUNION SCENE, THE FIRST SHOT SET IN 1958 IN *THE GODFATHER PART II*.

on the role with his characteristic immersion into the background for the role. (To prepare for his part as a baseball player from the south in *Bang the Drum Slowly*, De Niro journeyed to a small town in Georgia. He talked with the local people, learned their accents, observed their daily routine, listened to their music—even learned to chew tobacco.)

After preliminary instruction at Berlitz, De Niro studied with Romano Pianti, a speaker of six European languages and three Italian dialects, whom Coppola hired as Sicilian consultant on the script. Then De Niro left for Sicily. He began his journey in the capital city of Palermo, moving on to Trapani (where he visited Pianti's relatives), then to the coastal town of Scopello and Castellammare del Golfo. (Of course, he also visited the real town of Corleone.)

"I was always up front about what I was doing," De Niro said. "I feel it would be under-

EQUIPMENT FOR THE DIRECTOR.

handed not to say anything. I'm just an actor doing my work. I've found people enjoy helping, and if they understand what you're looking for, you save a lot of time and unnecessary suspicion."

De Niro also gained tremendous insight into the character of the Sicilian people and the historical tragedies that produced the families like the fictional Corleones.

"The people are wonderful and invited me into their homes. And yet, there's another side, another layer of logic that runs through the Sicilian communities and that relates to who *really* runs the community. An obvious example would be that in time of trouble, you might call the police, but they would turn to someone else.

"They have a tremendous disrespect for authority," De Niro said. "This you understand from learning a little history about the place. For centuries they've been invaded over and over again so that the only people they trust are members of their immediate family. Ultimately, everyone else is a foreigner. Suspicion runs high. And although they are very cordial to you as a tourist, you are still aware of this. Sicilians have a way of watching without watching; they'll scrutinize you thoroughly and you won't even know it."

When he returned from Sicily, De Niro continued his language studies but concentrated on the lines of the script, practicing endlessly with his tape recorder and his teacher.

"I find you just have to put in the time," he said. "I wanted to have those lines down so se-

curely that I wouldn't have to think about it. I probably understand more than I speak, but it's a hard language."

De Niro succeeded in mastering the language—or at least enough for his role—playing his part well enough to meet the high standards of the teacher, who listened with earphones, with rapt attention, to all his scenes.

"If you'd asked me if it was possible that an actor could master a language like Sicilian in such a short time," confided Pianti to Coppola, "I would have said, 'never, impossible.' But this De Niro has done it."

From Lake Tahoe, production of *The Godfather Part II* moved on to Las Vegas, for filming at the Tropicana Hotel. (Although the scenes were deleted from the final film, some would be restored for *The Godfather Epic* and *The Godfather Trilogy*.) Coppola shot in casinos from 4 A.M. until noon—the town's slow period. From there, the production shifted to Los Angeles, to sets built for both the 1958–59 sequences and the interiors of old New York. In the script, Frankie Pentangeli has taken over the Corleone residence in Long Island, so the interiors were re-created just as they had been on the Filmways lot two years before. From November 19 through the end of 1973, Coppola shifted production back

and forth between scenes set in 1959 and those set in New York tenements. Among
the sets built in Los Angeles were those for the massive Senate Caucus Room, the
famed venue that had been the site of so many important hearings about organized crime in the
1950s. The set was a faithful reproduction of the caucus room, but built to ⅞ scale.

Asked not long after the production if he was overwhelmed by the shifts in period during
the filming, Coppola replied, "No, because basically you still do one day at a time, one shot at a
time.

"It was good for me, because this was the time where there were the most coworkers with
whom I felt relaxed and whose work I genuinely admired, and yet who were still responsive to
where I was taking the film," Coppola said. "Primarily, I am thinking of Dean Tavoularis, the production designer, and Gordon Willis, the cinematographer."

Location shooting around Los Angeles included scenes of Duvall as Hagen and Gazzo as
Pentangeli shot at The Chino Correctional Facility near Los Angeles, which substituted for the
army post where the former Corleone *caporegime* was being held in protective custody. Filming at
the prison, accomplished in front of a captive audience of real prisoners, included an exquisite

3½-minute master shot of Hagen and Frankie, filmed after Gazzo recovered on set from a massive hangover.

On January 2, 1974, the production team arrived in Santo Domingo to film scenes set in Cuba. The presidential palace served as the palace of the Cuban dictator. The *Biblioteca Nacional* (National Library) became the American embassy, and the Hotel El Embajador was Roth's Capri Hotel and Casino. The Agua Luz, an amphitheater of colored "dancing waters," served as the superstructure of Capri's nightclub. (A company of Cuban dancers from Miami were brought to stage a re-creation of the famous Tropicana shows in the heyday of Havana showbiz.)

Unlike filming *The Godfather* on the streets of New York, in the Caribbean there was no attempt to disguise the production; crew members wore T-shirts em-

THE SENATE CAUCUS ROOM SET, A PERFECT REPRODUCTION OF THE REAL THING—AT ⅞ ORIGINAL SCALE.

blazoned with *The Godfather* logo, and trucks loaded with production gear were painted with large signs that read, EL
PADRINO, PARTE II.

In Santo Domingo, the production met its first serious
setback. Pacino, exhausted after nearly five months of nonstop
work and weakened by the seemingly constant deluge of rain in
the Caribbean, fell ill and was diagnosed with pneumonia (he was taken to the hospital immediately after filming the scene in which he discovers that his brother Fredo had betrayed the family, so the strain he displays in his performance is, in part, quite real). Coppola filmed around
Pacino as long as he could, but the production was delayed nearly three weeks before the actor
could rejoin the shooting.

Meanwhile, in New York, several months of painstaking construction had been under way
to transform an entire city block into a replica of Little Italy for scenes set between 1917 through
1923. Tavoularis selected East 6th Street, between Avenues A and B, for its basic architecture.
Buildings were aged and storefronts taken over and converted into Italian markets; cheese,
sausage, and poultry stores; tailoring and barber shops; fruit, vegetable, and fish stands; dry

goods, tobacco, and carriage shops; an immigrant employment center; and an Italian social club—all filling the street with colorful sights and pungent smells. The result was a long city block completely transformed into Little Italy of the early twentieth century—complete right down to the dirt on the street. (For scenes set a few years later, the street scene was modified slightly, the dirt removed, and carts replaced by vintage automobiles.)

Equally impressive were the hundreds of extras who would be needed when the crew arrived in late February. "For street scenes depicting Little Italy in 1918," *Variety* reported in March 1974, "Paramount, it appears, has hired most of the populace of the Lower East Side." In fact, to film the Festa of San Rocco, the production put out the single largest call for extras in the history of the New York office of the Screen Actors Guild.

Shooting in New York required another masterpiece of makeup effects by Dick Smith, for the scene in which Fanucci is slashed across the neck. Fanucci is not killed in the attack—which occurs while the young Vito watches—and runs away screaming, holding his hat to catch his own spurting blood.

To simulate a throat cut from ear to ear, Smith created a latex appliance that fit under actor Moschin's jawline. The appliance was already slit, then glued to his neck over flat tubing punched with holes. The tube ran underneath

ON LOCATION IN SANTO DOMINGO. UNLIKE THE 1971 SHOOT OF *THE GOD-FATHER*, NO EFFORT WAS MADE TO DISGUISE THE ON-LOCATION FILMING OF *EL PADRINO PARTE II*.

SETTING UP AN OVERHEAD SHOT OF THE RE-CREATED LITTLE ITALY. OLD NEW YORK ENDS ABRUPTLY AT THE END OF THE BLOCK WHERE 1974 MANHATTAN BEGINS.

Moschin's suit to a small pressure tank and another tank filled with Karo blood. Smith taped an electric valve to Moschin's arm, with a trigger in his palm to activate the pumping device. The gap in the appliance was carefully closed with sticky Karo blood and hidden with makeup; when the scene was shot, "all he had to do was yank his head back and push the trigger," Smith said.

Moschin, who did not speak English, was a favorite of the production crew. "We sort of communicated in my bad Italian," Coppola said, "yet I never had to explain anything. He is most patient. He was rigged and slit and shot and cut up for countless takes, and yet he always gave an imaginative variation. We were running late, and he was due back in Rome to start on a new picture or be sued. So we scheduled all his remaining scenes together, all of which were very difficult technically. But the crew had such professional respect for

DICK SMITH PRE-
PARES GASTONE
MOSCHIN (FANUCCI)
FOR THE SLASHING
OF HIS NECK, A
LATEX APPLIANCE
OVER TUBING THAT
COULD BE PUMPED
FULL OF KARO
BLOOD. "ALL HE HAD
TO DO," SAID SMITH,
"WAS YANK HIS
HEAD BACK AND
PUSH THE TRIGGER."

THE STREET FESTIVAL IN LITTLE ITALY, A MATCHLESS BLENDING OF PRODUCTION DESIGN BY DEAN TAVOULARIS AND CINEMATOGRAPHY BY GORDON WILLIS.

him that they worked, to a man, at optimum efficiency so that he did finish, just making the night plane to Rome straight from the set and with cheers and good wishes from everyone."

Beyond the demands of mastering a new language, De Niro had the equally daunting problem of creating a character interpretation that would be believable to an audience who knew Brando's Don from the previous film.

"Brando's creation of Don Vito Corleone exists and that is my guideline," De Niro said during the production. "It's interesting to work with the problem of playing a character as an older person. Brando played Vito as a man in his late fifties. For me, Vito is twenty-five years old, a Sicilian emigrant getting established in America. Going backward in time, I must find the threads of that man in his early life that created the power and warmth of the older Godfather."

Coppola realized that taking over what had become known as "the Brando role" was a mixed blessing.

"His assignment is incredibly difficult when you consider he's being asked to play one of the most famous actors in the world in a role for which he received tremendous credit," Coppola said. "He's being asked to have the audacity to play him as a young man, to evoke the character without doing an imitation of him. And, he must do it all in Sicilian, which he doesn't speak.

"Now inherent in those difficulties are the possible advantages," Coppola said. "Dealing with the character at the age of twenty-five gives him tremendous spatial distance. Learning and working in a foreign language could be a tremendous liability for an actor, but Bobby is such a unified, concentrated guy that he did it."

Without the assistance of elaborate makeup, De Niro chose to enhance this resemblance solely by suggestion.

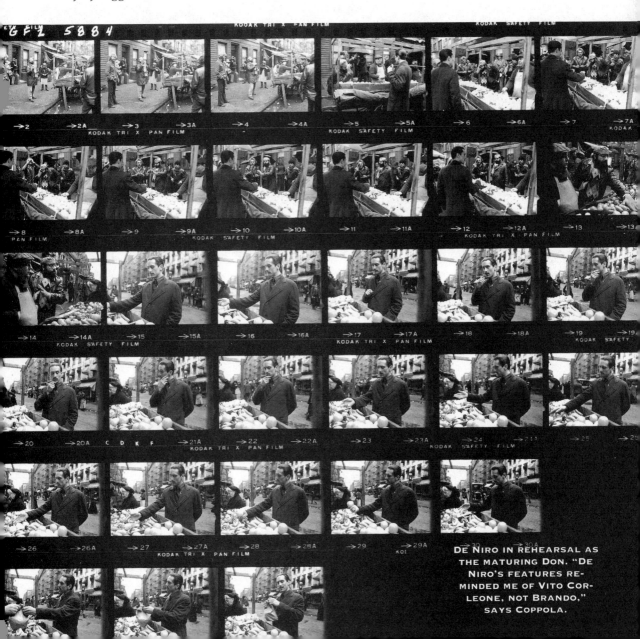

DE NIRO IN REHEARSAL AS THE MATURING DON. "DE NIRO'S FEATURES REMINDED ME OF VITO CORLEONE, NOT BRANDO," SAYS COPPOLA.

"It's like being a scientist or a technician," he said. "Audiences already know Vito Corleone. I watch him and I say, 'That's an interesting gesture. When could he have started to do that?' It's my job as an actor to find things I can make connections with. I must find things and figure out how I can use them, in what scenes can I use them to suggest what the older man will be like."

De Niro recognized that he would be compared with Brando, but he shrugged off the problem. "People will make comparisons, I suppose, but I can't really worry about that," he said just before *The Godfather Part II* was released. "He's him and I'm not him. I know what I am as an actor, and I'm not like anybody. I'll suggest things, that's natural and that's my job—to make audiences recall and feel the older Vito. It's a very special way to build a character—with him in mind. The character may be a continuation, but the actors, Marlon Brando and me, we're two separate people."

Before the production traveled to Europe, Tavoularis dressed another real street a few blocks from the Little Italy street—this for a 1958 scene. Scenes of the attempted murder of Frankie Pentangeli and the shootout that followed were filmed at 7th Street and Avenue B in Vasac's Bar and the intersection in front of the building.

To finish filming the flashback sequences of the young Vito, the production moved on to

Trieste and Sicily from April through early June 1974. To re-create Vito's arrival in America as a boy, Tavoularis mounted one of the most ambitious single location shots ever filmed, by transforming the Trieste Fish Market—"Il Grande Mercato Ittico all'Ingrosso"—into the Ellis Island Immigration Arrival Center of 1901. Before the cameras rolled, Tavoularis, art director Angelo Graham, and set dressers Bob Nelson and Joe Chavalier spent days "making up" the building to approximate photos of Ellis Island at the turn of the century. Powerful lighting was strung overhead, metal barriers built, benches painted, customs officials' desks installed, and partitioned police and medical offices constructed.

Meanwhile, the production team, in a near assembly-line arrangement, was busy selecting, primping, and dressing extras from among the local citizens. Because Trieste itself is populated by a melting pot of people of many nationalities, it was a simple task to recruit extras to play immigrants. For two days over the long Easter weekend, when the fish market was normally closed, the site was packed with more than eight hundred *comparsi* (extras), all of whom were willing to report for work at 6 A.M. on Easter Sunday for twenty-five dollars a day. They were clad in turn-of-the-century costumes carefully researched by Van Runkle, who was aided on site by a dozen Italian

COPPOLA SHOUTS DIRECTIONS FOR AN ESTABLISHING SHOT OF THE ELLIS ISLAND IMMIGRATION ARRIVAL CENTER—ACTUALLY THE TRIESTE FISH MARKET.

COPPOLA SETS UP THE SCENE OF VITO'S MOTHER AS SHE THREATENS TO KILL DON CICCIO TO SAVE HER SON.

wardrobe staff. The costumes included uniforms for U.S. police, immigration officials, doctors, nurses, and hundreds of immigrant poor—billowing voluminous floor-length skirts and shawls for women; baggy trousers, tight-fitting homespun coats, and wide-brimmed soft felt hats for the men; knickers and peaked caps for the small boys.

The next step was a visit to makeup chief Smith. Under his guidance, twenty expert shearers clipped away pounds of hair from the extras; for his careful inspection of extras' hair, Smith earned the nickname "Signore Cut Cut." Smith and his makeup crew painted dark shadows under eyes to give the effect of sickness and sleeplessness after a month's sea voyage. Simultaneously, a dozen hairdressers were setting the women's hair in period buns and coifs.

As they arrived on the floor of the fish market, Coppola critically inspected all eight hundred extras. "Take off that wristwatch," he told one youth. To another, "Your eyeglasses are too modern, change them." To another, he cautioned, "Hide those green socks." Still another was advised, "Smudge dust on your shoes, they look too new."

Mixed in with the Trieste extras were fifty young and middle-aged men with distinctly

American faces, who impersonated New York policemen, customs officials, and doctors. They were U.S. Marine sergeants, U.S. Navy petty officers, and young enlisted personnel of both services on loan from the U.S. Navy troop and ammunition transport ships, the USS *Raleigh* and USS *El Paso*, which were tied to docks a few hundred feet away from the fish market and fortuitously in Trieste for several days during annual six-month Mediterranean cruises. Of their combined 1,500 personnel, the film used as many volunteers willing to moonlight as actors as the supply of uniforms would fit.

Coppola directed the immigrants and officials into positions for the start of the scene. Prop masters supplied battered suitcases, sacks, blankets, packages of food, animals, and musical instruments for the immigrants; billy sticks for the police; and pens and rubber stamps for the customs officials. Above the chattering crowd hung two U.S. flags and signs reading MONEY EXCHANGE (in several languages), TELEGRAPH, and AMERICAN EXPRESS COMPANY.

All of this preparation resulted in two wide shots of the Immigration Arrival Center lasting only eleven seconds on-screen, along with several other closer shots of doctors and immigration officials at work—a total of less than two minutes of footage in the final film. But the preparation and expense were worthwhile to the director.

"Shooting out of the confines and artificiality of a film studio gives moviegoers a sense of actuality," Coppola said. "It is rewarding for the director, too, for there is a sense of reality, of space, of timeliness that he and his actors can dig into."

After Trieste, the production moved on to Sicily to shoot scenes of Vito as a boy and a grown man returning to Sicily twenty years later. Before principal photography wrapped in mid-June 1974, Coppola would film in several locations across Sicily—in steep canyons for the funeral procession for Vito's father, in the town of Forza d'Agro (which substituted for the village of Corleone), at a villa for Don Tommasino's home (the estate, Villa Palatantia, would be used in all three films), and at a backwater railway station for scenes of Don Vito and his young family visiting their ancestral homeland.

On his return to the United States, Coppola was asked if he had felt the same level of pressure he had experienced during production of *The Godfather*.

"No, this time I feel Paramount has been tremendously indulgent of me, and I think I've been good to them," Coppola said. "*The Godfather Part II* cost a lot of money, but the truth of the matter is that it's just a very big film—as the content of the script projected. Just the decision of saying we'll set up the Corleone home base in Lake Tahoe and we'll go to Las Vegas and we'll deal with Havana in 1958 and New York in 1918 and Sicily in the early 1900s—just stating that implied a certain scope, which dictated a big budget. Maybe I was wrong in mapping out such a big film, and I guess I'll be judged for that, but essentially Paramount really let me do it the way I wanted to—including all decisions on cast and staff—and for that I am very grateful.

"This has been the best experience I've had."

While Paramount exerted no budget or creative pressure—other than establishing the release date of the film—the simple constraint of time forced Coppola into what had become one of the most intense periods of his career. With hundreds of hours of footage at hand and a goal of producing a near 3½-hour film with two separate story lines, postproduction and editing dragged on weeks longer than anticipated. By late October, only *six weeks* before the film was set to debut, the film was not fully edited, sound rerecording was not complete, and the musical score was not ready. The first-time television airing of *The Godfather,* which was broadcast on NBC November 16 and 18 to near-record audiences, simultaneously helped spark enthusiasm for the sequel and at the same time increased concern about whether or not it would be ready for its December 12 opening. Knowing that exhibitors had paid $26 million in advance money to screen *The Godfather Part II* didn't help ease the tension at Paramount or American Zoetrope.

Yet Coppola remained relatively calm and open to suggestions for how to proceed.

"We were working 110 hours a week on *The Godfather Part II,*" said one of the assistant editors who worked on postproduction. "It was fun. It wasn't just work. I was amazed at Francis's total lack of proprietary ideas. If people said they didn't like it, Francis would say, 'OK, try something else.' He's very open toward his mistakes. He wants the movie to be good, and he doesn't care whose ideas make it good—and that's what gets people excited about working with him."

The film's length, the score, or sound recording were not at issue; as Coppola saw it, his problem focused on making the two story lines work together.

"I didn't want to go the easy way, which would be just to continue the story of Michael Corleone," Coppola recalled. "I decided to make a film about a man obsessed with his father's success on the eve of his own failure. A story of succession, juxtaposing the father and the son at approximately the same ages; the father is on the rise and the son in his fall. And that's hard to do. So, for a long time there, I had two films that didn't make sense together. They were shot in a different style; they had a different smell to them.

"My friend George Lucas told me, 'Francis, you have two movies. Throw one away. It doesn't work.' But I had this hunch that if I could ever make it work, it could be fantastic."

But it was not yet fantastic. Two weeks before the premiere date, a sneak preview in San Diego amplified the principal problem: The film shifted back and forth too often between the two stories—at one point in postproduction some twenty times. A postscreening gathering of the production team and Paramount executives—including Bob Evans—turned into a roundtable discussion of the film's strengths and flaws, and what could be done to fix them. The result was

THE SHOT OF IMMIGRANTS ARRIVING IN NEW YORK AND SEEING THE STATUE OF LIBERTY FOR THE FIRST TIME. ELEVEN-YEAR-OLD ORESTE BALDINI (CENTER WITH CAP) PLAYS THE YOUNG VITO ANDOLINI, SOON TO BE RENAMED VITO CORLEONE.

more than thirty changes, including condensing of the separate story lines into longer sections. The segments would be reduced to eleven major pieces, along with four other brief switches: a few seconds of Michael under the opening credits before the film opened in 1901 Sicily, and three brief switches in the film's closing minutes. Coppola, as he always managed to do, pulled together a final print literally days before screenings for distributors and entertainment industry reviewers.

The Godfather Part II opened December 12 in New York at the same five theaters where its predecessor had premiered two and a half years before. Critical response was strong—and eventually included many raves—but the earliest appraisals provided some far-from-enthusiastic comments. Vincent Canby of the New York Times called it "One Godfather Too Many." Time said, "Somehow, this beautifully made, intermittently exciting film never pulls us once and for all into its own world. But its ambition, vision, and artistic courage make it more marvelous than anything we might have expected from that ill-fated form, the sequel."

Perhaps critics expected a simple extension of The Godfather; if so, they didn't get it. The Godfather Part II was a different kind of movie—darker and not a romantic vision—in other words, exactly what Coppola had hoped for. And Coppola understood the reaction.

"People tell me they liked the opening wedding party in the original film better than the opening (First Communion) party for Michael's son in the sequel. Well, so do I. That was my point. I was trying to show how the family had lost its authenticity. I wanted to have scenes that would remind you of the first film and to show by their altered shape how much the family had changed."

However, the reputation of The Godfather Part II has grown over the years, and now it is considered by many film historians to be one of the great masterpieces of American cinema. Several early reviewers recognized the film's potential.

"I liked the book, loved the movie, and anxiously waited for the sequel to be made—thinking it could never match the original," reported Liz Smith in Cosmopolitan. "Well, this reviewer is delighted to say that The Godfather Part II is not only good, but damn near a work of art."

Wrote critic D. Keith Mano, "A sequel is never as good as its predecessor. This principle does not hold for The Godfather Part II. Godfather II is better than The Godfather. And the two-volume set represents a great American document. Francis Ford Coppola could go back to flesh flicks, he could spend the next thirty years in a sitz bath. His genius has been certified by a notary public. This, damn it, is filmmaking. Making. Period. Creation. Worlds do exist parallel to ours. For three and a half hours, Godfather II is one of them."

The acclaim to come was reflected in the Academy Awards for 1974. The Godfather Part II was nominated for eleven Oscars, including Best Actor (Pacino), three Best Supporting Actors (De Niro, Gazzo, Strasberg), Best Supporting Actress (Shire), Best Art Direction (Tavoularis, Angelo Graham; set decoration, George R. Nelson), Best Costume Design (Theadora Van Runkle), Best Original Dramatic Score (Nino Rota, Carmine Coppola), Best Screenplay adapted from other material (Coppola, Puzo), Best Director (Coppola), and Best Picture (Coppola, Frederickson, and Roos).

Coppola and Fred Roos were each nominated for Best Picture twice. The Conversation was also nominated for Best Picture, marking one of the few times in the Academy's history that two films by the same producer were nominated for Best Picture in the same year.

This time, there would be no competition. The Godfather Part II won six Academy Awards, including Best Supporting Actor, Best Art Direction, Best Score, Best Screenplay, Best Direction, and Best Picture.

Even Coppola, ever insecure about his accomplishments, found satisfaction in his sequel—perhaps buttressed by international acclaim and a half-dozen Academy Awards, including three he won himself.

"The way I personally feel about it now," Coppola said, "is that if *The Godfather Part II* hadn't been made, there would only have been a half a movie."

Over the next fifteen years, *The Godfather* and *The Godfather Part II* were never far from the public consciousness. Events every few years would keep the films in the news: In November 1977, the two *Godfather* films were reedited into chronological order and broadcast over four nights on NBC. With commercials, *The Godfather: The Complete Novel for Television* ran nine hours; over the nights it aired, an average of 40 percent of the televisions in America tuned in. (Released on videotape and laser disc, *The Godfather: The Complete Epic* ran 388 minutes.) When Paramount began to produce videotapes and laser discs of its films, two of its most popular releases were the two *Godfather* films. Both *Godfather* films remained in near-constant release in art houses and college film programs.

In the decade and a half that followed *Part II*, the life and career of Francis Ford Coppola, meanwhile, would include some of the highest peaks and deepest valleys that an artist, a husband, and a father could experience. In the fifteen years after the release of *The Godfather Part II*, Coppola would release monumental failures such as the disastrous *One from the Heart*, solid work as a director-for-hire including *Peggy Sue Got Married*, and successes pulled from the jaws of failure, most notably the seemingly endless production of *Apocalypse Now* that nearly cost him his sanity and his marriage. Coppola would face the possibility of bankruptcy, near financial ruin, and finally the ultimate personal catastrophe: In 1986, the Coppolas' beloved son Gio, his father's "best friend" and an aspiring filmmaker, was killed in a boating accident.

Through triumph and tragedy, Coppola

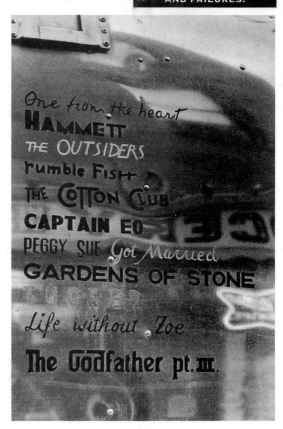

THE SIDE OF COPPOLA'S MOBILE DIRECTOR'S VEHICLE *SILVER FISH* WAS INSCRIBED WITH A LEGACY OF THE DIRECTOR'S SUCCESSES AND FAILURES.

would never escape the specter of the *Godfather* films. In interviews that explored his past or speculated about his future, he would always be asked: Would there ever be a *Godfather Part III*? Coppola would demur, he would hesitate, he would explain why another *Godfather* film would be unreasonable . . . but he never rejected the idea entirely.

"We talked about it from time to time," said Frank Mancuso, who was Paramount chairman in 1988. "But he would never say no to me. That gave me hope."

Finally, in 1988, the lure became too strong. Again, the combined incentive of money to bolster his sagging empire and the irresistible offer of broad creative control would bring Coppola back to the Corleones as producer, director, and cowriter of *The Godfather Part III.*

After being pestered for more than fourteen years about making another *Godfather* film, the final decision came surprisingly easily. After dinner at Mancuso's home, the chairman and Coppola continued their discussion in the driveway of Coppola's Los Angeles home.

"Frank said, 'What about you doing a sequel?' " Coppola recalled. "I said, 'You mean any way I want?' He said, 'Yeah.' And that was it."

For the third time, Coppola and Puzo worked together to create a *Godfather* script—as usual, splitting duties, but this time in close proximity to each other in a suite at the Peppermill Hotel Casino in Reno (successful progress on the script brought occasional rewards of time at the gambling tables). For the third *Godfather* film, Puzo and Coppola would bring the action forward to 1979 as a repentant Michael works yet again to make all of his family's investments legitimate. The plot wove together broad elements about Mafia intrigue and international business manipulation within the Catholic Church, along with Michael's attempts to renew his ties with his children and ex-wife.

"Michael has always been the master manipulator," said Coppola. "By the end of *Part II*, he had become very self-righteous and distrusted everyone. Now he is a man who wants to rehabilitate himself. Reflecting the mood in America at that time, Michael wants to take stock of himself honestly."

Said Pacino, "Over the years Michael has grown cold and alienated from those he most loves and is struggling to win back their trust and affection. In Michael's words, 'One's reach should exceed his grasp, or what's a Heaven for?'"

For the production of *The Godfather Part III*, Coppola was able to yet again reconvene most of the members of his production team: Fred Roos and Gray Frederickson again coproduced, this time with Charles Mulvehill. Gordon Willis shot the

THE ASSASSINATION OF DON TOMMASINO.

COPPOLA SHOWS FRANCO CITTI (CALO) HOW HE WANTS THE AS-SASSINATION-BY-GLASSES TO BE ACCOMPLISHED. THE TUBING (CEN-TER BOTTOM) WILL PUMP THE BLOOD TO THE WOUND.

film, Dean Tavoularis designed the production, and Carmine Coppola wrote new music, to be interwoven with the original themes by Nino Rota. For costumes, Coppola hired designer Milena Canonero, a two-time Academy Award winner who had worked with the director on *Tucker: The Man and His Dream* and *The Cotton Club.*

Most of the performers whose characters survived *Part II* returned as well— Al Pacino, Diane Keaton, Talia Shire, Richard Bright as Al Neri, and Tere Livrano (now Tere L. Baker) as Theresa Hagen. They would also be rejoined by old friends from *The God-father*: Franco Citti as Calo (Michael's bodyguard in Sicily), and Al Martino as Johnny Fontane.

To portray the Corleone children as adults, Coppola cast actress Winona Ryder as Mary and Franc D'Ambrosio as Anthony. New cast members included Andy Garcia as Vincent Mancini, the grown illegitimate son of Sonny Corleone and Lucy Mancini; veteran character actor Eli Wallach as family friend Don Altobello; Joe Mantegna as Joey Zasa, the ambitious wiseguy who assumed leadership of what had been the Corleone family business in New York; Don Novello as Dominic Abbandando, son of Genco and Michael's public relations adviser; and Bridget Fonda as photojournalist Grace Hamilton.

The first major blow of the production was the "death" of Tom Hagen. Duvall would not be back as the Corleone consigliere—his asking price was too high. His departure from the scene forced significant rewrites of the script, and Coppola hired George Hamilton to play a new character, investment adviser B. J. Harrison.

For this installment of the *Godfather* saga, principal production shifted to Italy's Cinecitta Studios, along with location shooting around Rome, New York, and Sicily. Principal photography began in Rome on November 27, 1989. Willis and Coppola maintained the same visual structure of the first two *Godfather* films; as Willis described it, "Point, counterpoint; light, dark; big, small—using contrasts can achieve a desired emotional response. This could be as simple as manipulating where characters appear on the screen or lighting a dark room with sunlight."

During six weeks of filming at Cinecitta, under Tavoularis's supervision, the crew erected massive sets on four enormous soundstages. The largest was Michael's lavish New York penthouse apartment; others included an Atlantic City luxury suite that was machine-gunned to pieces in a meeting of Mafia dons.

Location work brought the cast and crew to Rome's *Palazzo de Guistizia* (law courts) for the filming of a sequence set at the Vatican Bank. Other locations included a farm in Lunghezza outside Rome and the Santa Maria dell Quercia, a beautiful three-hundred-

SETUPS FOR THE MEETING OF THE DONS.

year-old church north of Rome, which became the setting for a meeting between Michael and Cardinal—later Pope—Lamberto (Raf Vallone). The colorful murals and ceiling frescoes of the sixteenth-century Villa Farnese at Caprarola, which had been planned as the papal summer residence, became the elaborate backdrop for the office of the archbishop who heads the Vatican Bank.

In Rome, the production suffered its most serious setback. When Winona Ryder arrived from the United States immediately after completing another motion picture, members of the production crew noticed she did not look well; that appraisal was amplified when the production's doctor declared she was suffering from exhaustion and was unable to play the role.

"I was so honored to have been chosen, and then to have done that to them, I felt terrible," said Ryder. "But it would have been worse had I stayed and either collapsed later on or done a really bad job, which would have been inevitable."

Ryder's departure was, as Paramount president Sidney Ganis put it, "high-anxiety time." The role of Mary was critical to the production, and Coppola and Paramount had limited choices for how they could proceed—rewrite or recast, both of which could necessitate costly delays. Instead, Coppola chose a solution comfortable to him. His daughter Sofia, visiting her parents and grandparents in Rome for the Christmas holidays, had not the slightest idea what was to come when the phone rang just as she was about to bathe. An assistant director was calling, asking if Sofia could report to Cinecitta to play Mary.

"I was like, 'Excuse me? Are you sure? I just want to take a shower,'" Sofia recalled.

It was a risky creative decision under the best of circumstances; although Sofia had appeared in speaking roles in three of her father's films (in addition to appearances as a newborn in *The Godfather* and a three-year-old in *The Godfather Part II*), she was essentially a novice actress. Her involvement in the film may have satisfied her father, but others in the cast and crew were troubled by the casting. While Sofia was well liked by those in the *Godfather* company—many of whom had known her all her life—they were concerned about the fate of the production, as well as the toll the part could take on an eighteen-year-old.

Eventually, the film proceeded with Sofia as Mary. As with many Coppola decisions, it was a risky gamble. This time, however, the gamble would fail.

In Spring 1990, the company relocated to Sicily for locations in Palermo and Taormina, filming in several of the same locations used for *Parts I* and *II* (the Teatro Massiimo in Palermo, site of the opera performed by Anthony at the climax of *Part III*, was undergoing restoration during the filming, so its interior and stage were re-created at Cinecitta).

The production would face another crisis in Italy, this one in the form of a real-life relationship between two of the principals. For several years, Diane Keaton and Al Pacino had struggled through an on-again off-again relationship. The main conflict seemed to be a long-term commitment; Keaton wanted one and Pacino didn't. The result was a strained relationship between the two that was soothed in part by misfortune: Pacino's beloved grandmother died during production, and Keaton accompanied him to New York for the funeral. While they were gone, they settled their differences and forged an uneasy personal truce that would last for the duration of the film.

In New York, Tavoularis again designed a street festival—this time as a backdrop for the murder of Joey Zasa. For scenes of Michael receiving his Order of St. Sebastian from the Catholic Church, the production also shot at the Old St. Patrick's Cathedral—the same interior location used in *The Godfather* for the baptism of Michael Rizzi.

During filming in Italy and America, Coppola used a favorite—and expensive—filmmaking gadget: an Airstream motor home equipped with the latest in video and film technology. Nicknamed the *Silver Fish*, Coppola had used the rolling facility since 1981, updating the equipment as needed. By the time production began for *The Godfather Part III*, the *Silver Fish* was equipped to allow Coppola to see through viewfinders of up to four cameras on the set, watch on Hi-8 video any scene already filmed—including preproduction rehearsals, edit scenes on video, listen to musical scores, communicate with the set through an intercom system, and use word processors to write or revise the script. With this last capability, Coppola would often revise the script three or

more times a day, sometimes producing new pages of dialogue before previous versions had even been distributed.

The *Silver Fish* was a veritable technological haven for the director, but some considered it a self-imposed isolation booth. At one point during production, Coppola did not appear on the set in person for days, instead choosing to direct the film entirely from inside the *Silver Fish*. His only presence on the set was a disembodied voice over the intercom.

Production continued through June, and as with *The Godfather Part II* the crush of postproduction would delay completion of the final product until only a few weeks before its premiere on December 20, 1990. Sixteen years after the premiere of *Part II*, critics and moviegoers had high expectations for the third *Godfather* film. There were generally upbeat reviews, but few raves.

Variety described Sofia's work as "the film's main flaw." Sofia was, wrote *Variety*, "ungainly, affected with a 'Valley-Girl' accent, and not an actress who can hold her own in this august company." The *Washington Post* described her work as "hopelessly amateurish."

However, despite the specific criticism, many reviews praised the film and were less harsh toward Sofia Coppola's work. Soren Anderson of *McClatchy Newspapers* called the film "magnificent," wrote Anderson. "It is filled with echoes and haunted by memories. Sofia doesn't embarrass herself, but doesn't distinguish herself either."

"This new sequel is another rich, broadly scaled work," wrote Michael Wilmington in the *Los Angeles Times*. "It has arias and grand moments to match either of its predecessors. But *The Godfather Part III* is never quite as sharp as its predecessors, its plot turns are muddled and the complex financial conspiracy that underlies the story never quite becomes clear, at least on its first viewing. And somehow, it never acquires the urgency the first two movies had. And yet, it is a wonderful movie."

After three films—the first a ground-breaking success, the second a cinematic masterpiece, and the third a not entirely satisfying but still solid follow-up—the inevitable question remains: Will there be a *Godfather Part IV*? Even after nearly twenty years of occasional involvement with *The Godfather* story, the usually decisive Coppola would remain uncertain about the future of the Corleones in his life.

"I really am not interested in gangsters," Coppola said, "but I like the Italian part. I've worked with some nice people on the *Godfather* films, and it's obviously part of my life now, but I always sort of resented that it took up so much of my life, and that it's about shooting people. I mean, I feel very lucky that I got to do it, and I think I was able to express some things about myself. I just don't want to spend my whole life doing that."

But he didn't say no.

COPPOLA
PREPARES
PACINO FOR
MICHAEL'S
DEATH
SCENE

The Godfather Films:
Cast and Production Credits

The principal production team and cast listed below are from the credits that appeared at the close of the three *Godfather* films, along with several additions. These production credits are not listed here in order of their appearance on screen; instead, to help explain who did what, they are grouped as much as possible by area of responsibility.

NOTE: In the credits for screenplay in the three films, Mario Puzo and Francis Ford Coppola are based on the writer who has the largest contribution to the particular work; thus Mario Puzo is listed first for screenplay credit for *The Godfather* and *The Godfather, Part III*, and Francis Ford Coppola is listed first for *The Godfather, Part II*.

* * * * * * * *

The Godfather
A Paramount Picture
An Albert S. Ruddy Production
Produced by Alfran Productions, Inc.
Running Time: 175 minutes
Released: March 15, 1972

Director . . . . Francis Ford Coppola
Producer . . . . Albert S. Ruddy

Screenplay . . . . Mario Puzo and Francis Ford Coppola

Director of Photography . . . . Gordon Willis
Camera Operator . . . . Michael Chapman

Production Designer . . . . Dean Tavoularis
Art Director . . . . Warren Clymer
Set Decorator . . . . Philip Smith

Editors . . . . William Reynolds and Peter Zinner

Makeup Artists . . . . Dick Smith and Philip Rhodes
Hair Stylist . . . . Phil Leto

Special Effects . . . . A. D. Flowers, Joe Lombardi, and Sass Bedig

Costume Designer . . . . Anna Hill Johnstone
Wardrobe Supervisor . . . . George Newman
Women's Wardrobe . . . . Marilyn Putnam

Associate Producer . . . . Gray Frederickson
Assistant to Producer . . . . Gary Chazen
Executive Assistant . . . . Robert S. Mendelsohn
Casting . . . . Fred Roos, Andrea Eastman, and Louis DiGiaimo
Location Coordinators . . . . Michael Briggs and Tony Bowers
Location Service . . . . Cinemobile Systems, Inc.
Script Continuity . . . . Nancy Tonery
Oaktree Productions:
    Unit Production Manager . . . . Fred Caruso
    Assistant Director . . . . Fred Gallo
    Unit Coordinator . . . . Robert Barth

Music . . . . Nino Rota
Conductor . . . . Carlo Savina

Additional Music
    Mall Wedding Sequence . . . . Carmine Coppola
    "I Have But One Heart" . . . . Johnny Farrow and Marty Symes
    "Luna Mezz' 'O Mare" . . . . Paolo Citarella
    "Manhattan Serenade" . . . . Louis Alter
    "Have Yourself a Merry Little Christmas" . . . . Hugh Martin and Ralph Blane
    "Santa Claus is Coming to Town" . . . . Haven Gillespie and J. Fred Coots
    "The Bells of St. Mary's" . . . . A. E. Adams and Douglas Furber
    "All of My Life" . . . . Irving Berlin
    "Mona Lisa" . . . . Jay Livingston and Ray Evans
    Baptism Sequence . . . . J. S. Bach

Production Recording . . . . Christopher Newman
Re-Recording . . . . Bud Grenzbach and Richard Portman

Sicilian Unit
Production Manager . . . . Valerio De Paolis
Assistant Director . . . . Tony Brandi
Assistant Art Director . . . . Samuel Verts

Post Production Consultant . . . . Walter Murch
Foreign Post Production . . . . Peter Zinner
Color . . . . Technicolor

Cast

Vito Corleone	Marlon Brando
Michael Corleone	Al Pacino
Sonny Corleone	James Caan
Peter Clemenza	Richard Castellano
Tom Hagen	Robert Duvall
McCluskey	Sterling Hayden
Jack Woltz	John Marley
Barzini	Richard Conte
Kay Adams	Diane Keaton
Sollozzo	Al Lettieri
Sal Tessio	Abe Vigoda
Connie Corleone Rizzi	Talia Shire
Carlo Rizzi	Gianni Russo
Fredo Corleone	John Cazale
Cuneo	Rudy Bond
Johnny Fontane	Al Martino
Mama (Carmella) Corleone	Morgana King
Luca Brasi	Lenny Montana
Paulie Gatto	John Martino
Bonasera	Salvatore Corsitto
Al Neri	Richard Bright
Rocco Lampone	Tom Rosqui
Moe Greene	Alex Rocco
Bruno Tattaglia	Tony Giorgio
Nazorine	Vito Scotti
Theresa Hagen	Tere Livrano
Phillip Tattaglia	Victor Rendina
Lucy Mancini	Jeannie Linero
Sandra Corleone	Julie Gregg
Mrs. Clemenza	Ardell Sheridan
Anthony Corleone	Anthony Gounaris

Sicilian Sequence:

Apollonia	Simonetta Stefanelli
Fabrizio	Angelo Infanti
Don Tommasino	Corrado Gaipa
Calo	Franco Citti
Vitelli	Saro Urzi

The Godfather, Part II
A Coppola Company Production
Released by Paramount Pictures
Running Time: 200 minutes
Released: December 12, 1974

Director	Francis Ford Coppola
Producer	Francis Ford Coppola
Co-Producers	Gray Frederickson and Fred Roos
Screenplay	Francis Ford Coppola and Mario Puzo
Director of Photography	Gordon Willis
Camera Operator	Ralph Gerling

Camera Assistant . . . . Bill Gereghty
Gaffer . . . . George Holmes

Production Designer . . . . Dean Tavoularis
Art Director . . . . Angelo Graham
Set Decorator . . . . George R. Nelson
Properties . . . . V. Bud Shelton and Doug Madison
Key Grip . . . . Bob Rose

Editors . . . . Peter Zinner, Barry Malkin, Richard Marks
Assistant Editors . . . . George Berndt, Bobbe Kurtz, Lisa Fruchtman

Makeup Artists . . . . Dick Smith and Charles Schram
Hair Stylist . . . . Naomi Cavin

Special Effects . . . . A. D. Flowers and Joe Lombardi

Costume Designer . . . . Theadora Van Runkle
Wardrobe . . . . Marie Osborne
. . . . Eric Seelig
Associate Producer . . . . Mona Skager
Production Manager . . . . Michael S. Glick
Assistant Director . . . . Newton Arnold
Second Assistant Directors . . . . Henry J. Lange, Jr.
. . . . Chuck Myers
. . . . Mike Kusley
. . . . Alan Hopkins
. . . . Burt Bluestein
New York Location Supervisor . . . . Ron Colby
Production Secretary . . . . Nanette Siegert
Casting . . . . Michael Fenton, Jane Feinberg, Vic Ramos
Location Auditor . . . . Carl Skelton
Location Coordinator . . . . Jack English
Location Assistants . . . . Randy Carter, Mona Houghton, Melissa Mathison
Research . . . . Deborah Fine
Unit Publicist . . . . Eileen Peterson
Script Supervisors . . . . John Franco and B. J. Bachman
Miami Coordinator . . . . Tammy Newell
Senate Hearings Advisor . . . . Ed Guthman

Music . . . . Nino Rota
Conductor . . . . Carmine Coppola
Additional Music . . . . Carmine Coppola
  "Senza Mamma" (F. Pennino Edition) . . . . Francesco Pennino
  "Napule Ve Salute" . . . . Francesco Pennino
  "Mr. Wonderful" . . . . Jerry Bock, Larry Holofcener, George Weiss
  "Heart and Soul" . . . . Hoagy Carmichael and Frank Loesser
Music Editor . . . . George Brand

Production Recording . . . . Chuck Wilborn and Nathan Boxer
Sound Montage and Re-Recording . . . . Walter Murch
Sound Effects Editors . . . . Howard Beals, Jim Fritch, Jim Klinger
Sound Montage Associates . . . . Pat Jackson and Mark Berger

Titles . . . . Wayne Fitzgerald
Subtitling . . . . Sonya Friedman
Sicilian Translation . . . . Romano Pianti

Foreign Post Production . . . . Peter Zinner

Sicilian Unit
Production Supervisor . . . . Valerio De Paolis
Unit Manager . . . . Mario Cotone
Assistant Director. . . . . Tony Brandt
Assistant Set Decorator . . . . Joe Chevalier
Casting . . . . Emy De Sica and Maurizio Lucci
Script Supervisor . . . . Serena Canevari
Production Assistant . . . . Bruno Perria

Color. . . . . Technicolor

Production Facilities . . . . American Zoetrope

Cast

Michael Corleone. . . . . Al Pacino
Tom Hagen . . . . Robert Duvall
Kay Adams Corleone . . . . Diane Keaton
Vito Corleone (as a young man). . . . . Robert De Niro
Fredo Corleone. . . . . John Cazale
Connie Corleone . . . . Talia Shire
Hyman Roth. . . . . Lee Strasberg
Frankie Pentangeli . . . . Michael V. Gazzo
Senator Pat Geary . . . . G. D. Spradlin
Al Neri . . . . Richard Bright
Fanucci . . . . Gaston Moschin
Rocco Lampone . . . . Tom Rosqui
Peter Clemenza (as a young man) . . . . B. Kirby Jr.
Genco Abbandando (as a young man). . . . . Frank Sivero
Mama Corleone . . . . Morgana King
Mama (Carmella) Corleone (as a young woman). . . . . Francesca De Sapio
Deanna Dunn Corleone . . . . Mariana Hill
Signor Roberto . . . . Leopoldo Trieste
Johnny Ola. . . . . Dominic Chianese
Michael's Bodyguard . . . . Amerigo Tot
Merle Johnson . . . . Troy Donahue
Sonny Corleone . . . . James Caan
Sal Tessio (as a young man) . . . . John Aprea
Sal Tessio. . . . . Abe Vigoda
Willi Cicci . . . . Joe Spinell
Theresa Hagen . . . . Tere Livrano
Carlo Rizzi . . . . Gianni Russo
Vito's Mother . . . . Maria Carta
Vito Andolini (Vito Corleone as a boy) . . . . Oreste Baldini
Don Francesco. . . . . Giuseppe Sillato
Don Tommasino . . . . Mario Cotone
Anthony Corleone . . . . James Gounaris
Marcia Roth . . . . Fay Spain
FBI Man #1 . . . . Harry Dean Stanton
FBI Man #2 . . . . David Baker
Carmine Rosato. . . . . Carmine Caridi
Tony Rosato . . . . Danny Aiello

Policeman	Carmine Foresta
Bartender	Nick Discenza
Father Carmelo	Father Joseph Medeglia
Senate Committee Chairman	William Bowers
Michael's Buttonman	Joe Della Sorte
Michael's Buttonman	Carmen Argenziano
Michael's Buttonman	Joe Lo Grippo
Impresario	Ezio Flagello
Tenor in "Senza Mamma"	Livio Giorgi
Girl in "Senza Mamma"	Kathy Beller
Signora Colombo	Saveria Mazzola
Cuban President	Tito Alba
Cuban Translator	Johnny Naranjo
Pentangeli's Wife	Elda Maida
Pentangeli's Brother	Salvatore Po
Mosca	Ignazio Pappalardo
Strollo	Andrea Maugeri
Signor Abbandando	Peter La Corte
Street Vendor	Vincent Coppola
Questadt	Peter Donat
Fred Corngold	Tom Dahlgren
Senator Ream	Paul R. Brown
Senator #1	Phil Feldman
Senator #2	Roger Corman
Yolanda	Yvonne Coll
Attendant at Brothel	J. D. Nichols
Ellis Island Doctor	Edward Van Sickle
Ellis Island Nurse	Gabria Belloni
Custom Official	Richard Watson
Cuban Nurse	Venancia Grangerard
Governess	Erica Yohn
Midwife	Theresa Tirelli

The Godfather, Part III
Zoetrope Studios
Released by Paramount Pictures
Running Time: 200 minutes
Released: December 20, 1990

Director	Francis Ford Coppola
Producer	Francis Ford Coppola
Screenplay	Mario Puzo and Francis Ford Coppola
Executive Producers	Fred Fuchs and Nicholas Gage
Co-Producers	Fred Roos, Gray Frederickson and Charles Mulvehill
Director of Photography	Gordon Willis
Camera Operator	Craig Dibona
Chief Lighting Technician	James Fitzpatrick
Production Designer	Dean Tavoularis
Supervising Art Director	Alex Tavoularis
Supervising Set Decorator	Gary Fettis
Assistant Art Director	Franckie Diago
Art Department Coordinator	Phillis Lehmer
Production Illustrator	Mauro Borelli
Property Master	Douglas Madison

Special Effects Coordinator . . . . Lawrence James Cavanaugh
Special Effects Supervisor . . . . R. Bruce Steinheimer

Costume Designer . . . . Milena Canonero
Assistant Costume Designers . . . . Richard Shissler and Elisabeth Beraldo
Additional Costume Designers' Assistant . . . . Ezio Maria Bruno
Wardrobe Supervisor . . . . William A. Campbell
Wardrobe Assistant . . . . Jacqui De La Fontaine
Makeup Supervisor . . . . Fabrizio Sforza
Additional Makeup Artist . . . . Antonio Maltempo
Makeup Artist for Keaton . . . . Tom Lucas
Hairstylists . . . . Giuseppina Bovino and Grazia De Rossi

Associate Producer . . . . Marina Geftner
Production Supervisor . . . . Alessandro Von Normann
First Assistant Director . . . . H. Gordon Boos
Second Assistant Director . . . . K. C. Hodenfield
Stunt Coordinator . . . . Buddy Joe Hooker
Script Supervisor . . . . Wilma Garscadden-Gahret
Research . . . . Anahid Nazarian
Assistant to Coppola . . . . Loolee DeLeon
Opera Advisor . . . . Anton Coppola
First Company Grip . . . . George Patsos

Editors . . . . Barry Malkin, Lisa Fruchtman, Walter Murch
Additional Film Editing . . . . Louise Rubacky, Glen Scantlebury

Music (composed, arranged, directed) . . . . Carmine Coppola
Additional Music and Themes . . . . Nino Rota
Music Supervisor . . . . Stephan R. Goldman
Music Editor . . . . Mark Adler

Casting . . . . Janet Hirshenson, Jane Jenkins, Roger Mussenden
Casting in Italy . . . . Aleta Chappelle

Sound Designer . . . . Richard Beggs
Sound Mixer . . . . Clive Winter
Boom Operator . . . . Allan Brereton

Additional Visual Effects . . . . Industrial Light & Magic

Italian Unit
Unit Manager . . . . Lynn Kamern
First Assistant Director . . . . Gianni Arduini-Plaisant
Production Manager . . . . Franco Ballati
Set Decorator . . . . Franco Fumagalli
Set Designers . . . . Maria Teresa Barbasso and Nazzareno Piana

New York Unit
Unit Production Manager . . . . Bruce S. Pustin
Production Coordinator . . . . Jane Raab
Chief Set Dresser . . . . Dan Grosso

Post Production Services . . . . Zoetrope Studios
Additional Sound Services . . . . Skywalker Sound

Color . . . . Technicolor

Cast

Michael Corleone . . . . Al Pacino
Kay Adams . . . . Diane Keaton
Connie Corleone Rizzi . . . . Talia Shire
Vincent Mancini . . . . Andy Garcia
Don Altobello . . . . Eli Wallach
Joey Zasa . . . . Joe Mantegna
B. J. Harrison . . . . George Hamilton
Grace Hamilton . . . . Bridget Fonda
Mary Corleone . . . . Sofia Coppola
Cardinal Lamberto . . . . Raf Vallone
Anthony Corleone . . . . Franc D'Ambrosio
Archbishop Gliday . . . . Donal Donnelly
Al Neri . . . . Richard Bright
Frederick Kelmszig . . . . Helmut Berger
Dominic Abbandando . . . . Don Novello
Andrew Hagen . . . . John Savage
Calo . . . . Franco Citti
Mosca . . . . Mario Donatone
Don Tommasino . . . . Vittorio Duse
Lucchesi . . . . Enzo Robutti
Spara . . . . Michele Russo
Johnny Fontane . . . . Al Martino
Lou Pennino . . . . Robert Cicchini
Armand . . . . Rogerio Miranda
Francesco . . . . Carlos Miranda
Lucy Mancini . . . . Jeannie Linero
Francesca Corleone . . . . Jeanne Savarino Pesch
Kathryn Corleone . . . . Janet Savarino Smith
Teresa Hagen . . . . Tere (Livrano) Baker
Albert Volpe . . . . Carmine Caridi
Frank Romano . . . . Don Costello
Leo Cuneo . . . . Al Ruscio
Enzo the Baker . . . . Garbriele Torrei

Bibliography

SOURCES

Margaret Herrick Library, Academy of Motion Picture Arts and Sciences, Los Angeles
Paramount Pictures publicity files and photo archives, Los Angeles
UCLA Library

PRODUCTION FILES AND NOTES

Production notes, photographs, and souvenir programs from *The Godfather, The Godfather, Part II, The Godfather, Part III*
Paramount Pictures publicity files and studio archives.

SCRIPT

Shooting script of *The Godfather*, dated March 29, 1971.
Margaret Herrick Library, Academy of Motion Picture Arts and Sciences.

VIDEO

The Godfather (laser disc), 1972.
The Godfather, Part II (laser disc), 1974.
The Godfather, Part III (laser disc), 1991.
The Godfather Epic (videotape), 1977.
The Godfather Trilogy (laser disc), 1991.
The Godfather Family: A Look Inside (videotape), 1991.
All laser discs and videotapes released by Paramount Pictures. *Marlon Brando Profile* (broadcast), 1996.
American Movie Classics Production.

INTERVIEWS

Francis Ford Coppola, unpublished interview with Paramount Pictures staff on the making of *The Godfather, Part II*, November 1974.
Margaret Herrick Library, Academy of Motion Picture Arts and Sciences.
Al Ruddy, interviews with the author, May–September 1996.
Dick Smith, interviews with the author, June and July 1996.
Dean Tavoularis, interviews with the author, July and August 1996.

BOOKS

Brady, John. *The Craft of the Screenwriter.* New York: Simon & Schuster, 1981.
Brando, Marlon, with Robert Lindsey. *Brando: Songs My Mother Taught Me.* New York: Random House, 1994.
Breskin, David. *Interviews: Filmmakers in Conversation.* Boston: Faber and Faber, 1992.
Chaillet, Jean-Paul, and Elizabeth Vincent. *Francis Ford Coppola.* New York: St. Martin's Press, 1984.
Chase, Donald, *Filmmaking: The Collaborative Art.* Boston: Little, Brown and Company, 1975.
Chown, Jeffrey. *Hollywood Auteur: Francis Coppola.* New York: Praeger Publishers, 1988.
Coppola, Eleanor. *Notes: On the Making of Apocalypse Now.* New York: Simon & Schuster, 1979.
Cowie, Peter. *Coppola.* London: Andre Deutsch Limited, 1989.
Evans, Robert. *The Kid Stays in the Picture.* New York: Hyperion, 1994.
Gelmis, Joseph. *The Film Director as Superstar.* New York: Doubleday & Company, 1970.
Goodwin, Michael, and Naomi Wise. *On the Edge: The Life and Times of Francis Coppola.* New York: William Morrow and Company, 1989.
Jacobs, Diane. *Hollywood Renaissance.* New York: A.S. Barnes & Co., 1977.
Kolker, Robert Phillip. *A Cinema of Loneliness.* New York: Oxford University Press, 1980.
McGee, Mark Thomas. *Roger Corman: The Best of the Cheap Acts.* Jefferson, North Carolina: McFarland & Company, 1988.
Puzo, Mario. *The Godfather Papers & Other Confessions.* New York: G. P. Putnam's Sons, 1972.
Schaefer, Dennis, and Larry Salvato. *Masters of Light: Conversations with Contemporary Cinematographers.* Oakland, California: University of California Press, 1984.
Zuckerman, Ira. *The Godfather Journal.* New York: Manor Books, 1972.

ARTICLES AND PUBLICATIONS

Box Office, Daily Variety, Hollywood Reporter, Los Angeles Herald-Examiner, Los Angeles Times, New York Times, San Francisco Chronicle, Variety, Wall Street Journal: Various articles, 1969–1989.

Gulf+Western Inc. Annual Reports, 1969–1976.

"Dick Smith: The Innovative Career of a Master of Makeup," *Theatre Crafts International,* John Calhoun, May 1993.

"Dynasty Italian Style," *California* Magazine, Stephen Farber and Marc Green, April 1984.

"*The Godfather* is Reborn," *TV Guide,* Edward Kiester, November 12, 1977.

"The Godfather of Makeup," *Horizon,* Donald Chase, May/June 1982.

"The Making of *The Godfather,*" *Time* Magazine, March 13, 1972.

"The Making of *The Godfather*—Sort of a Home Movie," *NY Times Magazine,* August 15, 1971.

"New York Florists Create Flowers for *The Godfather,*" *Florist* Magazine, October 1971.

"Playboy Interview: Francis Ford Coppola," *Playboy* Magazine, May 1975.

"The Story Behind *The Godfather* by the Men Who Lived It," *Ladies Home Journal,* June 1972.

"Under the Gun," *Vanity Fair,* Peter Boyer, June 1990.

Index

NOTE: References in the index to film production work apply to *The Godfather*, unless otherwise indicated as coming from *The Godfather, Part II*, or *The Godfather, Part III*.

THE GREATEST EPIC IN AMERICAN CINEMA.

IN TWO EXTRAORDINARY COLLECTOR'S EDITIONS.

A 25ᵀᴴ Anniversary Celebration.

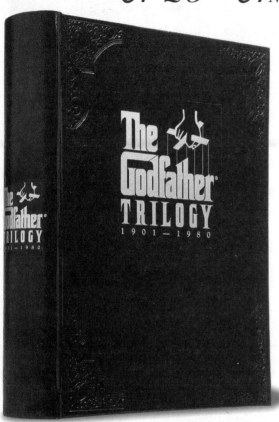

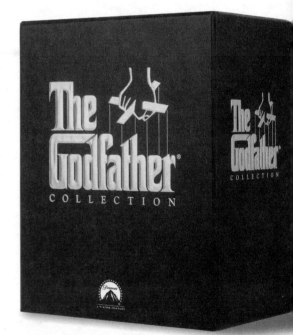

Francis Ford Coppola has interwoven the three Godfather films into one stunning production. This deluxe, leather-bound set also contains *The Godfather Family: A Look Inside* and a beautiful booklet filled with photography and Coppola's personal production notes and commentary on the Godfather films.

The Godfather and *The Godfather Part II*, plus Francis Ford Coppola's Final Director's Cut of the *The Godfather Part III* with 9 minutes of additional footage. Also available in widescreen.

$149.⁹⁵
Sugg. Retail

$66.⁹⁵
Sugg. Retail